NYMPHS AND THE TROUT

Nymphs

and the

Trout

FRANK SAWYER

ADAM & CHARLES BLACK
LONDON

First published 1958
by Stanley Paul & Co. Ltd.

This edition completely revised and reset

Published 1970
Reprinted 1974, 1977, 1979
by A. & C. Black (Publishers) Limited,
35 Bedford Row, London WC1R 4JH

© 1958, 1970 Frank Sawyer

ISBN 0 7136 1074 3

Reproduced from copy supplied
printed and bound in Great Britain
by Billing and Sons Limited
Guildford, London, Oxford, Worcester

CONTENTS

ILLUSTRATIONS

Drawings

REASONS FOR A SECOND VERSION

ONE CERTAINTY about fishing, the least certain of all sports, is the impossibility of knowing it all. Each individual fisherman, master-hand or raw beginner, knows a little or a lot more every time he fishes, from his first cast until his last. Some with special opportunities for observation, extra facilities for concentration, fewer distractions, and more massive experience than the rest reap a harvest of new knowledge which can be shared only through books.

Hence this second version (it is more than a mere new edition) of *Nymphs and the Trout*. Everybody knows that to the making of angling books there is no end, and that for some of them there is no readily perceptible reason. In the present instance the reason will soon be very obvious to all who are drawn into Mr. Sawyer's enthralling new odyssey through the under-water world and share his broadening view of a most skilful and attractive form of fly-fishing; a form, incidentally, in which the extra flexibility in tactics gives the fisherman opportunities to surmount environmental handicaps which are denied him in the older forms of fly-fishing.

It was my privilege to have some hand in editing the earlier version, so perhaps the greater scope of the new *Nymphs and the Trout* is as apparent to me as to anybody. Aside from the fact that the extension of nymph-technique to species (both game and non-game) other than trout has now been carried rather further, a whole series of new conclusions have now been substantiated and, of special interest to the practical fisherman, given significance as trout-catching stratagems. For it is, of course, the trout around which the whole sport of fly-fishing centres.

As has been said, no fisherman ever stops learning. Every visit to the river lifts some veil, confirms some theory, throws doubt on a preconceived notion, or offers some flash of knowledge the weight of which cannot be gauged except in the light of further experience, and perhaps trial and error. Even if a man does not fish at all his knowledge may grow as a result of reflection, like wine maturing in a cask. Sawyer's pen picture of G. E. M. Skues in extreme old age, unable to fish but still living within sight of a stream, still exercising his considerable intellect to extend still further what he had learned in a life which lasted more than ninety years, is an example of the endless quest of all anglers to penetrate further into the natural mysteries which govern their sport.

Compared with the Skues career, the passing of a decade of Sawyer's life may seem a small matter. In fact it has not been so. Sawyer has opportunities shared by few to see and interpret what goes on beside and within a river (his river, the Wiltshire Avon). Ten years of continued observation, repeatedly testing evidence and conclusions, have added greatly to the material of the original version. Yet nothing has been invalidated. In its way the second version, richer in deduction and corroborative fact, is a thorough vindication of the first.

It is also much more. It could be called a key to achievement, for by extending the proportion of productive fishing time in every fishing day, it must greatly increase the reader's chance of success. It could also be called a key to pleasure, because this is no dry treatise. All through it there breathes the cool and sunny air of the English summer, the sportsman's regard for wild life and, above all, good fellowship.

As such it is a book which had to be published. Many fishermen will feel that it is one which has to be read. Prediction is hazardous in both literary and piscatorial matters, doubly so when the two are combined, as none has better cause to know than an editor who is also an angler. Yet I predict confidently that this second version of *Nymphs and the Trout* will take its place beside the works of Halford, Skues, Dunne and Turing as one of the great illuminators of the most delicate of sporting arts, fly-fishing.   *Wilson Stephens*
The Field
December 1969

INTRODUCTION

Let us now praise famous men

IT WAS after reading two books written by the late Mr. G. E. M. Skues that I started to write about nymphs and nymph fishing myself. These were " Minor Tactics of the Chalk Streams " and " Nymph Fishing for Chalk Stream Trout ". Both books were loaned to me by my very old friend the late Sir Grimwood Mears. He knew Skues very well and like many others who had read his books, had practised the art of nymphing as advocated and expounded by this great writer. I remember so well when Sir Grimwood came to the Avon where I am keeper and I watched as he fished for trout with a Skues pattern nymph. I remember also his surprise when I showed him some of my own artificials and how they were constructed to give a quick entry to the water and so sink to the level of a feeding fish. I showed him too that fish could be caught. It was then he offered to lend me the two books, an offer I glady accepted.

I read both books thoroughly and later, when I intended to return them, I had a good talk with Sir Grimwood and told him, though I had found the books of considerable interest, I was not in agreement with all that Skues had written. He then suggested that I took the books home and read them again and to mark any passages which were at variance with my own observations. This I did and at the same time wrote a pile of notes, giving my own explanation, and let him have them. At that time I had no idea of publishing anything and so perhaps you can imagine my surprise and indeed consternation when he asked if he could send the notes I had written to Mr. Skues. My surprise was even greater when later on Sir Grimwood showed me a letter he had received from his old friend and I quote a passage from it. " Encourage this man Sawyer to write articles on this subject and I will arrange for publication ".

Now this, coming from so distinguished a writer and after he had read my review of his two books, was extremely gratifying, especially as he expressed a wish that I should visit him and have a talk in the near future. At that time Skues was living at the Nadder Vale Hotel, just west of Wilton, near Salisbury, and as this is no great distance from my home at Netheravon, I was able to go. This was in 1945.

The memory of this first meeting is still very clear. Skues was then nearly 90 years old. To me he looked a little fragile old man who wore a black skull cap to cover his extreme baldness and heavy lensed glasses to aid his sight. But though frail in body and aged in appearance I quickly found that his brain was very alert and this became more and more apparent as our discussion developed. Skues had been a solicitor and was trained to deal with matters far more complicated than fishing. His ability to sort out the corn from the chaff, so to speak, was brilliant, as also was his questioning and grasp of the answers. I had tea with him on this first visit and we talked for more than two hours.

I watched as with shaking hand, he took down notes from time to time in a minute and spidery writing which, good though my eyes were at that time, I found hard to read without the aid of magnification. I wondered then how he could have possibly constructed the most beautiful little dry-flies he had in his boxes and the various nymph patterns he had evolved through the years. Though he had a rod on a stretch of the Nadder he no longer fished, but it was obvious he still maintained a great interest in all that happened in the fishing world. All around him in his room was an immense collection of fishing books and sporting periodicals and apparently he had many more books in store.

Sir Grimwood was delighted to hear about my reception and of the conversation, and extremely pleased when receiving a further letter from Skues confirming his willingness to help in the publication of anything I wrote, and he was as good as his word. Through him I got an introduction to the late Mr. H. D.

Turing who was then the Editor of the Salmon and Trout Magazine and my first effort to describe nymphs and nymph fishing was published in this magazine. This was a proud moment for me. Though much of what I had written in this first article was at variance with his own observations, Skues had edited it and insisted on its publication.

Several times I visited him in following years until his death, and had quite a lot of correspondence with him. Many of his letters I still have. And I took it very kindly that he, the great authority on nymph fishing and delightful writer that he was, should condescend to listen to my own humble views and to do so with an old world charm which kept me from feeling shy and insignificant. I owe him much for his kindly attitude and for his introduction into the world of the writer and this I wanted you to know before reading what will follow. But I owe far more to my old friend Sir Grimwood Mears. It is true Skues opened the door for me into the literary realms of the fishing world but without the help I got from Sir Grimwood I would have been like a lost sheep.

I met him first in 1932 as he was fishing for trout on the upper Avon in Wiltshire where I am still the keeper, but ten years was to pass before I came to know him really well. It was because he was a fisherman that we were drawn together, for his interests in river life were like my own. When he suggested I should start to write articles for publication I told him I thought this task was far beyond my ability even though I had an urge to do this very thing. He insisted this was nonsense. He became my tutor, my friend and my idol, and to him I owe all the pleasure that has been mine since he, with his infinite patience and understanding, taught me the art of writing.

For more than six years I visited him regularly, almost weekly, at the Avon Hotel in Amesbury where he had retired after losing his first wife and there he instilled his own will into mine and gave me sufficient confidence to become an author. This is a debt I can only repay by continuing to write as he would wish and it is, I think, the greatest tribute I can make to his memory. He was a man who expected the same high standard in others as he had himself. He knew I was sensitive but in his gentle way he would guide me along, though I feel sure there were occasions when he almost despaired. Always he would greet me with a charm and courtesy which was so characteristic of him. Through him I met many people who have helped me onwards, and he gave me the courage I so badly needed to be able to feel at ease in any company.

Through him I learned of the world outside Nature, which was then the only world I knew thoroughly. He introduced me to the B.B.C. and so to broadcasting and to television. His faith in me gave me faith in myself and rather than let him think me a failure I did my best. So great was his influence over me that I have never written, indeed will never write, without seeing his image before me. He put out a hand to help me when I needed help badly and that hand will forever guide my own.

Sir Grimwood was a brilliant conversationalist and a perfect speaker, a man who thought clearly before uttering a syllable. He had a wonderful memory and was methodical in all he attempted. My work interested him greatly. As a fisherman and indeed student of Nature, I felt on an equal fring, for though he had cast his first dry fly on to the River Itchen by Winchester at the age of nine, his work had not allowed him the chance to learn all he would have liked about the river and riverside creatures. I was able to answer many of his questions and in doing so gave him pleasure. His life of fishing interested me too, for he could remember the days of fly fishing long before the eyed hook was invented and before there was tackle such as we are able to use today. He would speak of Halford, Francis Francis, William Senior, Lord Grey, of Skues and other great fishermen of that time, of the controversy which raged on the chalk streams about the dry-fly and the nymph. He was as methodical in his fishing as he was in everything but was one of the old school in wanting exact representations of all kinds of nymphs and flies with which I did not agree entirely.

I was with him when he caught his last trout on the Avon. He was then eighty-two and though gradually losing his eyesight, could still cast a delicate and accurate fly. In his life he had caught many fish and some of his dearest memories were linked with the riverside. This I could well understand for so are my own and not the least the fact that it was at the riverside I met him. He died in 1963.

Another of my great friends in those early days was the late Brigadier General H. E. Carey. It was in 1928 I met him, when I became keeper for the Officer's Fishing Association. He had been the honorary secretary for the Association for a period after the First World War and had then taken on the appointment again. He was a very keen fisherman and interested in all to do with the river and in experimenting with this or with that. Previous to my being engaged as keeper for the Association I had spent a couple of years as an underkeeper on a stretch lower down the Avon at Lake, Nr. Salisbury. This was then a first class trout fishery owned by the late Lieut. Col. Bailey. But it was regarded as dry fly water only. No-one used nymphs whilst I was there and the head keeper, Fred Martin, knew little about such tactics. It was there I met the late Lord Allenby who had a rod on this water and also the late Lord Grey who was then living at Wilsford Manor, and who still fished occasionally. He was then almost blind and though most fishermen used the dry-fly, he, Lord Grey, did at times fish with a single wet fly downstream and caught fish by touch. I had the privilege of accompanying him on two or three occasions but found that his interest was then more in birds than in fish. Though I learned a little about wet fly fishing, by touch, from Lord Grey, it was not until talking and fishing with Brig. Gen. Carey that I began to learn something of the nymph. One of the first things done by Gen. Carey on renewing his appointment as Honorary Secretary for the Association in 1928 was to suggest an amendment of the rules so that the use of the upstream nymphing technique could be permitted. The Committee agreed. Previous to this it had been dry-fly only, but the work of Skues had been read and Gen. Carey had constructed nymphs for his own use, based on the patterns Skues had evolved.

Another very keen Member of the Association at that time was Colonel G. E. Sharp who had written and published a book about the upper Avon water in 1910 called " Fly Leaves From A Fisherman's Diary ". He and Gen. Carey would often meet and discuss the Skues nymphing technique and I watched both in action. Years passed on. During this time, though I used a fly rod occasionally I did not fish much for trout. At that time my main concern was in killing pike and reducing the hordes of coarse fish and grayling, which filled all the best pools in the fishery. Both Gen. Carey and Col. Sharp were good dry-fly fishermen but both, I fear, lacked the good eyesight and quick reflexes one needs for nymphing. They fished in the manner advocated by Skues and caught fish if they took the nymph close to the surface. But many times when the artificial had sunk deeper they failed to appreciate the take and many a good fish was missed. I had many arguments with each and learned much by watching. The main lesson was that if one wished to interest the real nymph takers then it was necessary to get the artificial down to them and then to see the action of the fish in taking, and to be speedy in the hooking.

I knew most of the river flies by sight for they had been familiar to me since I was a boy old enough to understand. I knew some of the nymphs too, but realised that there was much I still had to learn. It was then I began to study the underwater life more thoroughly and to find out more of the natural history of the river flies. It became an interesting and absorbing occupation and I was encouraged by Gen. Carey. I collected different nymphs and took them alive for him to see and he spent many hours doing his best to copy them with artificials and then try them on the fish. I watched him tying these and as he fished them, and then started to make some of my own. For a while I persevered as he did, with silks, tinsels, furs and feathers, but to make these sink as I wanted meant anointing them with glycerine or with spit or mud. Gen. Carey had draped some lead around one or two of his patterns but this, though it had the desired effect in making the artificial sink, destroyed what artistry he had accomplished in his tying. It was then that I started to use very fine copper wire as a ballast and to build up a base; finally I dispensed entirely with silks, and used the wire to tie in and finish off the dressing. I found that in this way I could dress nymphs which not only had the desired weight to make them sink easily, but which in general shape and colour-ation conformed very closely to the trout's view of a natural insect.

Though I showed my nymphs to Gen. Carey and to Col. Sharp and explained the method of construction, neither was very impressed. They were both of the old school and I was a youngster. It is true each of them gave the nymphs a trial but failed to catch fish. I knew why, but had learned to know better than to say so. My eyesight had been trained to see fish under water and deep down, since I was old enough to be beside the river. I saw fish take my nymphs and I saw them spit them out again, with both fishermen unaware it had happened. Finally I despaired and left them to carry on with their nymphing at the surface. Gen. Carey wrote of some of his experiences in his book " One River ".

And so time passed on. Gradually I developed my own style of nymph fishing. This I practised mostly on grayling and caught many hundreds during the seasons which followed. My old rod became so limp and floppy with the numbers of fish it had to handle that I was forced to have a new one. I remember the occasion very vividly. My wife gave me the rod for a birthday present. It was September. I christened it in the afternoon with a total of eighty-three grayling a number of which were over two pounds. Grayling then were very numerous in the upper Avon and though you may think this was slaughter, fishing with a rod was a way of reducing them. There were many days when I caught far more than I could carry in comfort. For the catching of grayling I had devised a " bug " which proved to be very attractive, but of this later on. Sufficient now to say that in the catching of grayling I learned a lot of what happens beneath the surface when fishing a nymph and when, in later years, I started to fish more for trout in various places, the practice served me well. Though I had evolved nymphs and developed a technique of using them which was somewhat different to the methods of Skues, it was not, as I have said, until my old friend Sir Grimwood Mears, and Skues himself, started to show an interest, that I decided to publish more of my work. One thing led on to another.

My interest in the underwater activity of insects grew and then came a great desire to know for certain all the different families and species in their larval and nymphal forms. Skues gave me a letter of introduction to the late Mr. Martin E. Mosely who at that time was in charge of the Department of Entomology, British Museum (Natural History), with whom I carried on correspondence for several years, until in fact he died. Martin

Mosely was very helpful in many ways and identified many insects both in nymphal and aerial form which I sent to him. But he impressed on me that the only true way of finding out about these creatures was to breed them through the various stages oneself and this I started to do. I constructed what I called my fly hatchery. This was a long, narrow wooden box divided into a series of compartments each separated from its neighbour with fine perforated zinc through which a current of water from the river could pass from end to end. Each compartment had a glass top.

Already I had a rough idea of the different nymphs, and in the compartments I would place those I had collected from the river after separating them into the classes I expect to appear. For example Olives, Iron Blues, Pale Wateries, Mayflies, Blue Winged Olives etc., with various caddis. The nymphs I knew were all nearing the time for the change to duns and all appeared to be quite happy in their confined spaces. When hatching, the duns would climb or fly up from the water and then perch in an upside down position on the glass cover where it was a very easy matter to see and to collect them. In this way I was able to breed out nymphs to duns throughout the year. I learned much about them. I learned too that the colouration and indeed shape of the sexes could differ considerably and also that the colouring of the nymph was in no way an indication as to what the colour of the dun or the spinner was likely to be. Also I found that some of the most ugly looking nymphs would produce the most delicate and lovely duns. So far I had been satisfied to do my examinations with a hand lens. It is true this revealed a lot but for the more delicate structure and general anatomy I needed a microscope and so, using some of my savings, I bought one. The subject fascinated me. The microscope showed me things I had not thought existed and only then did I realise fully just how complex this study of insects could become. I realised too that before I could write with any authority on the subject of nymphs and nymph fishing that I had a great deal to learn.

Though he had been most considerate and helpful I knew I could not continue to send specimens to Martin Mosely for confirmation of genera and species and Sir Grimwood Mears suggested I bought a copy of Eaton's Monograph of Mayflies. This I was very fortunate in doing for complete copies of this excellent work were very difficult to obtain, even then. On reading this through and in studying the most excellent drawings I knew that here was a lifetime of work by a master and knew that my own previous efforts were just futile in comparison. So few I fear, realise just how much we are indebted to the studies of men like the Reverend A. E. Eaton. It is so easy to copy the work of others and to use such work for reference. But I already knew just what patience it needed. For me a new world had opened, for with my microscope and this first class book, I had an authentic means for the identification of many of the insects I knew by sight in the river, and those I bred through in my hatchery.

In this way and with studies of the nymphs in their natural habitat I became familiar with most of those to be found in the Avon and, as I found later, in most chalkstreams. This enabled me to place them in their various categories and indeed to assess their value as food for trout. Watching the nymphs moving in the water and about the bottom gave me many clues to the way they are seen by fish, the kinds seen most frequently, and those most likely to be taken as food. On these observations I based the construction of my artificials, and indeed the manner of fishing them.

Though the title of this book is " Nymphs and the Trout " it is not my intention to weary my reader with what can be read in many good books on river entomology, an outstanding example is " An Angler's Entomology " by J. R. Harris, which was first published in 1952. However, excellent though this work is in describing the various nymphs which can be found, the pity is that it does not include, amongst the wonderful coloured photographs, more of the nymphs which belong to the active and swimming group which indeed are the ones of most interest to the nymph fisherman.

It is with this swimming group that I will be dealing with in the Chapters which follow, though, to clarify the situation, some reference will be made to others as well. Also my study of the aquatic life has been extended to cover animals which are to be found in lakes and reservoirs, both in the British Isles and abroad and how the knowledge of such creatures can be put to good effect in the deception of trout and other fish. Since those early days I have been privileged to fish in many parts and in waters of all classes.

This foreword is almost through but I still have an important task to do for I cannot conclude it without recording my appreciation of the help, encouragement and privileges I have received, for there have been many others who have helped me besides those I have already mentioned. Foremost of these was the late Robert B. Marston who for many years was the Editor of The Fishing Gazette. He was introduced to me by Sir Grimwood Mears on an occasion when he came to Amesbury to fish on the lower Avon. He invited me to write regularly for publication in the Fishing Gazette and we became good friends. Each year for several following this, he would visit and fish the upper Avon water I look after, bringing with him his daughter Patricia, who was very keen to learn some of the arts of dry-fly and nymph fishing. Then there is Mr. Wilson Stephens who I met for the first time soon after he became Editor for The Field, a post he still holds. To him I owe a lot, first for his acceptance and publication in The Field of various articles I had written during the years, but mostly for his great interest and patience in editing and arranging the material for my two previous books " Keeper of the Stream " and the first Edition of " Nymphs and the Trout " and his masterly introduction. Since our first meeting we have fished together many times. Perhaps I have helped him a little with his fishing problems, perhaps not, but I always enjoy his company and am honoured to have him as a friend and collaborator. Another good friend and helper has been Mr. Ian Wood the late Editor of the Trout and Salmon magazine, to whom my thanks are due for his acceptance and publication of many of my articles through the years since the magazine started. My meeting with Ian Wood was arranged by that great character Mr. Howard Marshall who was one of the founders of Trout and Salmon. With him I have fished on various occasions on the Kennet at Hungerford and also on his own stretch of the Lambourne. Some experiences of this will be recorded later. He also came to fish on the Avon. Both he and Ian Wood are grand sportsmen to be with, and each interested in all to do with fishing and fisheries.

I am also extremely grateful to Monsieur Charles Ritz whose book " A Fly Fisher's Life " must have given great pleasure to many. I was put in touch with Charles Ritz by Robert Marston and I met him first when he came to the Avon in 1952 expressly to see me fishing for trout and grayling with nymphs. A versatile and " grande hombre " this man for whom I have great respect and indeed affection. Through him I became a Member of the Paris International Fario Club when this club was first formed, and where, at the annual dinners at the Hotel Ritz, I was honoured to be introduced by him to fishermen from all over the world. There I met some of the great champions of the casting world, Pierre Creusevaut, Jon Tarantino, Ben Fontaine and that great fisherman Lee Wulff, there also I met Monsieur de Boiset whose writings in France are so well known, and Monsieur Gagniard the Editor of the French Magazine Plaisirs de la Peche. And I made acquaintance with Prince and Princess Paul von Quadt in whose debt I will always be for the wonderful hosts they were to me when I visited Bavaria and fished their stretch of the River Argen, the late Monsieur Eduard Verne and his wife who made me so welcome on their beautiful river the Risle in Normandy. Yes, people have been kind to me, and there are others. I am indebted to Herrer Nils Farnstrom, the well known Swedish fisherman for being my host on a wonderful trip I had into Swedish Lapland the story of which forms a Chapter in this book. To The Northern Irish Tourist Board and their representative at that time, Mr. Daniel McCrea, for the opportunity I had to see and to fish throughout the province in those lovely Irish streams and lakes. I am most grateful to Alan and Jack Sharpe who took me fishing in Scotland, to Eric Combes for an exciting night after sea trout in Wales, and to Lionel and Mollie Sweet for a grand evening on the Usk.

Due to the kindness of my old friend Doctor Cecil Terry I have had some wonderful sport fishing as his guest on the River Kennet at Hungerford both at Mayfly time and in the autumn with the nymph. Days I have enjoyed, days I remember. He loves fishing for grayling in the autumn and several times has spent a day with me on the Avon in early October. I am sure

he will never forget the time when he returned to the Three
Swans Hotel in Hungerford with a bag of grayling he could
hardly carry which we had taken between us that day, he with
the dry-fly and I with the nymph.

Another to whom I am indebted is Professor Raymond
Rocher for the many translations of my work for publication in
France. I like to think he has learned a little from me about
fishing the nymph since his first visit to fish the upper Avon.
His enthusiasm always amused me as also his excitement.

Then there have been my friends in the tackle business. I
have mentioned Alan and Jack Sharpe of Aberdeen but I have
had much help from Mr. Julian Mills since he became managing
director of the long established firm of Farlows but mostly I
am grateful to the French tackle manufacturers Monsieurs Pezon
and Michel from whom I received a set of rods anyone in the
world could be proud to own, for these are the parabolics
designed by M. Charles Ritz and Pierre Creusevaut. I had the
privilege of visiting their factory in Amboise a few years ago
and appreciated the kindness and consideration I received
during my stay.

I now feel I must pay tribute to my wife for the patience she
has shown and continues to show. Many times I have been
forgiven for going off fishing when I know I should have been
at home doing the garden or maybe helping to decorate the
house, or doing other things dear to the heart of a housewife.
But the bug of fishing and all to do with fishing, had bitten me
hard when I was a boy, and this she knew when we were
married. She has never fished but enjoys watching others, and
even more, the wild life always to be seen by those who are
interested. She has borne with me in my joys and sorrows,
shared with me hope and disappointment, failure and success.
And it has urged me onward. She brought up our family, three
girls and a son while I, in perhaps a queer sort of way, was
doing my best to provide for them. I took them all fishing and
each mastered the art of casting fly or nymph. My son especially,
and I get far more joy in watching him catch fish now, than I
do in fishing myself. I started him off perched up on my
shoulders, when I would cast a fly or nymph to a feeding fish
and then hand him up the rod to do the hooking if the fish took.

Very early in life he appreciated the moment a fish had the artificial in his mouth and learned the precise moment to lift the rod to hook. This is something far more important than learning to cast a long line, though he can do this very nicely too. Girls and boy, each has given me pleasure even as they have had some enjoyment themselves. For that is the way of it. It is a grand feeling to see development, the grasp by others of ideas which might have taken years to perfect if left to their own resources.

To the B.B.C. I owe a lot for the opportunities given to me to appear on television, and for the chances I have had to broadcast on various things to do with fishing, and the natural history in the river valley. Through the medium of television and radio I became known to many and made many friends.

Finally, because I cannot mention everyone by name I wish to thank the Fishing Association who have employed me during the past forty-one years. Without the opportunities I have had whilst looking after this very lovely stretch of the upper Avon and the encouragement I get continually from the Committee and Members, I could have accomplished nothing. From the time I started in 1928 with Brig. Gen Carey until the present, the river and its life in the valley, has held a tremendous fascination for me. It has been my work it is true and perhaps not a work where the pocket becomes heavily laden, but a poorness in pocket has been amply repaid by a great richness in heart, and in my view, this is all that really matters. The Association have been kind to me. Through the years I have met many as strangers who have become my friends. I have had the privilege of fishing when and where I wish, and to be a host to many from all over the world who have been interested in fishing the nymph. The upper Avon is ideal water in which to show off such tactics to perfection and knowing every square foot of the bed of the stream as I do, I have had chances which are denied to the great majority.

In the Chapters which follow in this book I hope to be able to set out the style of nymph fishing I have used for many years which I have explained and demonstrated to a very large number of people. Some have mastered the art, others have tried and considered the technique beyond their ability, due to failing

eyesight or other infirmity. But I believe that the great majority
have found that nymphing for fish can be a most absorbing
and fascinating method of fishing, even as I did, and still do,
myself. And it is with the hope that still more will get the same
pleasure, that I have written the pages of my experiences.

Frank Sawyer
Netheravon, 1969

Chapter One

NYMPHS, A GENERAL SURVEY

Two approaches to imitation : A sporting definition : The
four main types : Evidence at the riverside : Exceptions to
the rules : The importance of delicacy : Unfounded suspicions : The best time.

MY STUDIES through the years have led me to the belief that if
one were to make artificials to imitate all the underwater
creatures on which fish feed then hundreds of different patterns
would be needed. Actually the representations of nymphs could
become as involved as it has with surface insects to such an extent
that it would be far too complicated for the average fisherman
to understand. For this is what has happened since the days of
Halford. Though I have great respect for the writings of the late
F. M. Halford and indeed for his great knowledge of aquatic
life, I feel he went far beyond what could be termed the requirements of the ordinary dry-fly fisherman and created compli-
cations which few have been able to solve to the present day. In
his book " Dry-Fly Entomology " Halford lists what he calls
his " Hundred best Patterns of Dry-Flies ". This is the hundred
best, so obviously he had made many more which did not deserve
mention. Indeed I think it is possible he created artificials to
imitate almost every fly one could find on the water or in the
valley nearby. Time has shown that this was unnecessary from
the point of view of the average fisherman, for less than one in
ten have proved to be of consistent value.

In all branches of angling, simplicity is an aim to be pursued,
and simplicity can indeed be adopted in both dry-fly and nymph

fishing, especially the latter. It seems obvious that Skues thought somewhat on the same lines as Halford when he started to create artificial nymphs for, in his book "Nymph Fishing for Chalk Stream Trout", he published a plate of no less than fifteen different patterns and gave details as to the materials he used to construct them. From time to time many other patterns have been described which represent the natural creatures from the human point of view. Exquisite without doubt, many of them are, but it is the fish, not the human who has to decide if they are attractive. So perhaps I look at things from a somewhat different angle. Through the years the fish have been the judge of any artificials I have constructed and in reasoning things out I have come to the conclusion that the view of the fish must have primary consideration.

Perhaps it would be as well to be quite clear as to what is meant by the term nymph. To me it describes the last stage during the underwater life of insects of the order Ephemeroptera which, except for the absence of wings and their longer tails and legs, they have similarities with the insects which they will become when they burst from their nymphal skins and become airborne. There are others it is true which are of different orders with which the term nymph could be used and so there can be some confusion. Also it seems as well to make this distinction because fish also take a big toll of some of the insects while they are in their larval stages, a stage actually which extends for considerably longer than that of the nymph. The difference between larval and nymphal stage is simply that of age and maturity, the nymph being the creature fully developed showing the folded wings in their cases and of course when they are fully grown. The larvae can be anything from the time it hatches from the egg on through the various dispars until the wing cases show plainly. So actually the same insect can be found in many sizes throughout the year. Its habits can vary accordingly. While it is necessary to take into consideration the fact that fish feed avidly on the immature insects, the technique of nymph fishing need not be concerned with it or indeed the construction of artificials. There is this to be said however. Even as the sub-imagos and the imagos (duns and spinners) have characteristics which can be defined by the human eye, so also have the nymphs. And I have proved on many occasions that there are times when fish will prefer one insect to another even though each are available in equal numbers. It is the same with nymphs. There are times when fish will feed exclusively on just one type and unless this is well represented both in the artificial and in the way it is fished, the angler has little success.

Though in my foreword I have suggested that much can be learned by the study of good books which deal entirely with river entomology, I feel it to be necessary to clarify the groups of nymphs which are to be found, and according to their life underwater. There are four of these groups:

1. Swimming nymphs. These are nymphs which move freely through the water and are continually active throughout the whole of their subaqueous life. This is the largest as well as being the most important of the four groups and the one with which we will be most concerned in the pages which follow.

2. Crawling nymphs. This is a group which prefer to move about on the river bed and crawl sluggishly amongst the vegetation on the bottom.

3. Flat nymphs. These are nymphs which have the appearance of being squat and flat which cling to the undersides of stones and debris and spend most of their underwater life in semi-darkness.

4. Burrowing nymphs. This is the mayfly group, whose existence underwater is spent mostly in burrows in the river bed where until the final stage, the actual nymph stage, they give fish very little chance to see them or to take them as food.

One might write for hours, for years in fact, before the subject of nymphs and their habits could be exhausted. Even then I am very doubtful if there is an author alive who could tell all that a man could learn at the riverside. Certainly it is not I, and therefore I say that if these writings stimulate your interest, then go to the riverside to check them and learn the deeper truths. Nymphs can be found in fair numbers throughout the year but the ideal time is from early summer on through till autumn, when, in point of fact, the temperature of the water is at its highest. I am not suggesting you go to the same lengths as I have myself in discovering and identifying the various creatures but

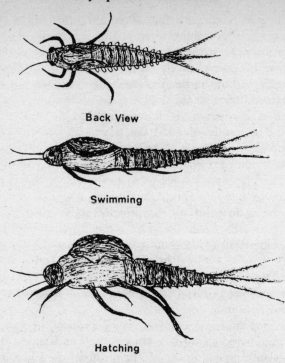

Back View

Swimming

Hatching

OLIVE NYMPHS IN NATURAL POSITIONS

an hour now and then spent in pulling handfuls of weeds from
the river bed, lifting out a few big stones, a log of wood perhaps,
or other debris to examine could be enlightening. You might also
dig out a section of the actual river bed and then there would
be the chance to see the insects in their natural environment.
Once seen the general structure of these aquatic insects become
imprinted on the memory and in evolving patterns afterwards the
images of the various nymphs remain in the mind.

If you select a few of the nymphs and put them in a glass
container you will see at once that they are very much alive.
You will also find out very quickly which are the types which
are represented in the four groups I have mentioned. Your main
attention will be directed to the types which swim and how
attractive they look as they pass through the water, the move-

ment will catch your eyes even as they catch the eyes of fish. The nymphs are never really still, for even when perched on the bottom or on vegetation there is always movement of the plate-like gills, or breathing appendages, which are either side of the body. And at once it becomes apparent that there is considerable importance in dressing an artificial version, to try and incorporate something which can give a suggestion of life. Trout, and other fish expect nymphs to look lively. It is generally accepted that the rows of gills I have mentioned as being along the sides, are for respiration, but they also give considerable aid to the insects in swimming. When the nymphs are in motion the gills appear only as a blur, and a fast moving blur. It is in representing something to suggest these gills that hairy fibres such as those on the herls of a pheasant's tail are so valuable. But though one can do a little to simulate life when building an imitation of a nymph, by far the greater part in deception is played in the presentation of the artificial. No matter how well a pattern is tied, or indeed what quality of material is used for the construction, the great thing is to be able to place it before a fish exactly where it expects to see a natural insect and so that, to him, it does appear to be one of the creatures on which he has been feeding. One cannot do this without knowing something of the habits of nymphs and of the trout in taking them.

Sometimes I have wished I could be a fish, preferably a trout, so that for a year or two I might live in a stream and find out more about the lives of the thousands of animals which inhabit the river bed and frolic amongst the plants which grow from it. But as this cannot be I must be content, as most of us must, in looking at what can be seen from the surface. It is very fascinating to peer into water for even as the sky changes when the sun or moon passes from east to west, so changes a running stream. What is seen in any hour of study must forever remain only as a picture imprinted on the plate of memory and if sufficiently interesting it will never be forgotten. Through the years there have been many advances in the ways one can view the underwater life but the greatest advance of all is with the use of the underwater camera. In years to come I feel sure the camera will reveal the truth of much which so far has been merely conjecture. It should be interesting for though many thousands of

men and women go fishing, not many have the time, or indeed
the opportunity to see more than just a fleeting glance of the
lesser creatures in the aquatic world and little time to spare to
ponder on how they are produced. Yet many millions of animals
must die before a fish can reach a size likely to give sport on a
rod or be large enough to be edible. There is the first. tiny life,
so small as to be quite invisible to us as it mingles with the water
at one end of the scale, and at the other end, the fish. In between
there is the multitude and all must play a part in the continuous
cycle of production.

Most of our trout flies spend one or two years underwater in
their larval and nymphal stages and during this underwater life
certain kinds are taken freely by fish. But there are many
different genera and species which have habits that are greatly
at variance. Some, as I have mentioned, spend their underwater
life in the river bed, some live under stones and other debris and
cling like limpets; others crawl about on the river bed and in
vegetation; and still more range freely and can swim like little
fish. Some of them prefer one type of water, some another, some
hatch into flies at the beginning of a season and others at the
end, with still more in the intermediary period. They are of
various sizes, shape and colouration, and when hatching to flies
each family has its characteristic method of approaching the
surface. For instance, the mayfly nymph, the largest of the
ephemeropterons, swims direct from its tunnel in the river bed
to the surface to hatch; trout or indeed other fish seldom have
much chance to see it in nymphal form until it is nearing the
surface to change to a fly. The mayfly nymph has been copied
and used by many but I am not in favour of this class of nymph
fishing. When trout take the hatching, mayfly nymph they will
also take the floating flies if one cares to wait a little while, and
to be honest about it, I do not consider it to be fair fishing.

But in converse to the mayfly we can take the olives, the iron
blues, pale wateries or spurwings, all very much the same in size
though varying in colouration. There are several species of these
genera and they have habits which are similar. The larvae and
nymphs of these are of the swimming group—that is, they can
move from point to point, by swimming freely through the water
like fish. They live on the river bed, on vegetation, and may be

found everywhere, at various depths. They may make journeys to the surface long before they are ready to hatch into flies and return once more to a lower level. They may move through the water whilst feeding, from one place to another and, in a score of ways, form an attraction the fish find hard to resist. Trout, and indeed other fish, know of the habits of this group of insects from a very early age, for insects such as these form a very big part of the diet of young fish. And so they hunt or position themselves accordingly, knowing what to expect. Those mentioned form most of the swimming group to be found in rivers, and indeed in the majority of lakes and reservoirs in this country. But there is another much larger swimming nymph of an entirely different genus which I will be describing in a later chapter which deals with nymphing in the mountains of Sweden.

As further examples of the ephemeropterons we have such flies as the yellow may dun, the turkey brown, the claret dun and the march brown both the spring and the summer types. And there are others which are in the same class. These are seldom seen by fish either in their larval or in their nymphal stages. They spend their life clinging to substances on the river bed, for the most part beneath them, and are seldom to be seen in midwater. When hatching to flies they crawl up the banks—on vegetation, or indeed, on anything which extends from the river bed to the surface. An artificial nymph of either would therefore be unfamiliar if fished in mid-water and I am doubtful if there is anyone in the world who could make one appear to crawl up a weed stem.

Then there are the types which crawl about on the river bed. It is true some of these can be seen and taken by fish but such cannot be fished in a natural way even if good copies of the natural are constructed. In this group are some of those mentioned above but other examples are the blue winged olives and the tiny Caenis, or fisherman's curse as it is commonly called. Both these hatch in a way not unlike that of the mayfly and if patterns could be made to simulate those insects just as they are changing into flies they might prove to be very attractive. But even as with the mayfly, when blue winged olives and the caenis are hatching, a floating fly, sparsely dressed, can give far more sport than a sunk pattern.

So far I have dealt briefly with the lives of nymphs in the order ephemeroptera but there are other creatures which can form a great attraction to trout and other fish in midwater and at the surface. Foremost of these are the Chironomids, a very large family which contains a great variety in both size and colouration. Though to be found, and indeed taken freely by fish in the running streams, those of a size which can be of greatest interest to the nymph fisherman, are inhabitants of the slower reaches of rivers, and of the static waters of ponds, lakes and reservoirs. Many of this genus prefer acid to alkaline water and can be found in their legions all about the British Isles. But, though extremely attractive for fish, the vast majority are much too small to be represented successfully by artificials. The exceptions are the big gnats and those known as buzzers, and these I will be dealing with in a later chapter. For some reason, quite unknown to me, the term nymph does not apply to the last stage in the underwater life of gnats and midges. Yet these hatch in a manner not unlike many of the ephemeroptera and cast a similar kind of shuck as eclosion takes place. It is only in recent years that I have made any detailed study of the larger types of chironomids and indeed made any effort to create artificials to represent them. But for the fact that we have several small artificial lakes here now, where such creatures exist, and form a big attraction for trout, I would not have done so. But I found, even as many fishermen have found when fishing the big lakes and reservoirs, that when a hatch of buzzers occurs the fish really come on to feed, but it needs a really good imitation of the hatching larvae to deceive them. Of this however later on.

Though there are a large number of other aquatic creatures which could be copied and fished successfully in the nymphing style I have no desire to deal with them. To get the most enjoyment from the technique I employ, it is necessary to use artificials which can be cast delicately and accurately with a light rod and line. Indeed delicacy in the whole outfit is the aim to be achieved or much of the joy and indeed the fascination of nymphing is lost. There is far more artistry in casting and presenting a dry-fly on the surface to a given point, than in fishing indiscriminately with a team of wet flies. It is because of this the dry-fly became

favourite with so many. But there is even more satisfaction to
be had in placing a tiny nymph in such a way that it can deceive
a fish into thinking it is alive for I feel that anyone who can do
this is accomplishing something far more artistic than those who
fish the dry or the wet-fly. This I know is a sweeping statement
but I believe it to be true. I would go further and say that
nymphing is a combination of the best points in both dry-fly
and wet-fly fishing but adding more difficulty and asking for
far more concentration on the part of the fisherman.

Regardless of many efforts to prove what an interesting and
fascinating sport nymph fishing can be, this method of taking
fish is still viewed with suspicion by some, still there is considerable controversy, and indeed in some waters the use of any kind
of nymph is forbidden and said to be unsporting. This is very
difficult for me to understand for I have had the opportunity to
look into the matter from many angles. Being a river keeper, it
is obvious that I would not be enthusiastic over a method for
the taking of trout if it was likely seriously to affect the stock,
or to give fishermen an unfair advantage over the fish. Even as a
gamekeeper does his utmost to make his birds give the maximum
sport to his guns, so I like rods to get as much enjoyment as they
can from their hours beside the river. Without question, there
are days, many days, throughout the trout season when the
dry-fly can give one the very peak of satisfaction—times when,
in fact, more fish can be caught with flies presented at the
surface, rather than by any beneath it. No one would want to
use a nymph then, but even as there are these dry-fly days, so
also are there times when the fish expect to see their food in the
water and not on it. Then, if sport is to be had, the correct
presentation of an artificial nymph is the only way by which
they can be interested or deceived.

Seasons differ considerably I know, but, generally speaking,
that is, in average years, I always think of the best nymphing
period as being during the months of July and August. These
are the two months when, excepting perhaps at early morning
or very late evening, dry-fly fishing is least productive. But it is
the time when many kinds of nymphs are very active. During
these few weeks the water in most rivers, more especially the
chalk streams, is at its clearest. Though shy, most of the fish are

on the look-out for underwater activity amongst the insects, and
with the sun high in a clear sky, feeding fish can be found if
one is careful.

Nymph fishing, if you are to be successful, is indeed a matter
of being careful. It is not just a business of throwing a nymph
to all the likely places and hoping a fish will take. You turn
yourself into a hunter and, with all the keenness of a stalker
after a stag, you pit your wits and your eyesight against the
faculties of the wild fish. It is not an art to be acquired in a
season, or, for that matter, in a dozen seasons, for to be truly a
nymph fisherman it is very necessary to know something of the
habits of fish and, even more, of the habits of the creatures on
which they feed beneath the surface. Many who are experts in
the presentation of a dry-fly fail at the start to cast a nymph so
that it appears lifelike to a fish, and I have seen first class wet-
fly fishermen scare far more trout than they catch. Nymph
fishing is indeed a technique of its own, and the casting of an
artificial so that it appears attractive and not disturbing is an
art one must learn only by experience.

Artificial nymphs can be used with deadly effect throughout
the whole season but I think it is only during the months of
July and August that the fisherman can obtain the highest
degree of sport, and the knowledge that he is accomplishing
something beyond the powers of the ordinary wet- or dry-fly
enthusiast. As I have mentioned, these are the days when the
water is usually at its clearest. There are days of sun blazing
from cloudless skies, when not a breath of air disturbs the surface
of the river; when it is possible to see every movement of a trout
in the water, and, conversely, for the fish to see every movement
of the angler, unless he uses the greatest caution in approach.
Truly these are the days when the utmost enjoyment in fishing
can be obtained, for trout already have had a severe hammering
with the dry-fly and most of them have gained a good knowledge of the fisherman and his wiles.

At this time the wild trout of a river are really wild; the
brilliant sunshine and the clear unruffled water gives them the
oportunity to see every artifice the fisherman may present. It is
not a time to expect many flies to hatch but the few which do
hatch leave the water very quickly. The clear dry atmosphere

allows them to change very rapidly from nymph to dun when they fly away without giving fish a chance to take at the surface. Yet fish are on the feed, continually on the look-out for nymphs moving in mid-water or below; and a feeding trout can be caught if he is offered a good representation of the food he is taking. And yet doubts remain about the methods by which such a trout should be offered an artificial insect, and about what form the artificial should take. At present the phrase " Upstream nymphing " covers a wide field and of course it is misrepresented. A nymph, in the opinion of some, but not in mine, can be any tying evolved which may catch a fish. In fishing it, so long as a man does not deliberately fish the water down-stream in wet-fly style, indiscriminately flog and search the water, then there is little one can do but trust to the conscience of the fisherman to use only artificials which can take fish in a sporting manner and during a period when the utmost skill is needed in presenting them.

Chapter Two

READING THE RIVER

Method in reconnaissance : How to visualise the bed :
Finding the feeding positions; What a fish can see : The
fisherman and the sun : Stalking and concealment : System
in seeking fish : The clue of tail movement.

A MAN who knows a river has a decided advantage, especially if
at the same time he has a knowledge of the habits of fish. Of
course, where water remains perfectly clear throughout the year
there are times when it is very easy to see the bottom, even in
the deepest parts, and so be able to judge the varying depths, but
in many rivers, particularly in winter or spring, it often is
difficult to see more than a foot beneath the surface. To the
unpractised eye the whole of this class of river looks alike, and
to find the depth a probe or a weighted string has to be used.

Certain classes of fish prefer certain classes of water. For
example, one would not normally expect to find a shoal of roach
and dace to be lying and feeding in fast running water or a pike
to be there digesting his kill, yet this same place may be ideal
for trout and grayling. It is pleasant to be able to walk along a
bank and visualise the bottom—to say to yourself : there's a pit
there, a boulder or a weedbed; here the water is deep or shallow
as the case might be, or there's an eddy or a back-water. You
see the track of the current snaking along, first this side, then
the other, then in the middle, a wave here, and a bulge there,
with ripples and whorls distorting the surface. For of course the
formation is truly portrayed for all to see. No matter whether
rough or even deep or shallow, weeded or bare, if there is

sufficient run on the stream the character of the bed is shown at the top.

Water cannot be compressed. It travels in a mass so that any obstruction on the bottom has the effect of lifting the water to cause a distortion at the surface. The faster the current the more clearly the bed is revealed. There is an old saying that " still waters run deep ". There is some truth in it, of course, as usually there is in these old proverbs, and this is one golden rule to observe. Where water in a river moves slowly it means that the pull of gravity has been obstructed in some way and that a build up of water has occurred. Deep waters are often the home of big fish. Where gravel bars extend across the river course they act as obstructions to the direct flow. Therefore in reaches upstream of such shallows the flow of the river is checked and slowed down considerably. To go on downstream it has to take a fall and here the speed of flow increases and in many cases the river widens. As it speeds along so one can see the positions of stones, boulders and weed-beds and there on the surface can be seen the tracks of the main currents.

Every running stream carries certain flotsam, particles of various kinds. For instance, bits of weed, sticks, dust, froth and bubbles float along and all can be seen to move in certain lanes. Perhaps there will be one main current, perhaps two or three, and here and there a jutting bank or sharp bend will interfere. It pays to watch this flotsam for it is in the grip of the stream and acts as a tell-tale. These same currents carry the varying creatures of the river and all such lanes are well known to the fish. It is not wise to be impatient when after fish with nymphs and a good study of all the likely places is desirable before moving farther upstream. Many a good fish has been disturbed from its feeding place by fishermen who have been too anxious to see what is going on around the next bend. Look once, twice, and yet again, is a motto well worth keeping in mind.

Each year I become more convinced that when trout take up a feeding position during the summer months it is with the primary intention of intercepting nymphs. If you catch a fish with a dry-fly at a time when to all appearances he is rising well to floating insects, you will find when you examine the contents of his stomach that quite eighty per cent of the food is made up of creatures he has taken beneath the surface. As the insects come near to the end of their underwater life so they give fish better opportunities to take them. Indeed there are times when they become easy prey. This the fish know and position themselves accordingly. If you know the kind of place a fish is likely to occupy, then half the battle in locating him is won, for it is on such places you concentrate your attention.

Nymphing trout are to be found in a great variety of positions and it is quite impossible to have any hard and fast rule to cover the approach to all of them. It is, however, important to be a good judge of depth and also to have a good idea as to the speed of current. I have taken trout with nymphs when they have been feeding near the bottom in over four feet of water and I have taken many when their tails and dorsal fins have been showing above the surface. Generally speaking a trout lying deep has his eyes focused on the bed of the river and has an area of view for feeding which extends to about four feet in front and at either side of his eyes. When near to the surface the area for taking is much more limited and an artificial must be placed fairly accurate and within a radius of about nine inches of the fish's head. These fish which lie well up in the water are usually looking for food floating just above them and show little interest in what is happening below.

The mid-water fish becomes the easiest victim, for this fish is truly alert to all which goes on around him. His eyes are watching everywhere, even for movements behind him. Should a bad, or short cast be made, the nymph should not be withdrawn hurriedly for a second throw without watching closely. There have been many times when I have taken trout which apparently had their first view of my artificial as it was sinking two or three feet downstream of their tails. These fish have swung round and downstream with a rush, to take without the slightest suspicion.

I know much has been written about what is called the " trout's window ", and years ago, as a sequel to some correspondence we had on the subject, Mr. Skues sent me his copy of " The Flyfisher and the Trout's Point of View ", by the late Col. E. W. Harding. Although I enjoyed reading this book I could not agree with Colonel Harding's estimate of a trout's point of

view. It seemed much too limited. It is true that trout are seldom
attracted to any creature moving outside a limited area but this,
I think, is simply because they are too lazy to range very far. It
is not because they cannot see beyond this distance because I
have proved many times that they can, and indeed see very
clearly. A cruising fish, that is, a fish hunting for prey, will see
insects on and in the water many feet away and will make his
way towards them. He has his beat and he hunts all the while
using his eyes to the best advantage. One who has a position has
chosen it simply because his food is being directed by a current,
or currents, into a narrow channel and brought to him. He
knows that he will get as much as he wants without moving
very far. No, I could not agree with the views of Colonel Harding
about a limited cone of vision. So many things have happened to
disprove it. I believe fish can see in water quite as well as we
can, that is look through it. But it is not so easy for them to see
out, especially when near to the surface.

Almost as important to the fisherman as a knowledge of what
a trout can see in the water is a knowledge of his awareness, by
sight and otherwise, of what is going on out of the water. No
man who does not know his safety zone for movement can stalk
his fish with complete efficiency. Many fishermen forget, or disregard, the fact that they are very conspicuous and easily seen
by fish while moving along a river bank. Caution in approach
is very important while dry-fly fishing, but it is even more
important when the angler is trying to catch fish with nymphs,
for unless you are able to spot your fish, or at least to form a
good idea just where it is in position, the odds are that the fish
will see you first and stop feeding, even if he is not scared to
cover.

In the past I have put forward the view that it is an advantage
to fish with your face towards the sun and this called forth comments from numerous people. These comments were based
mostly on the fact that wild creatures have difficulty in seeing
anything which may be between them and the sun. One correspondent spoke of the methods adopted by our fighter pilots and
of enemy aircraft pilots who invariably made their attacks with
the sun behind them. Others wrote of big game hunting and
brought forth many arguments to support their points. It is of

course true that animals and fish, and indeed ourselves, have difficulty in discerning movement while looking towards the sun and an angler approaching a fish with the sun behind him is much less likely to be seen than one from the opposite angle. But in fishing it is not solely the angler or his movements which cause the scare, but far more often the shadow of the line and the cast as it falls to the water and this is what the fisherman must keep foremost in his mind. Though we see the shadow reflected on the surface, a fish sees it right down through the water and on the bottom. Trout are wily at all times but more so during the bright summer days. One reason is that there are few flies on the water to keep their thoughts occupied and eyes peering forward. They are interested in what is taking place all around and quickly become suspicious.

Where one has a choice of banks the best answer is generally to choose the one where you can fish towards the sun. But where one is limited, as is often the case, to one bank only, then some thought is needed and before casting to a feeding fish it is an advantage to study the best way to place a nymph without there being the possibility of the shadow of line and leader falling across it. Perhaps, when reading this, there will come to mind memories of times when fish after fish has been scared. When in fact they have stopped feeding or have bolted for cover even before you have made a cast to them for this has happened to all of us. I well remember one such morning when I met one of our members who had become exasperated with this repeated end to his attempts. Trout were feeding well and he had been exercising extreme caution in approaching them. But the moment his line fell to the water the fish went down. As I spoke to him a sizeable trout showed plainly in midstream as it came near to the surface to take a nymph. He saw it and started to creep along through the herbage to get closer and in creeping to his position for casting he came in a direct line from the sun to the fish. " That is where you are making a big mistake " I said. " Come back here and try from this angle with a long cast, and try, if you can, to put the nymph down on the far side of the trout ". As he was making his preparation I told him why I had made the suggestion, and, saying he just had not thought about it, he pitched the nymph gently in to the far side of the fish and just upstream. Line and cast fell without scaring the trout and next moment it had taken and was hooked. My fisherman took a second in the same manner soon afterwards.

Things do not always work out so well. I have seen so many fish frightened and good chances missed through carelessness or thoughtlessness, that it is impossible to stress too strongly the great importance there is in concealment and approach at the riverside. Too many fishermen seem to forget they are in pursuit of wild life and of creatures which have a very highly trained instinct for self preservation. What I mentioned a while back about trout having difficulty in seeing out when they are near to the surface, may seem strange to you but I have found it to be very true. The nearer a fish is to the top, the more difficulty he has in seeing out at an angle. Movements on the bank, unless high up may be quite invisible to him and the farther he is away the less chance he has of seeing anything at all. But it is as well to remember this also. Just because a fish can be seen clearly there is no reason at all to assume that he can see you, even though you are in the open. A fish looking out has a view much different from yours looking in, so to speak; and his view, from the light ray angle, is the reverse of your own. Therefore it is not outside the bounds of possibility to think that on those days when you find great difficulty in looking into water and seeing fish, that it is comparatively easy for those fish to look out and see you. Even as it is possible for us sometimes to see every fin and spot, on at least half of a trout, when the angle is reversed a fish may see all that is happening in your area.

It is easy to advise a newcomer to dry-fly or nymph fishing first to find a feeding fish. But something should be added. It is necessary to find a feeding fish without the fish knowing he has been found, and then to take every precaution in trying to catch him. Movements should always be slow and remember, more especially if you are tall, that your eyes are at the top of your body, that it is of no use hiding your eyes while the rest of your anatomy is exposed to full view. Don't be too sure, however, that a fish recognises you as a human being and therefore something to dread. In some lights and positions it is more than possible that at times all he sees is shadow, or just a head and shoulders, which have more resemblance to a bird than a man, more especially when the arms are moving as when casting. Fish are generally more afraid of birds than they are of animals.

Often I am amused to see photographs of float fishermen perched on seats beneath umbrellas high up on a river's edge with a rod reaching out over the water which to a fish, must be as obvious as the bare mast of a yacht is to us. To me they appear as though, indeed, they are spectators at an aquarium watching tame fish, rather than anglers who have hopes of catching wild ones. It is a mistake to think that just because water is deep and cloudy all caution is unnecessary. Though we cannot see the bottom, fish can see the sky and anything outlined against it. Hundreds of times I have seen trout rising to take tiny flies in water so coloured that I could not see more than one or two inches into it. And to me it seems quite certain, if a fish can see out sufficiently well to note the movement of a tiny fly at the surface, he can also see moving objects that are thousands of times larger, though perhaps farther away. The larger a fish grows the more shy he becomes. This applies more especially where coarse fish are concerned, where a number of fish may be together in one shoal. Panic passes one to another very quickly. A frightened fish will never feed.

The higher ones eyes are from a river level, the easier it is to see into the water, and so, in this respect, a tall man has a decided advantage over a short one. Years ago I used to take my small son with me along the river bank and with him at that time I had an advantage of nearly three feet in height. Young as he was, he could see into water fairly well, and also spot fish. But such were the varying angles of light that sometimes he spotted a fish I missed, and there were others that I could see clearly which to him were invisible. So, when I saw a fish that he couldn't I lifted him up to my level, so that, in fact, his eyes commanded the same angle of light as my own. When he saw a fish that I couldn't then down I stooped till I was at his height.

Through the years I have learned much about light angles when searching for pike with a snare or harpoon. It is not enough to just wander along the river-bank in an upright position. When you are searching for fish you must look through the water to the bottom, and only by the help of the light rays is it possible to do this. At times a good view can be had near to the edge of the river, at others it is easier to see from a distance away from the water. Sometimes, you can see well from a higher level but to search a river from bank to bank, or at least as far out as it is possible to see, one should try views from varying angles.

If you have a choice of banks then it is much easier, but always remember the light from dawn to mid-day is much better than afternoon. In the morning I have always found it easier to see into water when I have the sun, or the position of the sun, on my right. In the afternoon it is the reverse. As you move along in your search try to take advantage of tree reflections. A tree on the opposite bank throws a reflection which cuts out the white surface light, and as you change position, so the reflection of bole, branches and foliage enables you to see a different part of the river bed. Sometimes one can see better by looking well upstream; indeed this is the best kind of light you can have, for then you can see your quarry long before he has a chance to see you and therefore can act accordingly.

When I search a water, my eyes first sweep upstream, while I lift and lower my head and body. Then I scan the area opposite and finally make sure there is nothing to be seen in the water downstream. Look first beneath your own bank and pay greatest attention to the places where experience has taught you are likely to be the positions of the fish you are after. It may seem strange to you, but there have been many times when I have been after pike, and have walked past clearly visible trout without seeing them; and the reverse has happened, though not quite so frequently. You get used to looking in certain places for certain fish and are apt to be blind to all else.

Though you may be looking closely for trout it is seldom their position is located by a full view. Often fish are so well camouflaged when lying on the bottom or on weedbeds they would escape notice but for some movement they make. Sometimes such movement is caused through a fish lifting or turning to take a nymph or other creature, or perhaps in rising towards the surface. But the main thing which can catch the eye is the wagging of the tail and the beating of the ventral fins. The tail is never stationary if a fish is on the feed. Once this movement is seen and the tail located the remainder of the fish seems to come into view as if by magic. Movement plays a very big part in attracting the eyes of both hunter and quarry and I cannot stress this too strongly for it plays a very big part in successful nymph fishing. Even as the movement of the tail of a trout will attract our eyes, so the movement of an insect will attract the eyes of a fish. The truth of the matter is, that until there is some movement there is no indication of life. To bring out the point more clearly I would like to draw your attention to looking at a tree or bush in full leaf. You look at all of it, then suddenly your eyes are attracted to where a bird has hopped from branch to branch and that point immediately becomes your focus. That bird hopping attracted your eyes in much the same way as a tiny nymph could attract the eyes of a fish as it moves through the fronds of a weedbed, or as it leaves the river bed to make a journey to the surface. It brings about a focus point in much the same way as happens when one sees the movement of a fish's tail in a place where all else is still.

A trout, though feeding well on nymphs, may not show his location frequently. He can take scores of natural insects without once breaking the surface. But now and again he may take a floater. He may bulge or hump the water. You might perhaps see a wave, a swirl or a flash from side or tail, just enough to tell you his position and that he is on the feed. But it is as well to remember. If he can take natural insects without showing himself at the surface, he can also take an artificial if it has sunk to a depth of more than six inches without giving much sign that he has done so.

Riverside trees can be good view points. I know one can hardly expect fly or nymph fishermen to go clambering up trees to search for feeding fish, but scores of times I have done so when in search of pike. I well remember a pike of about 6lb. We had seen and lost him quite half a dozen times on different occasions. He had a lie in some dead water behind a big weedbed, where, when he had filled himself with trout, he would find himself a comfortable place and rest like a log on the bottom, plain for all to see from the bank, and in such position that he saw all who wished him ill. Just downstream was a big withy tree which almost spanned the river. When alarmed down he would rush to this shelter and though we hunted from the bank and climbed the tree to find him, it was no good. He seemed to disappear. So one morning, after spotting him in his favourite lie, we left him while I climbed the tree. Though quite fifty paces away, I could see him clearly and could follow him distinctly as he came rushing downstream after my assistant made an attempt to enter the water to snare him.

Down he came and swung round immediately below me and then sidled gently towards where a fringe of pinky roots from the tree hung to the river bed. Under these he went and settled. I could see part of his back, but had I not known it was he, the camouflage would have been perfect. It was a very simple matter to clamber down to within reach and run my harpoon through him. Trees can be helpful, as this one instance proves. I can also remember another tree episode which started badly but ended well. One of our members had been after a fair-sized trout in midstream, when his fly caught high up on a nearby tree. It was a fly he valued and rather than break and lose it, he decided to climb up and release it. While high up he glanced to see if his fish was still rising. It was, but beyond it he spotted another close to the opposite bank which was quietly feeding under water. He left the mid-stream fish, crossed the river and after a good battle landed his best trout of the season on a nymph.

Chapter Three

TECHNIQUES IN NYMPH IMITATION

Learning from experience : Some requirements of artificial patterns : Resemblance not enough : The importance of movement : The movement of metamorphosis : What a microscope revealed : Some consequent hypotheses.

THE GREAT joy in trout fishing comes with the knowledge that one has deceived a fish into taking an imitation of the natural insect on which it happens to be feeding. If the fisherman is a fly-tier there is added pleasure, for in the occupation of making an artificial, he will be filled with the anticipation of seeing his creation accepted by a trout in mistake for the insect he has been at such pains to copy. In imagination he will be by the riverside, see the trout moving without suspicion towards the hook his nimble fingers have so artfully concealed, see the mouth of his fish open and close, and in advance get the thrill as, in his mind, he lifts the rod to drive home the hook point. But it does not always work out that way. During my life as a nymph fisherman I have made many different artificials. Though I have had some success with my patterns, I have also had failures and many of my dreams at the vice have never materialised. But in making the various patterns and in trying them on the fish I have had considerable pleasure for there is nothing to be ashamed of in being beaten by fish. Failure is but an incentive to success and the harder a thing is to obtain the greater is its value. Or so I think. Though a good copy of an insect is essential, this is not always enough, one should know what the fish expect this insect to do, and be able to show it to them in this light.

I once made some copies of the blue winged olive nymphs
and, when comparing them under the microscope with the
natural insect in water and ignoring the hook, had difficulty in
telling the two apart. I was exceedingly pleased with my efforts
and, as plentiful blue winged olives were then hatching about
the river, I tried them on the trout. The blue winged olive is an
insect which excites fish almost as much as does the mayfly and,
similarly, are very fond of taking this insect just as it is breaking
the surface and hatching from the nymph. But I thought I would
try these in much the same way as I fished my other patterns.
I had tied them so that they could have a good entry to the
water and, on being presented, they immediately sank towards
the bottom. Though one fish made a move towards one of my
casts, six or seven more totally disregarded the placed nymph.
I failed to get a single fish to take either of the patterns I had
made.

This puzzled me for a while and then it occurred to me that
the blue winged olive swims to the surface in a jerky, undulating
movement; that once it has risen to hatch it seldom returns to
the bottom but often floats for a long distance down a stream
all the time wriggling as it endeavours to burst from its shuck
and withdraw its legs, wings and tail, in the change from nymph
to dun. Good though my patterns had seemed to me they lacked
the very thing which trout were looking for. These fish knew
there was something wrong and that what I was offering was in
no way edible. I then also knew what it was and went home to
construct other patterns. The trout wanted something which
showed life near the surface of the water. They should have it.

I used exactly the same materials for a body as I had for the
previous patterns, but instead of adding a few turns of copper
wire to the hook to make it heavier, I dressed my new copies as
though I were making a dry-fly. My rejected patterns had been
finished with a soft hen hackle at the head, but these new ones I
dressed with a cock hackle and then cut off the fibres so that
they stood out sparsely and rigid from the thorax. My one idea
was to make an imitation that would sink just through the
surface film, and appear to the trout as though it had spread its
legs and tails in an effort to hold itself up in the water. My
finished efforts pleased me.

When cast lightly, like a dry-fly, the artificials did as I wanted, and sank just beneath the surface; and, in sinking, the stiff cock hackles spread one from another with the action of the water and appeared like moving legs and tails of the nymph I had copied. Six trout took my offerings. I could have hooked them all, but I did not want to. I had had sufficient pleasure in deceiving them. It was, sad to say, only a passing triumph. Though I tried this same pattern many times afterwards it was never again consistently successful.

Since then I have tried many different arrangements to try and evolve a good pattern of this particular nymph but have come to the conclusion that such an effort is beyond me. It is the wriggle, or struggle of this nymph in trying to hatch which causes the attraction for fish and I have found this can be better typified with a floating pattern, rather than with one fished beneath the surface. And now when the blue winged olives are hatching well, I use a sparsely hackled red spinner pattern, which is often successful when the weather is calm and bright, and at late evening. On blustery, or wet cloudy days I have found a small pattern tied in a somewhat similar manner to the March Brown is very effective. In this the brown partridge hackle is the main attraction I think. The shade and shape of the body is of far less importance. The pattern should only be sparsely hackled. Just enough in fact to keep the fly on the surface. Skues recommended the use of an orange quill when the blue winged olives are hatching. Though I have tried this on many occasions it has never been really good here on the upper Avon. I much prefer the partridge hackle and others who have tried it have been of the same opinion.

The blue winged olive is not, as I have mentioned previously, one of the nymphs which are to be seen frequently by fish and I think it unlikely that it is known to them in the larval or nymph form as a food. This may have some bearing on the fact that they do not take an artificial copy very readily beneath water. They are poor swimmers. They belong to the crawling group and when hatching in open water have none of the easy movements so characteristic of the swimming nymphs, and which can be so readily imitated. Trout seldom take them in mid-water, but the attraction comes when the insects reach the surface film and are hatching. Fish know all about this, I feel sure, for once the insects reach the surface there is no returning for them. If they cannot hatch quickly they may float along for a considerable distance at the mercy of stream and fish. The slow rolling rise of a trout to blue winged olives is well known for this is a fly which is very widespread and one which hatches in great numbers in many waters. Some writers refer to the rise in the terms used by Skues, as being " kidney shaped ". I often wonder why, for this type of rise is not just characteristic of fish rising to this one type of insect. The same kind of rise is made to many others. In a way it is a rise which denotes the take of an insect which the fish know has no possibility of escape. In a way it is elongated, for often head, dorsal and tail of a fish will break through the water to make a queer shaped rise form. To me the sight of trout doing it has at times become maddening. Of all the nymphs of the ephemeroptera I think the blue winged olive incites a trout most urgently and if you care to study one as it is being carried along in the stream prior to hatching, the reason is plain to see. The nymphs rise to the surface in a series of undulating, jerky glides and when they reach it they make frantic efforts to hatch. It is less than true to say they wriggle, struggle is the right word for it, with legs and body performing all kinds of actions which cannot fail to attract notice. On some occasions the insects hatch quickly—almost the moment they reach the surface film—and take flight at once, but there are other times when, even though they break the nymphal skin, they just cannot shed it, and they float along with the shuck on their tails.

Though I have seen many thousands of river insects in the process of hatching from the nymph to the sub-imago or dun, it was not until quite recently that I was able to obtain positive proof as to how the transformation is carried out. I was examining a live mayfly nymph in water under the microscope when it decided to hatch, or to put it more clearly, to transpose to a sub-imago. Though I had done so much work with nymphs years ago I had never been sure how this metamorphosis took place and like many others before me had come to the conclusion that just prior to hatching, the nymphal envelope becomes loose and between it and the sub-imago integument there is certain air or gas. It was this I was studying at the time and wondering how the air could be obtained and how it could be secreted between the two skins. Knowledge of this looseness suggesting trapped air has been exploited many times in the construction of artificial wet-flies and nymphs and is often suggested with the employment of tinsels along the body. I had thought, as perhaps others had thought, that this air could be compressed by the insect at a time when it wanted to hatch and so bring about a fracture of the skin. Perhaps it does help in this way.

Though I was using a low magnification which enabled me to see the whole thorax and head of the mayfly, my focal point was on the thorax and just between the wing cases. Both wing cases began to swell suddenly as though from some exertion beneath and then a longitudinal split appeared in the nymphal shuck between them. The wings started to rise and to unfold and then I could see the front legs of the nymph being thrust downwards and the head of the fly coming up through the split. Moving quickly I lifted the hatching nymph with a pair of forceps and dropped it into a jar of formalin nearby. There it died immediately. Many times I had wanted to get an insect in the half-way stage of emergence, and at last I had it, with chances to carry out detailed examination at leisure.

Under a high-powered lens I made discoveries which interested me considerably. Through the loose and partially slipped shuck I could see all the appendages of the sub-imago, the six legs, the three setae and the antennae, with the wings still folded. Though I knew that the legs and setae of the sub-imago are much longer than in the nymphal form, I had thought these grew after the nymphal envelope had been shed. But here I discovered, in the short time which had elapsed between the start of the hatching and when I dropped the insect in formalin to kill it, that the legs and tails had extended telescopic fashion, and I could then see why. As all the appendages grew in length so they acted as levers to push the nymphal skin off. The semi hatched nymph had died with the body in a slightly arched position, the tail end bending downwards.

Here then is the secret of hatching which had remained hidden from me for so long and it explains what I had considered to be a mystery. It is the swelling wings which exert pressure to break the nymphal envelope, not air or gas, as I once thought. The front legs lengthen to push the shuck clear of the head, then simultaneously the other legs grow longer together with the tails, to lever the rest of the overcoat free. It was very obvious that the whole integument was quite loose and separated from the sub-imago. Though I have never witnessed the latter stage of hatching under magnification, I feel that in most cases these insects have little difficulty in withdrawing all appendages from their sheaths and so be completely free. Seeing the actual lengthening under the microscrope whilst the nymph was alive and then being able to make more leisurely observations on the dead creature was proof enough. But, to set my mind at rest and indeed to get more detailed information, I decided to measure the legs and setae of another mature nymph. I compared these measurements with those of the one I had killed before it could complete its metamorphosis. This was both interesting and enlightening, for the measurements confirmed my observations. The tails, or setae, had extended to three times as long, the hind legs had trebled, the middle pair were double and the front pair four times as long. A comparison afterwards of these measurements with a freshly-hatched mayfly showed them to be almost identical. The lengthening of all limbs and setae is done during the transformation.

As yet, I have not been able to confirm that the same thing happens with the smaller flies of the ephemeroptera. But as they all have a somewhat similar structure to the mayfly I think this must occur. The only insect I know which experiences some difficulty in the change from nymph to dun is the blue winged olive some of whose habits I have already described. Here I think the trouble is with the setae. In this insect dun, the fibres of the tail do not extend much beyond the length of the nymph, so that most of the leverage to free the shuck is exerted by the lengthening of the hinder pair of legs, once the head and wings are free. This might account for some of the struggling done by the nymph at the surface whilst hatching.

I think it possible too, that the lengthening of the appendages of a nymph when hatching to a fly, is governed to a large extent by the weather conditions. In cold or wet conditions the time taken in extending the limbs and the tail would be longer than in a dry and warm atmosphere. It would account for the fact that duns hatch and fly away much more quickly in dry, warm, weather, than when it is cold and wet.

Chapter Four

MORE ABOUT NYMPH IMITATION

Difference in size: Possibilities in simplification: More
species than patterns: Contrasts in colouration: Wire as
a basis: The effect of translucence: Business patterns and
some others.

NATURAL NYMPHS vary greatly in size according to genus and
species. Some, as for instance those of the caenis, are less than
one quarter of an inch in length from nose to the end of their
tails, while mature nymphs of the mayflies are at least one and
a quarter inches long. But the group of ephemeroptera with
which we shall be mostly concerned is of the families which
seldom exceed half an inch in length from nose to tail, and
therefore artificials to represent these can quite easily be fashioned on hooks no larger than No. 1. In making an artificial
nymph there are several important points to consider. First the
general appearance, shape, colouring and translucency. Secondly
it must be made to enter quickly without any addition afterwards to make it sink. Thirdly, and this is essential, so that it
can be cast both accurately and delicately as the occasion
demands.

I am basing my general nymph fishing technique and artificials on the period which follows mid-summer which I think
to be the most sporting time of year for this method. Therefore
I am considering only the natural insects which may form a
food supply for trout during these few weeks. This mid-season
fishing does therefore rule out a large number of the ephemeroptera as being suitable as representatives in the nymph box,

and leaves but two or three families whose nymphs are active throughout this period. It is members of the swimming group which then provide the main attraction for trout and grayling and during this time these are represented by five different families. These are pale wateries, olives, spurwings, pro-cloeon and cloeon. To most fishermen these names are familiar but it is possible that there could be some confusion over the name " spurwing ". These, of which there are two species, a large and small, may be better known as the small and large blue-winged pale watery, a name given to them by Skuès. It was after I had done considerable work in identifying these species in the Avon, and writing some papers about them, that the name " spurwing " was adopted to describe the genus, by Turing, who I have mentioned as being a late Editor of The Salmon and Trout Magazine. But actually from the point of view of artificial nymph construction, the name pale watery is better, for this conveys the fact that the creatures are somewhat similar in colouration, at least from the body angle, from which the name pale watery is derived. Cloeon can also be termed in the same context as having a pale watery body appearance, but the pro-cloeon has a body more of the shade of the olives. As I wrote in my foreword, the study, and the definition of river and lake insects, can be complex, for unless one is familiar with both the Latin and scientific names, and also the names given to the certain groups by fishermen, description is very hard to accomplish for the layman.

To some fishermen, the names of the insects the artificial fly or nymph represents, has little interest, to others it is important, so one has to strike a happy medium. At one time, as I think is the case with all who start making artificial flies and nymphs, I was obsessed with the idea of making exact copies of all the animals I thought might be taken by fish as a food, with the result that I had scores of different tyings, and indeed needed a considerable stock of materials to construct them. In all, to imitate the majority of the swimming nymphs which should be mature and active during the summer months one would need, in theory, about ten different artificials, all varying in sizes, and colouration. I made these, and tried them with some success on the fish, but gradually it became apparent that fish had a preference for one or another and, after a process of elimination, and a blending of materials from one into another, I found it was possible to reject the majority and concentrate on those which were consistently accepted. When I wrote the material for the first edition of " Nymphs and the Trout " I had already brought this system of elimination into operation and, in this, suggested but three different patterns, which I had proved to be effective. But since then I evolved one pattern to take the place of two of these, and so simplified things even more. This pattern, which I christened The Grey Goose, is a blending of dressings to bring about a general representation of the pale wateries, in which group is included the spurwings, and the cloeon. Whether or not it is accepted by trout in mistake for one, or for all, is of course, impossible for me to say, but of this I am confident, when such creatures are hatching in quantities, together, or as a single species, the grey goose artificial is attractive. This same pattern, tied in various sizes from oo to size 1 can meet the requirements at all times when the pale watery group is hatching or active. The general shape and colouration conforms very well with that of the natural insects as viewed by fish. The size of the different species is taken care of by the different length of hooks.

My pheasant tail pattern which had become so well known as a " Sawyer Nymph " needed no alteration. This pattern has been proved everywhere throughout the world and will, I feel sure, continue to hold pride of place as an effective artificial. This I evolved to represent the trout's view of the several olive nymphs which are active during the summer months. It incorporates the pro-cloeon as well as having some semblance to the nymphs of the iron blue, the nymphs of which are mostly active in the spring and autumn, though a few might be taken during the summer. I feel the success of the pheasant tail is indeed due to the fact that it might well, in the different sizes, be mistaken by fish, for one or another of at least a dozen nymphs, of various genus and species. As I have mentioned earlier, simplicity is an aim to be desired. There is enough confusion as it is with many things to do with fishing, and it is not my desire to add more.

Perhaps you will have noted the phrases I have used to convey the fact that the patterns have been constructed from what I

think is the view of the fish, and not that of the human. Though
I give full credit to fish in being able to differentiate between
general colours and sizes, I am quite sure that in the brief time
they have in between seeing, and taking an artificial, it is not
possible for them to see a mixture of several different materials.
What is more I came to the conclusion many years ago that they
see colours in a different way than we do ourselves. This of
course is something impossible to prove. The red of the pheasant
tail body and wire tying that I use could not possibly be mistaken
by us for an olive, or greenish yellow colouring. Yet fish take it
readily when creatures with this latter colouring are hatching.
Much the same thing with the grey goose. It is not an exact
copy in colouring, as we know it, but fish are deceived by it. For
many years I have used cock pheasant tail fibres for the bodies
of mayflies with a red cock's hackle to represent legs and wings.
This has no resemblance whatsoever to the colouring of a mayfly
as we see it, but it brings fish far more readily than many artificials which have been dressed as seen by the human.

I have made these points simply because you might think the
materials used in the construction of my nymphs are somewhat
at variance with the general colouration of the natural insects.
This is quite true, and I hope my explanation is sufficient. I
have constructed from the trout's point of view, and not from
my own, as regards colour. In all other respects the tyings are
based on my own observations. You will note that none of my
patterns have anything included in the dressing to suggest legs.
When swimming nymphs are indeed swimming, they do so with
the legs tucked in closely to the body, to, in fact, bring about a
streamlined effect. The tail is the propulsion unit with these
insects, which acts to propel, and also to steer. Some of the
naturals, as for example the "spurwings", are better equipped
than others in this respect, and in consequence can move more
freely through the water. The tail of an artificial nymph is therefore a desirable feature, but not completely essential, because I
have caught many fish after the tails have been broken off and
only the body has been left.

Now as to the dressings. The materials used are quite easy for
most, who are interested, to obtain. To represent the olives etc,
my pattern of the pheasant tail can be constructed on three

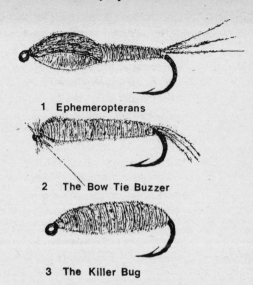

1 Ephemeropterans

2 The Bow Tie Buzzer

3 The Killer Bug

SAWYER PATTERNS FOR ARTIFICIALS

different hook sizes, No. oo, No. o and No. 1, and I make no claim that the use of pheasant tail fibres for a body of nymphs, or flies, is original. But what I do claim is the manner of base building, ballasting, and the tying in of the pheasant tail fibres, with fine copper wire, of a colouring to suit and tone in with the general dressing. Artificial nymphs tied in my way are not difficult to make, and the simple instructions I am able to give should be sufficient for anyone with nimble fingers, to follow. First grip the selected hook firmly in the vice and then give the hook an even covering from bend to eye with fine red-coloured copper wire. The wire we use is little thicker than a human hair and this one can obtain at little cost from various sources. It is used for the windings in small transformers, dynamos, or electric motors. After the hook has been covered and the wire locked so that it cannot spin around the hook shank, wind the wire in even turns to the point where the thorax of the nymph is to be constructed, and there build up a hump. Then wind the wire back to the hook bend and let it dangle. Wire is much easier to use than silk as it will not spin off or loosen if the tension is relaxed.

The wire with its red colour forms the base for the dressing and at the same time gives additional weight to the hook. I dispense entirely with the use of silk and use the fine wire to tie in the dressing. The wire is now dangling from the hook bend. Take four centre fibres of a browny-red cock pheasant tail feather. Hold the fibres by their tips and then tie them on with the wire so that the fine ends stand out about one eighth of an inch from the hook bend. They form the tails, or setae of the nymph. Then spin the four fibres of the pheasant tail on to the wire so that they are reinforced, and then lap fibres and wire evenly to the hook eye. Hold the wire firmly, separate the fibres from it and then wind the wire to the point behind which the thorax is to be made. Bend the fibres back and fasten for the first lap of the thorax, then forward to the eye of the hook again. Fasten here securely with half a dozen turns of wire and then cut away spare fibres.

Our finished effort should have a very pronounced thorax which suggests the bulging wing cases, and a body which tapers neatly to the tail. With the tail fibres spread, all is complete.

It will be noted by those who follow these instructions that the upper part of the thorax which imitates the wing cases, is much darker than the rest of the body. This is brought about by the lapping back and forth of the butt ends of the pheasant tail fibres. If wire and fibres are wound evenly on the hook, the spare ends should have the dark tone which is a feature in the butts of these fibres. This gives a very natural appearance to the thorax. The fibres of pheasant tail vary in length, and indeed texture, from the butt of the feather to the tip, so when dressing a nymph one can select lengths most suitable for the size of the hook, bearing in mind that when the body is made, the dark part is ready to use for lapping.

When wet this pattern has a translucent effect and one can see the red of the wire showing through the pheasant tail fibres. The artificial, so constructed, has a very good entry to water and will sink deeply when required. The hook point is not muffled or guarded in any way by hackles or by the dressing, and a slight lift of the rod will drive it home.

My second pattern, is as I have mentioned, to represent the pale wateries. This also is of simple construction and should be made in three different sizes as suggested for the P.T., No. oo, No. o and No. 1. I use fine copper wire in the construction of all my nymphs but use different colours according to the demand. For the base of this pattern The Grey Goose, I use a golden coloured wire and also this same colour for tying in the dressing. For the tails, and the body and thorax, I use herls from the wing feather of the ordinary farmyard grey goose. Only a few of the wing feathers are suitable and only the parts of these which have a lightish grey, green, yellowish appearance. The construction is somewhat similar to that of the pheasant tail. Take out four herls from the wing feather, tie these in so that the tips can form the setae for the nymph, and then dress in the same manner as with the P.T. At the butt end of the herls the colouring is darker, as with the pheasant tail fibres and this, lapped backwards and forwards, can bring about a well defined thorax and wing cases. As with the first artificial, the colour of the wire is one of the features. The gold shows through the dressing and is very marked, at the head end.

Both of these dressings change their general colouring when wet.

These then are what I would like to call my two business patterns for use in the chalk streams and other waters where there is an abundance of the kind of nymphs I have mentioned, but in Chapter 21 I have mentioned the construction of a nymph when fishing in north Sweden. This we still dress for I have found that a smaller version of it is very effective in the lakes and reservoirs in the British Isles. This as I have mentioned was christened the S.S. and the name has continued. It is tied on size 3 and 4 hooks. Originally it was called a grey goose, but I have no wish to confuse this with the one evolved to represent the pale wateries. It is true the basic dressing of the S.S. is of herls from the grey goose wing feathers, but these are all of a much darker shade, of those actually, which come from the primary wing feathers. The Grey Goose herls are from the secondaries. The construction of this is much the same as with the grey goose, the difference being that a dark red wire is used instead of gold. In sizes No. 1 and No. 2 this pattern is taken very readily when the claret dun is appearing in the stillwaters.

I now come to the dressing of what has come to be known as the Killer Bug. This, as I have mentioned elsewhere, was a

name given to it by an American friend. I devised this originally to kill grayling in the upper Avon but in later years found
it to be very effective when fished for trout in reservoirs and
lakes. Also in a much larger version for salmon, and sea trout.

Once again this is of very simple construction, so simple
indeed that anyone looking at it could be forgiven for thinking
it could not possibly deceive a fish. These we construct in sizes
varying according to the requirements, from sizes No. 3, No. 4,
5 and 6 for lake and sea trout, to others on hooks of size 8 and
10 for use after salmon. Generally however it is the former, and
smaller sizes, which are in greatest demand.

To make this bug, grip the hook firmly in the vice and then
give the hook a double even covering of wire, colour of this not
important but normally we now use red. This can be much
heavier wire than used in the construction of the nymphs. When
the double covering has been done leave the wire dangling at
hook bend. Then start at the eye end of the hook and lap in
securely a length of wool. The colour and the texture of this is
important. I call it wool, but actually it is a mixture of wool and
nylon, produced and carded for mending purposes. The manufacturers of this product give their name as Chadwicks and they
list the colour as being 477. Actually it is a natural and not very
easy to obtain. However this is by the way. After locking in the
end of the wool, give an even winding to the hook bend, back to
the eye, and then once more to the hook bend, so that in fact the
base is covered with a triple layer. Then, holding the wool
tightly, use the wire to tie it in securely at the hook bend with
about four turns. Then cut off both wool and wire neatly. The
colour of this bug changes completely when it is wet and I feel
sure it is this, that causes its attraction for so many kinds of
fish. Though I have constructed these bugs with many other
colours of wool, none have been so effective. More detail of the
Killer Bug and the way it is fished will be in the Chapters on
grayling and lake fishing.

I now come to the last of my creations and the manner of its
tying and arrangement. Though I made this some years ago I
did not consider the pattern had received sufficient testing until
quite recently. It is constructed and arranged to meet the
requirements of lake fishermen mostly, or for use in waters

where the big chironomids known to so many fishermen as
" buzzers " may be found in quantity. The excited rise of fish,
especially brown trout and rainbow trout, when this class of
creature is hatching, is so well known, that I need dwell but
briefly on it. Sufficient to say that when the fish are really set
on taking the hatching larvae, it has been extremely difficult to
interest them in artificial flies, nymphs, or lures. It is not so much
that there is difficulty in making copies of these buzzer nymphs,
or larvae, for this is fairly easy. The difficulty has been in how
to arrange the construction and the way it is fished, so that it
can conform closely to what is expected to be seen by the trout.
This I think I have at last accomplished, and it is my pleasure to
introduce what has been christened the " *Bow-tie Buzzer* ". This
was a name given to it by one of my friends who fished it in
some of the big reservoirs in the West Country of which I will
be writing later. I think the name is descriptive, and likely to
remain in the minds of fishermen. As I have written, it has taken
me several years to arrive at the conclusion I have now reached.
During this time I made a lot of study of the habits of these big
chironomids, especially during the very last stage which is when
they hatch into winged insects. They have a manner characteristic of all gnats and midges in the order of Chironomidae when
moving through water from place to place, or when hatching.
It is hardly true to say they swim, for the movement through the
water is brought about by a series of contractions of the body,
a kind of looping along, when tail and head are brought together
and then spread out again.

There are times when the creature will spin completely
around, and times when it can hang motionless excepting for a
movement of the cilia, or fringes of fine hairs, which is at the
head, and which indeed is an important feature when considering imitation. When changing to the perfect insect, these buzzers
rise in their looping manner to the surface, sometimes from very
deep down, for they can live in varying depths of water, sometimes in water very deep. When at the surface they spread their
celia, and sometimes also the appendages at the tail end, and
hold themselves in the surface film. The actual hatching is not
unlike the metamorphosis of the mayfly previously described. The
shuck splits between the wing cases and the long legs thrust it

clear. The legs of this creature are contained within the shuck which envelops the whole body and cannot be seen as free limbs until after hatching has taken place. It is whilst hanging in the surface film, or whilst being suspended in the water beneath it, that these buzzer nymphs are so attractive to the fish. The looping, spinning, and general struggling at the surface when hatching, shows almost continuous movement, which can be easily seen by fish from a long distance. But these fish know there is no real hurry to take and they do so in a most leisurely manner with a rise form not unlike that adopted when trout are taking the blue winged olives. One feature is the continuous buzzing or movement of the celia which is a fringe of minute white hairs at the head. These are never really still.

In the last stage just before hatching, these larvae or nymphs, have a very translucent appearance, similar I think, to the nymphs of the ephemeroptera.and caused by the looseness of the nymphal envelope, and with these chironomids there is importance in taking this into account when constructing an artificial. These big gnats, though all called buzzers, can vary in colouration, the majority are of a browny-reddish-yellow, but some are mostly green, with others almost black. Whether this is due to types, or to environment, I cannot say. There are a very large number of species of chironomids but these three colours are the major ones to keep in mind when dressing artificials.

The pattern I am about to describe is a representation of the browny coloured one which effect is brought about by a mixture of red and yellow. For this I use but one hook size. This is size No. 3. Grip the hook firmly in the vice and then, using a fine gold coloured copper wire, spin on a single even layer along the hook from eye to bend and leave the wire dangling. Then tie in a strip of silver foil, or tinsel and spin this evenly on the hook up to just behind the eye. Fasten and cut the remainder free. Then select four or five fibres of red cock pheasant tail. Tie these in so that the fine ends can act as a short tail. Then wind fibres and wire together in neat spacings which show the foil in ribs, to the hook eye and there extra windings can be done to form the thorax. Fasten in securely with three or four turns of wire and the tying is complete. The red feather, gold wire and silver base all blend to give the right colouring and translucency. But

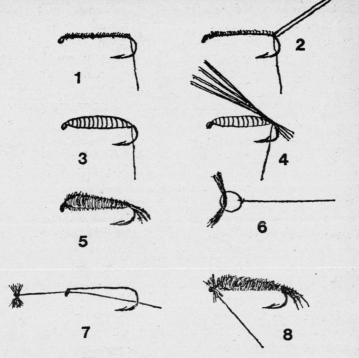

CONSTRUCTION OF THE BOW-TIE BUZZER

this is only the first part. Though the actual nymph is constructed one of the main features is missing. This is the white fringe, or celia

I tried incorporating this in dressings but without much success until I hit on the idea of making it entirely separate. I knew it to be important, very important, that some kind of movement could be simulated and so instead of tying in a white fringe at the head of my nymph, I arranged it so this could be carried on the end of the leader, or cast. It is very simple really. All one needs to do is to thread the nylon point through the eye of the hook, make a slip knot in it, and then attach a tiny piece of white nylon wool. This can then be cut down to the correct size with a pair of sharp scissors and if knot and nylon is quite secure, it cannot be pulled through the hook eye.

I always use down eyed hooks on which to tie my nymphs and it is the same with the buzzer, but in threading this on to the nylon point of the leader, I do this up, instead of down, as I do normally when threading on the usual nymphs and flies. This is so that when the knot, and the tiny piece of white nylon, is drawn into position, it sits in the eye of the hook, at the top of the head. And it serves a second important purpose. When hanging in the film of the surface or just beneath it, these buzzers are mostly vertical and so, when cast correctly, the artificial does this too. But a third and equally important feature in this arrangement is that the nymph can move very freely on the leader, it can in fact spin around the cast if a slight draw on the line is made, and in this way, give a definite movement, and one which is quickly sighted by fish. The loose fringe to represent the celia will also move in a very attractive manner, even when the actual nymph is hung stationary. And so a combination of almost everything is accomplished. All it means is that one has to carry a short length of white nylon separately. The actual arranging of this takes no longer than in knotting on a fly or nymph, in the usual manner. Some experiences in the manner of fishing the buzzer will be given in later chapters.

I have found, when armed with the five patterns of nymphs etc., that I have been able to take fish in every water I have been privileged to fish. In the lakes and big reservoirs I have had far greater pleasure with these small creations than ever I have got when fishing lures. It is nice to think fish take the artificials for what they are supposed to represent, but of this it is of course impossible to be certain.

All the above patterns may be obtained through my wife at our address: Mrs. M. O. Sawyer, 325 Lower Street, Haxton, Nr. Netheravon, Salisbury, Wiltshire.

Chapter Five

PROBLEMS OF FAST WATER

Factors of flow and weed : The vulnerability of " bulging "
fish : The need for keeping contact : The upstream pre-
requisite : Hatches from weed-beds : A lesson for fishery
managers.

THOUGH, GENERALLY speaking, it is possible to find nymphs of all
types in a given reach of water, the habits of the families differ
considerably. Olives and pale wateries, both of the order Baetis,
prefer the shallow, well-aerated parts of the river and seldom
are to be found in any great numbers in water which exceeds
three feet in depth. On the other hand spurwings, cloeon and
pro-cloeon like the deeper, slower-moving water and all thrive
best during drought years, when in fact the temperature of the
water is higher than normal. Olive nymphs and wateries live
almost everywhere about the shallows in the gravel, on the
gravel and also in and on the various types of vegetation. They
favour ranunculus mostly and always great numbers are to be
found in the short young growths at the upstream ends of the
weed-beds. In this respect they are like their cousins the darker
olives of spring and like the iron blues, all of which belong to
the Baetis group. But whereas the spring nymphs have the
opportunity to crawl to the surface on the trailing fronds of the
ranunculus the summer insects for the most part have to swim.
The fronds of the ranunculus have rotted away and in moving
from the short young growths on the river-bed to the surface
these summer nymphs give the fish a better chance to take
them.

Trout are often seen rushing about, " bulging ", and at times apparently rising, while on a weed-bed. And there are other occasions when the fish are tailing—routing into the short weed growths to find nymphs clinging there. You see part of the tail above the surface, sometimes waving, sometimes still. Then on occasions the fish will make a rush to one side or the other to leave a bow wave plain for all to see. Usually it is olives which these fish are after. Many writers have said tailing fish cannot be caught. This I have disproved time and time again. Tailing trout are looking for insects in the weed-beds. Their eyes are searching for movement in or very near the vegetation. It is useless to try to tempt these fish with a dry-fly or with a nymph which floats above them. I have tied my artificials so that they will sink quickly and have found, if I drop the nymph just upstream of a tailing fish, let it sink to the weeds just in front of his nose, then it has the necessary attraction.

Catching trout with nymphs in fast running water is far more difficult than in the smoother meandering types. Trout take artificials very well in the faster water but the fisherman is handicapped in various ways and here I think the full art of the nymph fisherman is called into play. Firstly, it is far more difficult to see a feeding trout in the turbulence; secondly, it is not easy to watch the floating cast and, thirdly, the hand which controls the line has much work to do in gathering the slack to keep the remainder straight.

Of the three points raised the last-named is of most importance, for when fishing upstream, unless one can keep in immediate touch with the nymph, then the hooking of fish becomes extremely difficult. Fast water is, of course, ideal for wet-fly fishing when a team of flies can be cast across and then allowed to swing downstream and play across the current. One has a tight line all the time and in the majority of cases when a fair-sized trout takes, he hooks himself. If not, the slightest twitch of the rod tip will set the barb. However, wet-fly fishing and nymph fishing are two different arts. Downstream nymph is never very profitable and one can get far more enjoyment and satisfaction by fishing in the proper way.

When fishing upstream in fast water one should give continued thought to the habits of the natural insects and to the trout's point of view. An artificial can then be presented so as to raise no suspicion. Always you find the best trout at the tail of a run—in position where the insects converge into one narrow current and where, at the point selected, the trout can have the best chance of securing prey without having to exert energy in moving far to either side.

Just, for example, imagine a part of a river where there is a good fall in level and the water is speedy. The surface is rippled and broken as the water passes over the uneven bed. Here and there across the shallow, one can see places where currents converge into narrow runs. Perhaps the water is passing between weed-beds or boulders—perhaps the bed is ditched and deeper, perhaps an outcrop from the bank, a root or a tree stump, directs the water into a kind of funnel. Into this funnel the insects are swept as they are caught in the stream and there the trout waits patiently. As you crouch down and watch, there shows the gleam of a silver side, a flash of white as the jaws open and close, a boil near the surface or perhaps a head showing above the water as a floating insect is taken. You have marked your fish and it is certain that in that spot he will remain until he has finished feeding, or until he has been frightened.

Upstream the nymphs are active. Hatching time is near. As they leave perches on weeds or gravel so they are caught in the fast moving water and are swept along in a gradually converging lane to the fish waiting at the narrowest point of the funnel below. His eyes are concentrated on that one place where the helpless nymphs are sweeping along and if you want to catch him that is where your artificial also must be. It is useless to attack such a fish as this anywhere than from below. If you cast across the current the artificial keeps near to the surface and immediately is swept to one side. A trout seeing this happen becomes suspicious at once. He knows it just is not possible for an insect to swim across fast water. If you approach him from upstream a similar suspicion is aroused, the trout sees the nymph as it hangs in the current and knows at once that something is wrong, for nymphs cannot battle against such a stream as this. The only possible way is to throw the nymph upstream and into the centre of the run so that it can sink quickly and so that the water can carry it in a natural manner to your would-be victim.

That is how it should be done. All very easy to write, but in practice it is not so simple.

On a mayfly river one often sees the multitude of nymph shucks which float downstream after every hatch of fly. Unless you look very closely it is very difficult to tell whether some of them are just shucks or if indeed they are nymphs floating along in the surface film. Many people say they have seen trout rising and taking empty shucks. Not having seen this myself I am inclined to be doubtful, as generally speaking I feel sure a fish has sufficient good sense to know the nymphal envelopes are of no food value. However, I have mentioned mayflies merely as an example. The majority of insects which hatch from water do so only after casting a skin and this skin, or shuck, is sufficiently buoyant to float.

Mayfly shucks are easy to see, yet amongst them, if you care to look closely, are the nymphal overcoats of smaller insects all being carried along in the current. During the summer months there may be shucks from several different types of fly, all small, of course, and with these it is even more difficult to ascertain if the shuck is full or empty. If it is full, of course, it cannot be a shuck. But I would feel highly delighted if I could evolve an artificial which would appear before me exactly as an empty nymph skin does in the water, for immediately I would say— here is a nymph pattern no trout could resist. But would a fish show the slightest interest, I wonder, if I fished it in the surface film and allowed it to drift without other movement than that imparted by the current? I am quite certain that no sensible trout would give it any more attention than he does to the scores of shucks which pass over him continuously.

Our point of view of a nymph is from above. We look on to the backs of the shucks and on nymphs, with the darkness of the river-bed as a background. Therefore, unless we are very close, small movements go unnoticed. But the trout are looking upwards towards the sky where shuck or live creature is clearly defined, and so the slightest sign of life is plain for them to see. You may, perhaps, think I have been a long way round to get to my point. Well here it is. Elsewhere I have made reference to Nymph Fishing for Chalk Stream Trout, by G. E. M. Skues. I so do again. In it he writes of nymphs floating inertly in the

surface film. By inertly I interpret the meaning to be without
movement and never yet have I seen a live nymph floating in
the film without seeing some movement of legs and body. A
movement quite sufficient to attract the eyes of a feeding trout.

Seldom have I been successful in trying to interest trout with
nymph patterns which float semi-submerged—just awash so to
speak. Perhaps Mr. Skues' success with the inert nymph, as he
calls it, was due to the fact that he constructed his nymphs in
a manner very similar to the way I make my dry flies. All his
artificials are hackled—have fibres which suggest legs. As they
float near the surface there is a certain movement of the fibres
even as there is with a sparsely-hackled dry-fly.

When weed-growths are extensive, most of the nymphs have
the habit of using the long trailing fronds as a means by which
they can crawl to the surface to hatch. Many times I have seen
really good hatches of fly coming away from a big weed-bed,
yet, except for the occasional trout sucking off nymphs from the
weed stalks in some inaccessible position, no fish have been on
the move. It might have been quite different. These fly were
hatching. They were ready to hatch and had all the tops of the
weed been cut away then many of them would have floated on
the surface for a few moments and, in doing so, would have
attracted a few trout out into the open to feed. This hatching of
flies from weed-beds is a point well worth considering when
weed-cutting or trimming out. We have to remember that these
insects hatch merely to complete their life-cycle—to mate and
to lay eggs. Even as they do their utmost to avoid being eaten
while in their subaqueous stages, so also do they try to hatch
without floating longer than they need upon the water.

This is just the instinct of self-preservation and I feel sure
these insects know of the danger they run in staying too long on
the river surface. Therefore, if given the opportunity, the
nymphs creep unobtrusively up the weed stems to break the
surface, and there they hatch into duns while perched in
security. Trout have little chance to see them and none at all to
take. I have mentioned the possibility that these insects know
of the danger lurking beneath the surface. There must have been
times when you have been waiting for a trout to rise; one of
those days, perhaps, when the hatch of fly has been sparse. And

I expect you have watched flies drifting downstream and then, just as you expected the fish to rise and take, the creatures have taken flight. I have seen this kind of thing happen often enough to be almost positive that it is not just coincidence—that in fact the insects have seen, or sensed, the fish waiting in its feeding position. They fly away in an endeavour to escape destruction.

When arranging the river for fishing I have tried many ways to cut weeds to suit all purposes, and at last I have come to the conclusion that one cannot improve the old idea of leaving bars across the river providing, that is, that the long trailers are cut off well beneath the surface. Between the bars, the river-bed can be cut cleanly, and if possible the gravel kept free of all mud. For instance, on a shallow which has a fair fall in level, a series of weed-beds can be left in bars with about fifty yards of clean, open water between them. Each bar should not be more than fifteen feet in width. In this way one can create ideal conditions for fly life. They can live and thrive in the short well-aerated growths and when it comes to hatching time the fish are given a chance to take both the hatching nymphs and the duns. The fisherman has also been considered. If he does manage to hook a fish he has a very fair chance to land it in the open water between the bars.

At one time, we tried leaving weeds in long strips down the centre of our water on the Avon, actually cutting two-thirds and leaving the remainder down the middle. Other shallows we formed into runs of perhaps five or six feet wide. These looked very nice, because each carried a fast stream of water. But the great trouble was that, though good strong currents were provided, all the fly hatched from the strips of weed we left and the runs only fished well when spinners were falling.

Then other points became apparent. Those long strips were almost useless for fly production. As I examined them I found larvae and nymphs in abundance at the up-stream ends, where in fact the weed-growths were well aerated, but these gradually petered out to almost nil after about fifty feet, what was more, the long strips of uncut weed acted as mud traps and in a very short time the gravel silted up. Though fish rose very well in the runs to spent spinners many a good fish was lost after being well hooked, for when fishing a midstream run, unless one takes immediate action to hold up a trout's head after hooking it, the chances are that he will turn into the weeds and there become entangled. Even if you free him from one place he still has to be taken downstream and, often enough, you have to admit defeat.

Chapter Six

NYMPHS, FISH AND FISHERMAN

A chain-reaction under water : A rhythm of activity before
hatching : Why trout " go off the feed " : Finding takeable
fish : An example near home : Some others from the French
chalk streams.

WHEN THE change from nymph to dun is only a few hours away
the insects stop feeding, and sometimes are quite content to rest
for long periods without moving from a selected position. While
they are doing this the trout have little interest. But there are
occasions when these periods of rest are broken by times of
violent activity.

Perhaps the creatures become impatient while waiting for
conditions which are satisfactory for them to leave the water.
Atmospherics may play a big part, for quite suddenly the insects
will awaken from a kind of stupor and a mass movement takes
place. The mature nymphs flit from weed-bed to weed-bed, some
rise to the surface and float downstream for long distances in
the surface film, while still more rise from the river-bed and
swim about like tiny fish. Then, just as suddenly as they com-
menced, the movements stop. All nymphs cling tightly to their
perches and there remain until a similar impulse starts off a
mass movement once more.

Trout have more knowledge of the habits of the creatures
than man can ever hope to gain. While a movement of nymphs
is taking place the fish are alert and feeding, but when the
insects decide to rest so also do the trout. Thus there are days
when, for a while, trout appear near to the surface. Then sud-

denly they go down for no reason that is obvious to us on the
bank. Flies may be floating over the position occasionally and be
disregarded because at the time the trout has little interest in
anything on the surface, his thoughts being concentrated on
what is happening below. Down he goes to the bottom, there
to wait until the nymphs become restless again. He may stay
there but a few moments, or it might be for an hour or more.
If we want to catch him we also must wait our chance.

Much of course must depend on the depth of the water and
whether it is sufficiently clear to be able to watch what is happening. If a fish is in shallow water, of a depth of up to 18in.,
he can still be attracted to an artificial provided the nymph is
fished so that it sinks down to within a few inches of his nose.
In the deeper water it pays to wait until the fish has lifted once
more from the river-bed, and is on the fin again, near to the
surface. During the hot days in July and August the nymphs
mostly wait until the cool of late evening before hatching into
flies, and usually it is during the preceding hours from about
midday that the periods of restlessness occur. It is quite
impossible to give a true answer to the problem as to why they
become so agitated. It might be that the creatures are preparing
for eclosion by loosening their nymphal skins, and that this can
only be accomplished by occasional violent exertions. Why they
all choose to do it at a given time and for a certain period is
something I cannot understand. All I can say with certainty is
that when the nymphs become active trout will feed and when
trout feed the nymph fisherman has his chance.

When you know something of the habits of nymphs it gives
a clue as to where you can expect to find a feeding fish. In a
rise to duns, a fish gives away his position by breaking the surface
periodically; in fact one can see the floating flies disappear into
a hollow in the water. But a trout can and will feed greedily for
considerable periods on underwater food, without making any
disturbance at the surface at all. I well remember an afternoon
in late July. As I walked along the left bank of a deep, slow-
running reach I saw trout after trout, each in a small pocket
amongst the weed-fronds. There they were, about a foot or so
beneath the surface, and each was on the feed. I watched two
of them move first to one side then to the other, and could see

their mouths open and shut as each unlucky insect was secured. Nothing was hurried about their movements, and, with a passing thought that they were taking mature nymphs I went on downstream. Neither of these fish had risen. By this I mean neither of them had broken the surface, and had a fisherman been sitting watching the water in the hope of getting a trout with a dry fly I feel sure he would have said there was not a feeding fish in the reach.

As it happened there was a fisherman doing exactly that. As I rounded a bend, there on the opposite bank one of our members was sitting with a rather forlorn expression on his face. The sun was blazing from a clear blue sky and not a breath of wind stirred the surface of the water. He looked tired and hot and even as I asked the question, I knew what the answer would be. No, he hadn't done any good. Only an odd fish had moved since lunch. I told him of those I had seen upstream. Could he fish a nymph? No, he had never tried and he had no nymphs with him. Would he care to try if I got some artificials? He answered that he was eager to.

My house was quite near and in a few moments I fetched a few patterns and joined him on his side of the river. The trout, I felt sure, were taking the small spurwing, and, after adding an extra 4 x point to his cast, I tied on an imitation. Together we moved upstream and came opposite to where I had noticed the lowermost fish. His position was near to the other bank in a tiny pocket of open water about the size of a table top. But the light from that side was different and try as I would, I could see no sign of the trout. My companion looked sceptical when I told him I felt sure the fish was there and on the feed, and I know it was only half-heartedly that he threw the nymph into the pocket as I suggested he should do. The nymph had sunk but a few inches when I saw the floating cast draw slightly under. " Yes ", I said involuntarily. But he made no move to lift his rod. There came a twitch of the cast and line and that was that. He saw the line twitch and tightened hurriedly, but too late.

It was my fault, I should have told him what to expect. We moved upstream to the next fish, a matter of about twenty yards. The position of this trout was very similar to the previous one, just a small pocket amongst the weed fronds. It was near the middle of the river and I could just discern the fish as it lay poised in the water. I tried hard to get my companion to see it, but he could not. " Here, you take the rod and show me how it should be done." But I refused his offer. " No, you try again," I replied, " and if I say ' yes ', you tighten, and at once." He could throw a good line and the nymph pitched gently and accurately into the pocket. The fish moved forward and I saw a gleam of white as his jaws opened and shut. Again came my " Yes ", and this time the reaction was instant. Home went the hook. The fish was on. I'stayed with him for about an hour and in that time he took two brace of sizeable trout and lost two others which were also good ones. When I met him a week or so later he told me he had caught another later and that the afternoon had been one of the most enjoyable he had ever spent.

There is a saying that they order some things better in France. The feeding habits of trout are not among them. For the dry-fly fisherman there are periods of apparent inaction there as here, when no rising fish breaks the surface, and all activity takes place beneath it. Thanks to M. Charles Ritz I was able to try out on two chalk streams in Normandy the ways of fishing the nymphs which I have learned on my native Avon. He took me to the water of M. Verne on the Risle.

Monsier Lambiotte another of my hosts was outside the door of the rod room as M. Ritz and I reached the house, and to my delight, on catching sight of each other, these two old friends started shouting and waving like a couple of excited schoolboys. My heart warmed at once. If these two distinguished men could so far forget themselves in their joy at going fishing together again, then I had no need to worry. Both were as eager as I to be on the river and we soon had our rods ready. My ordeal had still to come. These fishermen wanted to see me take trout with nymphs, and my thoughts were in a whirl as I walked with them along the bank. M. Verne, would join us next day.

The Risle is a chalk stream and said to be the best in France, famed like our Test in Hampshire. Indeed, it is as broad there at Valleville as the Test below Romsey or the Avon at Christchurch, and beautifully clear. For the time of year there was considerable flow of water, far more than in any of our rivers

in October. The Risle Valley is wide, again something like our
Test, and the scenery everywhere is wonderful. Conifers grow
on the hillsides on either side of the valley, sweeping up and up
to the great plateaux high above. On the lower ground are
thousands of fruit trees—apples, pears and peaches.

Few flies were hatching and it was some time before I saw
the first rise—and the fish was only a little one. We wandered
about, each looking for a rising fish, and then, right out in mid-
stream, in one of the widest parts, which I later found was the
very famous Acclou reach mentioned in Charles Ritz's book, I
saw the head of a decent-sized trout show for a moment above
the water. It rose again in the same place, and then I knew
that here was a chance to catch my first trout in Normandy. I
cast my nymph, conscious that the others were watching, and
quick as a flash the fish took it. That trout took even faster than
a small grayling in the Avon, so I tightened in rather a hurry
and then got the thrill I always feel when the hook goes home
to stay. Soon afterwards the keeper netted him, a trout of just
over a pound.

Here was my first fish from Normandy and a really beautiful
one it was; deep and fat, with a small head, curiously humped
shoulders and bronze with big dark red spots along its sides.
Shortly afterwards I got another and, lovely as was the first, this
was a real beauty. I was then quite prepared for the quick take
and for the fight these fish put up. The second took twenty yards
of line out in one mad rush, and as he made a mad plunge and
swirl at the end of his run, I thought I had hooked a fish of
3 or 4 lb. He fought well and deep after this, and then I was
surprised to find he was only a two-pounder. This fish also had
the curious, humped back, which I can only think is developed
to withstand the fast water.

Next morning little was doing on the river. I took three small
trout and a chub, of which there are many in the Risle—some
big ones, too, up to 6 or 7 lb. The French also have far too many
of my old enemies, the pike, some up to 30 lb. I suspect. I spent
some time amongst the weed-beds and grubbing in the river-
bed. The main food of the trout seems to be snails and shrimps.
Usually where there are plenty of snails there are few small
flies, and it was the same here. I would say that more insects are

to be found in half a mile of the upper Avon than in five miles of the Risle, although the Risle is twice as big.

That afternoon, after a lunch which made me feel at peace with all the world, we went fishing again. I took three more trout and thus, I think, firmly convinced my hosts that, when the right pattern is fished in the right way, nymph fishing can give good sport when a dry-fly is unproductive. Two of these trout had disregarded M. Lambiotte's best presentation with dry flies, and he and M. Ritz were delighted to see me take them, one after the other, on my nymphs. M. Vernes told me of a trout, a good fish he said, which he wanted me to catch. To its haunts we went. Sure enough a fish was rising there occasionally. He was cruising about an eddy under the far bank and it meant a cast of well over twenty yards. It was a hopeless place for a dry fly, for there was a stream of fast water in the middle. But with a nymph—well, it might be done. I studied the position for a few moments and then started to fish. Three times I threw the nymph and placed it as I thought, accurately, and then even as I was beginning to despair, there came the moment I expected.

The floating cast was drawn gently beneath the surface. I lifted the rod gently but firmly and my heart gave a leap. It was a good fish, another humped backed beauty of just over $1\frac{1}{2}$ lb., and after an exciting three or four minutes I had him on the bank.

Next we went to fish the Andelle at Radepont, which meant a journey of about sixty miles. The window of my room in the little fishing Château commanded a view of one of the streams through the park and this ran so close to the house that one could throw a fly on to it from a downstairs window. M. Lambiotte told me that when he had General Bedell Smith, the American Ambassador to Moscow, staying with him as a guest, he looked out of his window upstairs one morning, just after dawn, to see the General outside this lower window in the wet grass, in his pyjamas, casting for a fish which apparently he had been unable to reach from his bedroom.

Soon we had our rods ready. Few flies were hatching and we wandered along for some distance before we saw the first rise. I got this fish with my second cast but it proved to be a small one. Then, from a view beneath an overhanging branch of a chestnut tree, I saw the rise of a good fish in a backwater, a place where the water whirled away from a pool to strike the roots of the tree and so make an eddy. It was an ideal place for a good trout. My hosts watched as I cast, once, twice, three times, but nothing happened. Then the fish rose again quite ten feet farther upstream from where I saw his first rise. Then his nose appeared again, a bit nearer to me, and I knew then why I had failed to interest him in my nymph. This fish was cruising round and round the backwater, looking all over the eddy for flies and hatching nymphs. I had been casting my nymph behind him. I said as much to my friends and waited a moment or two. Sure enough, he rose again at the bottom of his beat, within easy reach of me and exactly where I expected him. I forgot everything, where I was and who was watching. My nymph pitched into the water about a yard upstream of the last rise, and almost at once the cast drew under. I tightened and the hook went home and I knew that once again I was into a good fish. He fought like a demon, but after a few minutes of suspense M. Ritz had him in the net. He was a lovely fish, just short of 2 lb. and a good one for the Andelle. The Andelle trout are more like those of the Avon, and not humped backed like those in the Risle.

I got other trout that day. In one place I took three, none larger than 1 lb. They rose one downstream of the other near the bank I was fishing from. Each I took with an upstream cast and where both my friends could see the takes and just how quick one has to be to hook a fish when fishing upstream to them with a nymph. Here, as on the Risle, there was a great shortage of flies, but the rising trout were taking nymphs—active nymphs— playing about just beneath the surface. I was offering them something they expected to see. That first day on the Andelle I caught twelve trout, and it was a day on which dry-fly fisher- men did no good. All twelve took a pheasant tail.

While in Normandy on this visit M. Ritz took me to see the lovely little river Charentonne and I have always regretted not taking advantage of an invitation I had to fish it on this occasion. This was mostly due to our meeting with an American visitor who was having great difficulty in his casting. It was very obvious that he was a beginner and obvious too that he had been given a stretch to fish where trout were plentiful. He was excited and would rush along the bank to flog away at every trout which rose and put them down one after the other. We watched him for a while and then M. Ritz approached him and spoke to him in French, offering to give him some help with his casting and suggested that I might help him too. The reply, in real American, astonished me. " Buddy," he said. " I can catch these gol-darned fish without any help from you or the tall feller, these are just babes to what we have in the States." With that he went off at a run to where another trout had risen. We did not wait to watch him. It is so seldom one meets an ill-mannered trout fisherman. M. Ritz is a first-class caster and top-rate tutor. In a few moments I am sure he would have shown this man how to cast a line properly and in doing so the pupil could have enjoyed a good day's sport. As it was I feel very doubtful if he rose a single fish.

Chapter Seven

CONTRASTS IN TROUT BEHAVIOUR

Rewards of close observation : Effects of wind and weather :
A sequel to a broadcast : When spinners lay eggs under
water : Defeat by a heavyweight : Late season contest at
an eel trap.

SOMETIMES FISH on one side of a river behave very differently
from those opposite. I first became sure of this one afternoon
in early July some years ago. It was rough and showery, also
cold for the time of year, with the wind blowing directly across
the river from the bank I was fishing from. As usual, when we
get a day like this in July, a really good hatch of olives and
wateries were on and fish feeding well.

As they hatched most of the flies drifted across with the wind,
and there, in a steady and seemingly endless procession, they
floated downstream in a narrow lane under the far bank. I was
surprised that more fish were not taking advantage of the concentration because, though not rising so frequently, there were
just as many fish scattered about mid-stream and under my
bank, as under the other side. The water was of medium depth
with an even flow over and through the weedbeds. I had taken
a brace of fair trout and a grayling from under the opposite
bank when in midstream I saw the head of a really good trout
appear. Then, close to my own bank another good fish moved.
Both were in easy reach. As I waited the one in mid-stream rose
again and immediately I threw my dry-fly to him. There was
no response. Again I cast and yet again, a dozen times, or
more, each time putting the fly gently over the position I imag-

ined the fish to be in. But, though he showed twice more while I was fishing him, my best efforts received no attention that I could see.

Without moving I cast to the second fish beneath my bank. Again no response, yet, like the midstream one, he continued to rise. I changed my fly and tried both with the new pattern, then changed a second and a third time. Still there was no response. My first pattern had been accepted very well by the fish across the river, so I put it on again with a new cast point. But when I cast this to the fish under my own bank and in midstream it was still the same old story. Neither would have it. While I was musing a trout started to rise regularly under the far bank. Going opposite to him, I put my fly over him and at once he took. So also did another a little farther down. I tried two other fish which moved in midstream but neither would take and in rather a pensive mood I returned to my former quarry. These were moving occasionally but though I put my fly over both, it was again without the result I wanted. As I watched, a natural fly floated over the position of the mid-stream fish and I waited to see the head appear. Nothing happened. I continued to watch. Another fly drifted, wind blown, over him without being taken and then I saw a third fly pass over the trout under my bank. Until then I had not thought of putting on a nymph. It was no weather for nymph fishing, in addition to which fish were rising eagerly to a good hatch of fly. Then a thought occurred to me. The hatch of fly was taking place all over the river. Though there was a concentration of floaters under the far bank it was simply because they had drifted there with the wind after hatching.

This turned out to be the solution. The fish on my side of the river and in midstream had taken to nymphing after having flies blown away from their noses as they were about to take. One after the other, the two I had tried for so long with the dry-fly, took the nymph first cast, both good trout. I tried others and each fell to the nymph. There have been other similar occasions since that afternoon, and the knowledge I gained then has given me many a trout.

One big trout lived in the Avon just upstream of Middle Woodford Mill, near Salisbury, and the owner of the fishery had given permission for him to play the star role in a B.B.C. recording. My part was to catch the trout, while my old friend Sir Grimwood Mears gave a running commentary. It was nearing the end of May. I had watched this fish rising well in the same place during the two preceding afternoons and knew he was a good one. Mayflies had disappeared as the big head showed above the water and I could visualise my artificial being taken without suspicion when we were ready. But alas for the best-laid plans. Though we waited over three hours for him to rise he failed to show, and at last we left for another part of the river.

I was disappointed, as you can imagine, and possibly the disappointment showed on my face. " Come along and try for him later on, Sawyer, if you would care to," our host told me as we were leaving. As I thanked him I made a mental note that at some time I would try for him with a nymph and so get even with the fish for failing me in time of need. It was, however, about the middle of July before I got a chance to visit this water again and I suppose it was silly of me to expect to see the trout in the same place after so long. Yet somehow I had a feeling that the fish was still there and I sat on the hatches just hoping.

An hour passed while I enjoyed the wild life around, but not a fish moved in my sight. Then, just as I came to the conclusion that I was wasting my time, I saw an underwater movement near to the concrete winging of the left bank, just upstream of the hatches opposite the place at which I was sitting. That it was a fish I felt sure and peered more closely into the water. Just then the light changed as the sun came from behind a cloud. My heart gave a bound. My feeling about the fish had been right for there, busily feeding underwater, beside the wall, was the big trout I had come on purpose to find. Possibly he had been there all the time I had been waiting.

Now, I pride myself on never getting excited while after a fish, yet the sight of this big trout on the feed, within cast reach of me, caused me to have a fit of trembling. Indeed my hand shook so much that I had difficulty in changing the fly I had on for a nymph. The fish was no record breaker. I estimated him to be about 4 lb., certainly no larger than others I had caught.

The sun continued to shine, brightly and I could see him plainly as he worked gently along the wall, flushing, as I then thought, the nymphs from their positions, and then taking them as they swam away. Without moving I gradually lengthened line and made ready to cast. But I should first have looked behind me. Usually I do when not excited. My hook caught in the top of a bush and I had to creep over various obstacles to release it. Twice more I did the same silly thing and then at last pitched the nymph to the place where I wanted it. Down it went to where the fish was in position some two feet beneath the surface. Just as I expected him to open his mouth and take he turned away and resumed his hunt along the wall. Again he did the same thing. He would swing out and follow the nymph along, with me tense and waiting for that white flash of the opening and closing of the mouth. He did it again and I decided to change the nymph for another pattern. Although attractive, something about the pheasant tail was not quite right. I cast a new pattern with the same result, then another, but he was still not taking.

By now I was even more jittery than I had been at the start, but suddenly it occurred to me that perhaps he was not nymph-ing after all, but instead was taking egg-laying olive spinners. I had in my nymph box a pheasant-tail bodied nymph with white tails. It is, however, impossible to say whether these white tails allayed any suspicion, because in every other feature the nymph was a replica of the one I had tried first. The big trout turned out from the wall as the artificial drifted past him and as his mouth closed I tightened. Away he went upstream in a mad rush and I, letting the reel run, ran over the bridge and up the bank following him. The water here is about six feet deep, and on the bed were strong growths of lily. He fought strongly. Time and again he bored down into these lilies yet always I managed to get him out. My thoughts went back to the day in May when Sir Grimwood Mears and the B.B.C. men had waited so patiently for just such an occasion as this. What a recording it would have made. Five minutes passed with the fish beginning to tire. Two or three times he leapt and splashed at the surface. Yes indeed, he was a four pounder, maybe more, a deep, well-conditioned fish.

He turned on his side. " He's beaten. He's coming into the landing net ". I could almost hear these words as I reached

forward with rod held over my left shoulder and with the net
in my right hand. One just should not think of anything on such
occasions as these. Perhaps I was too eager to hear the imagined
" and now he's in the net ". Just as I thought I had him, the
little hook lost its hold. There I stood, rod in one hand, net in
the other, while the beaten fish sank slowly down and out of my
sight. It was bad luck that I lost him, but I had the satisfaction
of knowing he had been deceived and had learned a lesson
which will in future stop me from being too eager to get a big
trout into the landing net. The story does, however, bring out a
few points worth consideration. Had I not known that the fish
was in the locality it is more than possible that after about ten
minutes watching, I should have moved upstream or down in
search of another. Yet that trout was there and feeding when
eventually I saw him. He could quite well have been there from
the moment of my arrival, for during the whole time he did not
come near to the surface or make any disturbance which could
give away his position. Patience in waiting and watching was
rewarded. It pays to watch and wait when nymph fishing,
and more especially in the locality of hatchways and hatch
structures.

As to my conclusion that the big trout was taking female olive
spinners which were laying eggs beneath the water on the concrete wall upstream of the hatches, had I landed him I feel
positive that an examination of his throat would have proved
the point for, when I looked afterwards at the wall, I could see
submerged spinners crawling about on it, and watched others
as they pitched near to the surface and crawled down to join
them. The majority were those tiny spinners of the July dun,
but closer examination proved that all three species of the
summer and autumn olives were there, the small one, the
medium sized and the large one which hatch in greater numbers
much later in the season. They are all very similar in colour and
have almost white tails.

With their transparent wings folded neatly down on their
backs, these spinners, beneath the surface, have an appearance
not unlike nymphs. The main difference is the two long, light
coloured tails, which, when submerged, appear as a single
thread and quite easy to see. These olive spinners prefer the

concrete or stone walls around hatch structures, weirs, etc., for usually the water is well aerated and the face of the stonework is an ideal place on which they can stick their eggs. There is every possibility that the eggs will keep clean and well oxygen-ated and that eventually they will hatch. This the flies know. Trout know the preference of the insects for such places and what could be more natural than they take advantage of easy meals.

When I first saw the big trout moving along the wall I thought he was flushing nymphs, as I have seen others do from time to time, and catching them as they swim away. Instead he was brushing the wall with his nose and front fins to create a wash sufficient to dislodge the egg-layers and then taking them as they started to float to the surface. This accounts for his very leisurely manner. He was not interested in the slightest in any-thing floating on the surface. His eyes were just concentrated on the wall and I feel I could have spent hours floating a dry-fly over him without getting any response. Indeed, while I was after him, a few duns passed over his position, and once a cin-namon sedge floated along, struggling as they do when just hatched, but it received no notice that I could see.

Sometimes trout which work along walls for spinners will wear the skin off the end of the nose in taking insects from the stone-work. This makes them quite easy to see for the bared patch shows up very white in the water. As mentioned, any insects which are dislodged by a feeding trout will float to the surface or be carried in the stream. Though these spinners can live for a long time submerged, they cannot swim.

Another instance of egg-laying spinners occurred at a later date. It was nearing the end of September and the end of our trout fishing season. I had been running an eel trap at Gunville Hatches where the set controls the flow of the Avon in the middle part of the fishery. Several mornings following I had been there to shut off the water, take out the eels and clear the debris from the grid of the trap, and, at almost the same time each morning, four big trout had come up out of the hatch pool to feed on the concrete apron behind the hatches. All four were exceptionally good fish and two were near three pounds each. Neither took the slightest notice of me as I moved about and worked in the trap. They remained in the foot or so of water which covered the concrete apron until I lifted the eel trap hatch again to send the water flowing in a fast stream into the pool. I watched them all and knew quite well what they were after, for here is one of the best egg-laying sites we have for olives. At early morning the spinners came in by thousands to pitch on the hatch structure and then creep down into the water to lay their eggs on the wingings and apron stonework.

There are five big iron hatches here. Two of them did not fit snugly to the bottom and the pressure from the impounded water upstream caused a very fast flow to sweep beneath and on to the concrete apron. Here the big trout took their positions, occasionally fighting, one with another, for the choicest place. There these fish took the olive spinners as they crawled into the fast water, lost their foothold on the bottom and were swept towards the pool. Each was as busy as a bee, swinging first this way, then that, dropping back a bit, then surging up again. These fish were really on the feed.

One of our members at that time was Lt. Col. Patrick Badham. He was a Major then and a very good fisherman. He wanted but two fish to complete his fifty brace of trout for the season, and here, I thought, were some worthy ones which would interest him. We agreed to meet early on the following morning and at about half past seven he called at my house. At eight o'clock, my usual time, I closed the eel-trap hatch and together we stood by to watch.

Only a few moments had passed before the first fish came up over the lip of the apron from the pool. Then, one after the other, the other three surged into position and all started to feed, a big one and a smaller one in each of the two fast streams issuing from beneath the badly fitting hatches. Major Badham had tied some nymphs with white tails as I had suggested he should do, and he also had some sparsely hackled red spinners. He was excited. The fish were feeding badly and were not more than five yards from where we were crouching low above the eel-trap and where, with the morning sun just showing above the tree tops in the distance, we had a perfect view of what they were doing.

Dry-fly was hopeless in a case like this. None of the fish had any interest in what was happening above them and took no notice of the Major casting, or of me watching. The eyes of the fish were concentrated into the fast run in front of them, to where the insects were being washed to them. Time and again the nymph dropped in front of the nearer of the two big fish and was swept to him. I was positive he took twice and had I held the rod, I know I would have tightened. Each time I saw the mouth open to take and then the head shake as he spat it out again. I also saw the check of the floating cast but this my companion missed. He argued that the fish had taken something else and then, to pacify me, he decided to tighten whenever he saw the jaws of the fish move in the vicinity of where his artificial should be drifting. Three times he did this but each time at fault. One gets a certain tenseness at times like this. I knew what would happen even before it did. The fourth time he tightened, the trout had the nymph in his mouth but, instead of flicking the rod back to fix the hook, the Major gave a pull backwards, with the line almost straight from reel to fish—very definitely a thing he would not normally have done. A break was inevitable and away went the trout with a nymph and half a yard of cast.

It was difficult fishing. The current was all at the bottom. As the nymph was cast it would sink slowly down until reaching the fast water, and then be caught in the current and swept along in advance of the cast and so quickly that it was quite impossible to know just where it was. Quickly putting on another 4 x cast and another nymph, the Major tried the second of the three pounders, with the firm intention of lifting whenever he saw anything to indicate that the artificial had been taken. Several times he made a mistake when the trout took a natural (it is so easy to record these things when the other man has the rod). Then, as he lifted his rod to make another cast, the hook went home—but in the wrong fish. What had happened was that the nymph had swirled wide of the big one and straight into the mouth of one of the smaller fish feeding about two feet to the left. He was well hooked. Up into the air he went twice in succession and in a moment alarm spread to the other two. All three rushed into the pool together. But one came out again and into the landing net. He was a nice fish, just short of 2 lb. but very unlucky to be caught. Though extremely interesting, the morning had not gone just as we had planned and there was no further opportunity that season to catch the big ones.

Chapter Eight

CASTING AND HOOKING

Preparing the wind: An accelerated tempo: Need for
quick reflexes: A drill for the approach: What to look for:
Importance of hand work: Control under water: Timing
the strike: The mystery of the sixth sense.

IF A FISHERMAN is to give himself a fair chance when nymph
fishing, he must prepare his mind in several ways. Two, at least,
are exceedingly important. First, the tempo of events at the
decisive moments is quicker than in either of the longer established forms of fly fishing, and there is no time to catch up with
the proceedings once one has fallen behind them. The imagination must always march in step with what is going on underwater, so as to prevent the angler from being taken by surprise.
Secondly, he must be ready to respond to different indications
than those to which he would react when fishing dry or wet fly.
The evidence of his eyes, upon which his hands will act, will be
of a more fleeting nature. He must, above all, tell himself, before
even his nymph is cast, what he hopes to see and where he hopes
to see it after the cast is made.

Anticipation is, therefore, the key to success in nymph fishing
for all quarry, whether they be trout, grayling or other kinds
one wishes to catch. Grayling especially call for very quick
reaction. The secret, if there is such a thing, lies in making your
fish do just what you expect him to do, this at a time when you
have all nerves well under control and muscles ready to respond
smoothly to commands from the brain. This is easier to advise
than to accomplish. It takes a considerable time, if indeed it

can ever be done, to conquer one's nerves and to act as a fishing machine. I know that I shall never have a complete mastery. There are some days when I am extremely jumpy, when the sudden take of a fish causes all well-meaning intentions to go astray and my hands to lose their precision in action. I can think of many hundreds of fish I have deceived and then missed through carelessness, and I regret that there have been many others which have escaped with one of my nymphs and perhaps trailing a part of a cast.

Hands, eyes and brain must all play their parts in unison. First find your fish, if a grayling then it is almost certain he is on the feed and this too, is often the case with rainbow trout. If it is a brownie, a few moments of observation will tell you if he is likely to become a victim. Remember you are after a wild creature and creep stealthily to a position where the light can give you the best chance to see the head of the fish and an area of about two feet in front of him. Judge the depth of the water and the pace of the current. Remember that the slower a current the faster a nymph will sink. Forget all your dry-fly and wet-fly practices. The correct presentation of a nymph is a separate technique. With the dry-fly the aim is to place the fly accurately and delicately ON the surface and not more than a foot in front of the rising fish. If cast properly it settles gently on the water without disturbance and you wait for the head of the fish to appear as a signal that he has been deceived. This signal is quite plain to see. You get a signal when a fish takes a nymph beneath the surface but this can only be appreciated fully when the eyes have been trained to understand and interpret the underwater movements of a fish.

With a nymph the most important thing is to concentrate on the fish if it is possible to see him which is often the case in clear unruffled water. Watch the head of the fish and more especially the mouth. Try to pitch the nymph INTO the water well to the front and so that any ripples caused by the entry will not distort your view of the quarry. Already you will have judged the level at which he is poised and also the speed of the current. As the artificial sinks and drifts so you are prepared for the take and the hooking. Such presentation is quite simple and it is not difficult to deceive trout and grayling with nymphs.

But, unless you can see the fish take, or some indication that he has taken the artificial, it is only by luck that you will catch more than one in a hundred, and then only because the fish has hooked himself.

Now a word or two about hand work. In both dry-fly and nymph fishing both hands must play their respective parts, more especially when fishing directly upstream. In this it differs considerably from the general wet-fly style when most of the fishing is done downstream, where the flowing water will straighten the line. While one hand has control of the rod, the other must control the drift of the line to prevent there being slackness between rod tip and artificial. Your rod has three main duties to perform. Firstly to place the nymph in the desired position. Secondly to hook the fish, and thirdly to control it and play it out so it can be landed. It can do neither of these things unless held and guided properly. Of the three, hooking is by far the most important.

Since there is very little time in which to perform this action, and since even this small moment is further reduced by the period taken by rod and line to communicate the fisherman's intention to the hook, a swift and economical action is demanded. A sideways flick of the rod tip, by a hand held ready to give it, is better than an upward " strike " which can be a cumbersome business. There is no need to say more about this vital matter now, because it is covered in the chapter on Tackle which again emphasises the need for speed and for an outfit which is built to convey speed.

Assuming that the nymph has been accurately cast, its control in the water is the next most important consideration. When gathering in the slack line take care not to impart a drag of the nymph before being prepared, or a fish may take, before you have your rod ready to hook him. A natural insect can swim only at a certain speed. If you accelerate your artificial beyond this speed it will immediately cause suspicion in the fish's mind. In one way and another the fish must be deceived into thinking your offering is alive and one of the creatures he is in the habit of eating. An artificial, no matter how well constructed is, in itself, a very poor imitation of a natural. Without just that little something to simulate life, a fish may disregard a good copy of an insect even as he does a hundred other small inanimate things which come to him with the current.

Even so, it is not always necessary to drag a nymph to make the fish take. Where the water is slow running the eyes of the fish are often attracted by the action of the artificial as it sinks which is one of the reasons why all my patterns are ballasted. Sometimes, when casting across a current, the play of the water on the submerged cast, or leader, is sufficient to give the appearance of animation. But in all cases, to have the best chance of hooking the fish the moment it takes, it is essential that the line has no slackness and the rod is held under control to give instant action the moment the tip is flicked.

It would seem difficult to forget the part played in hooking by the hook, but few fishermen think seriously about this. I use forged hooks whenever possible and prefer the Limerick type with a down eye and with the point in line with the shank. Sneck bends may give an advantage with dry or wet flies and perhaps if I used them more often I would find they hook well with nymphs also. The main thing is to have a hook which can be disguised as much as possible and yet at the same time have enough gape to enable the point and barb to go home and stay home. Also an artificial nymph must swim on an even keel. Natural nymphs do not wobble from side to side, neither can they swim on their backs. An artificial nymph must look as much like a natural in the water as it does out of it, in fact more so, for the eyes of fish are extremely keen.

It is very easy to see when suspicions are aroused in a fish if, of course, you have a good view of him. You watch as the trout is attracted and makes a move forward to take and then at the very last moment, you may see him put on the brake, so to speak. The fins become rigid, stuck out from the body, and then he shies away with body curled and eyes moving as though thoroughly frightened. He may not bolt for cover at once, but the chances are if you persist with your pattern and show it to him a second time, he will immediately bolt for the nearest cover. When I find a fish like this I know something is very wrong in the presentation, or in the construction of my artificial. Usually I leave such a fish for a while and then return to show him something smaller and on a finer cast point. A tiny bit of weed hanging on a hook will cause suspicion to be aroused but usually, it is because the nymph has been swimming in a manner at variance with the naturals, this being caused by a bad balance in the dressing or by a hook which is not suitable.

You can learn a lot about the reactions of fish when watching them in clear water and this helps one to understand quite a lot of what may be happening when fishing " blind ". By this I mean when casting to fish which are not visible to you from the bank. Both trout and grayling, indeed a number of other fish too, can be taken with nymphs even if you cannot see them.

I call this blind fishing from the one angle only, for though it may not be possible to see the fish there are a number of other things which call for great attention and good eyesight. Much of the more fascinating part of nymph fishing is lost when you can't see your quarry but nevertheless blind fishing calls for considerable concentration and precision in action and a skill which surpasses the high art of dry-fly. Though I refer to it as blind fishing it is not with any intention of conveying the idea that one can go indiscriminately flogging the water in a sink and draw method just hoping a fish will take. It is necessary to be just as selective as with a dry-fly and to try only for those fish which from a rise form, bulge, or other indication, appear to be of a takeable size.

Skues wrote so much about this type of fishing that his book " Nymph Fishing for Chalk Stream Trout " may be said to be based mostly on it. His success with nymphs undoubtedly was with fish feeding near the surface, some of which he could see, others he could not, and with patterns which deceived the fish into thinking they were taking insects which were nearing the end of their underwater life and preparing to emerge as flies. Though he stresses the fact that it is not often possible to interest a nymphing trout with a dry fly, what he did not make clear is that a fish taking floaters well, will also take a nymph even more readily. The eyes of a rising trout though interested mostly on what is happening on the surface are also keen enough to see movement beneath it. If you care to watch one you can soon learn that should a nymph move beneath the surface in a trout's vision whilst a fly is floating over him, the fish will most often take the nymph in preference.

The nymph fisherman then has the advantage over the dry-fly man in that the fish is more likely to take an offering beneath the water than upon it. But the advantage gained in one way is lost in another. A fish taking floaters readily can usually be caught with a dry-fly pattern. The dry fly man has the advantage of being able to see the head of his fish appear as he takes, or at least a rise form which gives all the indication necessary. Indeed he gets a signal very plain to see and if the fish is missed, well it is just too bad. Actually this fisherman has but one thing to occupy his mind—just one indication to tell him his fish has been deluded into taking—a rise form. One thing is very certain —fish cannot take a fly from the surface without breaking it, and so telling you that he has done so. Underwater it can be very different. While after fish which are plainly visible, one learns just how a nymph is taken and it becomes increasingly obvious that sometimes the indication shown is so slight that without very keen attention, a trout can have your nymph in his mouth and spit it out without your knowing a chance has been missed.

One develops an awareness which is not even a sixth sense. It is something which cannot be explained. You see nothing, feel nothing, yet something prompts you to lift your rod tip, some little whisper in your brain to tell you a fish is at the other end of your line. But this feeling only comes if you are intent on your work, for though it may not be possible to see through the surface, it is possible to visualise the position of the fish and to anticipate his actions.

But until this uncanny awareness develops all of us must rely on more perceptible effects. For nymph fishing I stress the importance of a well greased line, or a line which floats well, and I suggest also that it is an advantage to grease the butt part of the leader to within a yard or so of the nymph. Line and this heavy part of the cast should ride high and be always visible, for this can act as the tell-tale. The part to watch closely is where the cast enters the water, the point where it breaks through the surface in what appears to be a small hole. Should a fish take which cannot be seen, his take is registered as the cast checks and draws downwards.

Because you cannot see a fish is no reason to assume that the

fish is unable to see you. Even when the water is perfectly clear
and unruffled, the angle of light often makes it extremely difficult
to see more than just the surface, though a fish can see out quite
clearly. Accuracy and delicacy are, therefore, just as important
as when a fish can be seen, perhaps more so. But having made
the cast then a close watch for the sign, or signs, that a fish has
taken your artificial, must be made. Sometimes two, or even
three indications all happen together and these leave no doubt
in your mind. There could be a swirl in the water, the flash of a
fish's side and the draw of the cast all taking place together
which leaves no doubt whatsoever. But far more often one has
but one indication and this is so slight that unless you are prepared for it and expecting it to happen, it may pass unnoticed.
Whether fishing directly upstream, obliquely, across or below,
it is very unusual for a fish to take the nymph on your cast without moving that part of it which is floating. When I fish blindly
I concentrate on the point, on that tiny hole I have mentioned,
where my cast disappears beneath the water and tense myself in
anticipation and ready to flick aside my rod tip the moment the
tell-tale shows. Though, as I have said, it is unusual, trout,
especially rainbows, and really big ones, can take a nymph and
spit it out without any indication showing on the floating cast.
This happens far more often in static water and usually when a
fish takes as he is heading directly towards the rod.

A trout, though feeding well on nymphs, may not show his
location frequently. He can take scores of naturals without once
breaking the surface. But it pays to watch any stretch before
searching along it. Now and again he may take a floater. He
may bulge or hump the water. You might perhaps see a wave,
a swirl or a flash from tail or side, just enough to tell you his
position and that he is on the feed. When a trout takes a swimming nymph he does so quickly. The opening and closing of the
mouth is no leisurely affair, as, for instance, when he is sucking
in spent spinners or rolling to hatching chironomids at the top.
He is after something he knows is lively. He moves quickly to
intercept, but whether this movement is forwards, or to one side
or other, or even behind him, the moment he takes the nymph
his swimming motion ceases. He closes his mouth, then checks
forward motion with his fins. As he does this so he sinks lower in

the water. This underwater activity of the fish is communicated immediately to the floating cast and if you know and expect the movement which is imparted, then there is a very good chance that the fish will be hooked. Here is my interpretation. As the trout closes his mouth on the nymph the part of the cast on the surface stops in its drift. There is a slight check. Then, as the fish sinks with the nymph in his closed mouth, so the cast draws into the tiny hole where it goes beneath the water. To be certain of hooking, one should tighten the moment the cast checks in its drift, just as the fish is sinking to draw more down with him.

If you wait longer than this it is true you will get a movement which is far more definite, something which leaves no doubt in your mind that the fish has taken. Usually this is too late. You can be as quick as a flash with your rod but get no connection. The twitch and definite draw you get and which show plainly on cast and line, is no indication that a fish has just taken but simply that he is making an effort to get rid of your nymph. As he sinks, so he tastes and feels. A moment is quite sufficient for him to know he has been deceived. His mouth opens even quicker than he shuts it to take the nymph and with a shake of the head he spits out the offending morsel. Odd fish can be hooked, for some have difficulty in getting the nymph free, especially if the point of the hook has pricked in, but these are exceptions. Many times I have talked with fishermen about this very important point in nymph fishing and on numerous occasions have taken the rod to prove my words. I may possibly have good eyesight, but it is only because I expect what I see that my hook goes home as often as it does.

Eddies and backwaters are common in most rivers and in many of them good trout have defied the best endeavours of fly fishermen to catch them. There are the fish, often quite easy to see, moving leisurely about, tempting and tantalising, with eyes ready to detect a struggling fly and extremely quick to see the movement of a nymph. Cruisers they are called, and cruise indeed they do, more often than not in anything but the direction you expect. In my experience, far more are frightened than caught. Usually they are large, but I think if left to the dry-fly purist, the majority are more likely to die of old age than from a rap of the angler's priest.

Some can be caught with a dry-fly it is true. The fish often will take floaters readily if one can but present them properly. But the snag is in showing a fish an artificial which appears similar to the insects he is eating. Usually these eddies and slack waters have a scummy film over the surface and in this scum winged flies are trapped and nymphs have great difficulty in hatching. It is the scum which defeats the fly fisherman in most cases. The artificial becomes a sodden mass the moment it touches down, while the cast cuts a lane through the film which immediately becomes apparent to the trout. But these trout are not looking for dead things, indeed they pass beneath dead natural flies with no more regard than they give to an artificial. They look for flies trapped in the scum whose wings are quivering and whose legs are moving rapidly in vain attempts to extricate themselves.

It is not possible to make an artificial dun quiver and give the other suggestions of life the trout expect to see. And often enough, when one is trying to place a fly exactly where it is desired, the quarry is frightened. There is no knowing just where the fish is going to be when cast and fly fall to the surface. With a nymph one has a decided advantage. It can be fun and greatly exciting, more especially when a big nose appears through some scummy part in half a dozen different places within a few moments.

Although such fish appear to rise frequently, much the greater part of their prey is nymphs. These eddies act as a trap. Nymphs are swept into them and then find great difficulty in finding a clear area of water where they can hatch. Time and again they will rise to the surface and wriggle desperately to break through the scum, then drop down into clear water and swim to another place. Should one manage to get its thorax through to the air and hatch, the wings of the fly immediately become imprisoned. These big trout know all about scummy films. They hunt here and there, this way and that as fancy takes them. Their feeding is unhurried, for neither nymph nor fly has much chance to escape.

An artificial nymph deceives them very easily. If it is made sufficiently heavy it will quickly cut a way through the scummy

surface and clean itself in the clear water below. The fine end of
the cast sinks also and merges with the water. If the trout is near
when the nymph breaks through he will take at once as it is
sinking. This is just what he expects to see and it causes no
suspicion. If he is not in the immediate locality a slight movement of the nymph, imparted by the rod, will be enough to
attract his eyes even if he is a yard or more away. All the nymph
fisherman has to do is to know when his nymph has been taken.
Before trying for a trout under these conditions it is wise to
regrease both line and cast butt. The rest should be easy for
generally the take is very decided.

Through the years I have had great enjoyment in fishing a
nymph in preference to the dry-fly and while at the riverside
have often discussed the method with fishermen who had not
brought themselves to accept the method. Well do I remember
one such man who was fishing an eddy where a big trout was
moving repeatedly. He was so intent on his fishing that my
approach was unnoticed and for a long time I watched as he
cast. A good fisherman, as I had every reason to know, but a
dry-fly purist to whom the use of a nymph was little better than
sacrilege. Several times he changed small flies without result,
then finally he snapped off his fine cast-point and put on a big
red sedge. Apparently he had come to the conclusion that he
was getting drag and possibly having had previous experience
that slight drag movement of a big sedge has attraction, he cast
this across the river on a tight line. The big fly skittered along
the surface and there came quick slashes as the trout took. When
he had it on the bank I spoke.

"Oh, hello, Sawyer," he said, " didn't know you were watching. He was a sticky beggar, but he made a mistake with the red
sedge. Have you done any good?" I showed him the two brace
of nice trout I had taken with nymphs.

"How did you get those?" he asked. "On one of those
beastly nymphs of yours, I suppose."

He deserved full marks for catching his fish, for indeed the
effort had been a good one and made after careful thought. But
his last sentence was a challenge, coming as it did from a man
who had used a red sedge of such ample proportions, and I
answered rather shortly: " Yes, Colonel. On a horrible bit of

pheasant tail tied on a ooo hook and with 4 x points. For the life of me I can't see how you can be so disparaging about my nymphs and yet be pleased to catch a fish on a monstrous sedge you let drag to attract him."

He looked rather surprised at my outburst and then was thoughtful for a moment or two. Then he laughed. " By Jove, Sawyer, you are quite right. By all the standards of dry-fly fishing, I am nothing better than a damned poacher. That's not the first fish by many I have taken like that, and when you compare your little nymph with my fly, I apologise. I'm afraid I haven't looked at it from that angle. D'you mean to say you got those trout on that tiny thing? Mind if I come along and watch you get another?"

This all happened a number of years ago. Today the Colonel is a keen and enthusiastic nymph fisherman who much prefers to throw a tiny nymph to trout feeding in eddies, rather than to hammer them with an assortment of dry-flies.

There is, as no doubt you have realised, a moral to this story. I am sure there have been few dry-fly purists who, at one time or another, have not deliberately attempted to deceive a good trout by dapping or dragging a fly, and I am equally sure many a fish has been caught and killed after taking a waterlogged specimen. There are others who have little compunction in fishing downstream. Yet often it is these very fishermen who decry the use of a nymph and say the technique is unsporting. To me it is a queer state of affairs. A sportsman is one who, in his own mind, is quite satisfied he has attained the peak of his sporting opportunities and has, at the same time, given due consideration to his friends. If one is so minded, a trout can be poached with a dry-fly just as it can with any other of the imitations we use.

To end this chapter, already a long one, here is a brief consideration of what may have happened when things do not work out as planned. In such circumstances the prime essential is to identify accurately the factor which has gone wrong. Often it is something which, because one takes it for granted, has not entered our calculations at all

The inquest generally begins with that familiar riverside remark : " No. Can't get them to look at anything." How often I have heard these words when trout refuse to rise to an artificial fly, especially at mayfly time. But they are far from factual. The trouble is that trout look all too closely and, what is more, see all too plainly the snare that is laid for them. You have known these difficult times and so have I, so also has every other fisherman. Many times you see a fish rising to take every natural fly which floats to him, yet he disregards your very best endeavours to present an artificial in his zone of vision.

Though more likely to occur when fishing a dry fly, this same thing occurs occasionally when fishing the nymph. You see fish after fish which are interested and will move towards your pattern and then turn off. Various thoughts flash through your mind—wrong pattern or colour perhaps, too large or too small, the fish have been pricked and are educated, the cast point too thick, and other thoughts. You change your fly, there being nothing much else at present that you can do; still no response, change again and yet a third time. Finally you move to the next fish, hoping things will be different. But it is the same story. You try yet another but none will take. Strange, you think. Why, the fish were taking very well only an hour previously and once more you put on the artificial you were using then. Another hour passes, perhaps longer, then suddenly a fish takes, you are so surprised that you just prick him and he is gone. You cast to another. The response is immediate, he takes with confidence and so also do others over which you spent time and thought a while ago.

One mayfly day I was after such a fish as I have previously described. Time after time he rose to take naturals but mine had not sunk into the quiet dimple he was making. It was rather a difficult position near a high bank. A short cast, it is true but it meant my using the left hand, which I have never yet taught to do the things I can do with my right. I had tried and tried, then finally, being more awkward than usual, the fly hit the top of the rod and broke off. Away it sailed free, to fall perfectly in front of the trout. I saw the fish lift and glide gently up to take without the slightest suspicion.

It was not just coincidence that he should decide to take just then. There had been very little appreciable alteration. To all outward appearances everything was just the same as it had been formerly. Not a cloud in the sky and not a ripple on the water. The only difference was that my fly was floating untethered to my cast and here I think, is the answer to this problem.

That was a long time ago but many times since then I have been convinced that there are days when fish can see the leader point attached to the artificial much more clearly than on others. And there are periods during a single day when this can happen. When thinking about it, I found that the same thing applies to me. In some lights I can see the point of even a 5 x leader at a distance of over twenty yards. Often too, when I have been watching others fishing, I have been able to see line cast and fly, or nymph over fifty yards away. On these days and during the periods when I can see the leader so well, I find it is the same with fish, even though their view is the reverse to my own. You might make a few observations yourself and this may prove to you, as well as it was proved to me, that the days to catch fish are those when you have the most difficulty in seeing your line, leader and fly on the water. Try the extremes. A bright sunny day and a dark and cloudy one.

I have come to the conclusion that success is far more likely to come with a change of leader point than with a change of artificial. We are limited to the fineness of the nylon or gut we can use because of its strength. But we are not limited to one certain colour. Ofter a dark coloured cast point will succeed when a lighter one fails. After all, why shouldn't a red or a yellow leader point be as successful as a red or yellow fly?

Chapter Nine

SPEED IN THE TACKLE

Obtaining instant contact: Precision preferred to distance
in casting and hooking: The danger of overweight: lines:
The concept of pitching the nymph: The works of the
disengaged hand: How to strike.

PROPERLY USED, a good practical dry-fly outfit will provide the
performance which nymph fishing demands. But there has been
a tendency for specialisation in some modern rods and lines
which could mean that a fisherman is handicapping himself
when he turns to the use of a nymph. Fishing the nymph makes
certain demands; and it is as well to be sure that one's tackle
can meet them. Some tackle, needless to say, does so better than
others.

When I see the tackle some fishermen use, I wonder if we are
not overdoing it a bit and just letting our pride in long distance
casting over-rule the more essential part of fishing. An expert
fly-caster can throw a fly a fair distance with a length of string
tied to the end of a bean stick, possibly much farther than a
beginner who has a first class and expensive dry-fly outfit. We
now have fast action rods which, together with heavy balanced
lines, give the angler a chance to throw his artificial to great
distances. In wide parts of a river years ago, a fish rising under
the opposite bank was considered to be out of reach and left to
the rods fishing on the opposite side. But now it gives the angler
an urge to show his skill in casting and to get a fly or nymph to
the position. There he will stand flogging and flogging away as
though taking part at a casting tournament and seemingly

oblivious to the fact that his chances of catching the fish are indeed few. Though one can throw a long way with a short rod and heavy forward tapered line, a short rod and weighty line bring difficulties when it comes to the most essential part, the hooking of the fish and the control of such fish afterwards.

My experience of watching others long distance casting, whether with dry fly or nymph, is that at least fifty per cent of fish are missed, twenty per cent pricked, fifteen per cent the hook goes home and the cast breaks, ten per cent are hooked well and lost in weed-beds or snags before control can be established. The remaining five per cent may give certain satisfaction when they are landed but I think one should look at it from another angle. Roughly ninety-five per cent are badly frightened, some may rise again shortly but with far more caution, but others may stop taking food from the surface for a considerable time and perhaps for the remainder of the season. Indeed, in the endeavour to satisfy a craze for long distance casting, much sport is being spoiled for fishermen who can approach to within comfortable casting distance on the opposite bank.

What point is gained? None that I can see, and much is lost. Many a time I have stood, watched and listened. I have seen fishermen work themselves up into a frenzy and tire themselves out. Flies and nymphs by the dozen have been left in the grasses, sedges and bushes behind them, cast points become as frayed and broken as nerves. There are the " damns " as a fish stops rising, stronger language when a fish is missed and almost maniacal actions when the victim escapes as a break occurs. I have been just as foolish myself, but now have come to understand the limitations of my eyesight and the extreme distance I can make my hand and eye co-ordinate to drive home the hook while the fish had its mouth closed on my artificial. Personally, if I wanted to catch fish at great distances, I would use a long light rod and a lightweight line. Possibly hollow glass will provide the rods that we need in the future and an action to enable a long, light rod to throw a really light line as far as one can see to hook a fish properly.

To lift and tighten a line in a split second one must have a leverage to correspond with the length of line one has on the water. At 20 yards an 8ft 6in. rod comes to its limit, and for every 6 feet after this one needs an extra 6 inches of rod. Or so I find. Otherwise one has to alter considerably the moment to tighten. The timing for hooking with an 8ft. 6in. rod has to be speeded up until at, say, 25 yards or 26 yards. To hook a fish when its mouth is closed, one should start the tightening of the line before the fish has turned down with the fly or opened his mouth to take a nymph.

There is, however, another important point to be considered. A speedy action rod is useless if it has to counteract the drag of a heavy line. The more line one has on the water the greater the weight the rod has to pull. If one tied 6 feet of cotton to a little finger and gave that finger a twitch, the cotton would move from end to end in a flash. A similar length of cord would need a decided pull and even then the movement would be sluggish.

Nymph fishing, more than any other method, brings out the need for fast action because a fish underwater can eject an artificial much more quickly than one taking a fly at the surface. And all fishermen know just how quickly a trout can get rid of a dry-fly. To be successful the whole technique of the fisherman has to be speeded up. Lightness of tackle is essential but there are many points to consider. First the rod. If you use a light line and are to throw it accurately and delicately you need a full action rod, that is, a rod which has an action right through to the butt and indeed into it, but if you wish to have instant reaction to your brain that rod must have a fast action tip which will give movement to your line, cast and nymph the moment you flick your wrist to drive home the hook. Again, while nymph fishing you have the opportunity to catch really big trout and therefore your rod must be sufficiently strong to hold and play them.

I know it cannot have been easy to make such a rod as this, yet I possess one designed especially for me by the well-known fisherman and author, M. Charles Ritz, of Paris, and made by Pezon and Michel of Amboise, France. Years ago, G. E. M. Skues used an American Leonard rod for dry fly fishing which he called his W.B.R., the World's Best Rod. I think I have the world's best nymph rod for it does everything I want when used with a suitable line. M. Ritz has, in my humble opinion, perfected the parabolic action and provided a sweet rod for

casting with a fast tip to hook and hold a fish. The Sawyer
Nymph as he has called this rod, is a split cane, 8ft. 10in. long
and weighs 5 oz. It is expensive it is true, being three pieces with
two tops, but all good rods are dear. With it I would be proud
and confident to fish anywhere in the world and feel greatly
honoured to have the rod named after me. On it for many years
I used a No. 1 and No. 2 Kingfisher D.T. line and with this
could place a nymph so that it deceived fish up to twenty yards
distance. Beyond this distance I seldom try, as it is not fair to
force a rod to do more than it is capable of doing with ease.
Often now I use an Air Cel No 4 H. E. H., which is much about
the same weight though more bulky in diameter. This type of
line saves trouble in greasing quite so often, but a light smear
along the first ten feet is always desirable.

Using light lines is of course far more difficult than the heavy
ones and good presentation calls for perfect timing with the rod
even though it is a full actioned type. This question of rods and
lines has occupied the thoughts of many during the last half-
century; experts who are far more capable of dealing with such
matters than I am. But I speak of my own experiences and of
the observations made while watching a very large number of
fishermen. It is possible that I look at fishing from an angle
rather different than that of others. And I would like to stress
the point that the successful catching of fish with dry-fly or
nymph goes well beyond the ability to cast a long and accurate
line. Often a very indifferent caster will catch far more fish than
his companion who is an expert. Fishing is not mechanical;
there is much more to learn than just the mechanics of a rod
and line. I know many first class clay pigeon shots, and a
number of expert riflemen. All are very good on the ranges, but
with very little knowledge of Nature. If they had to hunt to
provide a living then I fear the larder would be more often
empty than full.

What point is there in being able to put a fly or nymph to a
trout's position if you cannot hook him when he takes the artificial, or, if as is more often the case, the fish is frightened. Those
heavy lines and rods which make casting easy make hooking
difficult. Many a really good rod has been ruined with the
weight it has been expected to lift and to throw, tempers become

frayed because line and fly refuse to float for any length of time
without being regreased or oiled and generally speaking one
loses far more than is gained.

To be consistent as a game shot you need a good gun. But
the most important part of the gun is its trigger action. Here is
where precision is so necessary so that there can be no variation
when the time comes to release the shot. Even as the triggers are
the essential part of the gun, so the tip is the essential part of a
rod. Brain and hand has to control the action of both but when
this action is known to be positive there can be no blame
attached to the tool. The pressure of a finger to discharge a shot
is almost the same as the wrist action on the butt of a rod which
brings the tip into play to hook a fish. If both actions are carried
out smoothly it makes all the difference between a hit or a miss.

When speaking or writing of presenting a nymph to a feeding
fish, I prefer to use the word pitching, rather than casting. Pitching does more to convey the action one should adopt when
nymph fishing, for the correct entry of an artificial into the water
does much towards its success beneath. Pitching becomes very
necessary when after fish in fast water and also where they are
lying deep. One cannot expect to interest a quarry unless the
nymph is placed deep enough to come into his range of vision
and where he expects to see it. My patterns are constructed so
that they sink well, but, heavy as they are, the sinking is greatly
restricted if the artificial is tethered to heavy cast points laid in
a straight line on the water. Nylon and gut both have certain
buoyancy, an advantage certainly for dry-fly fishing, but a
disadvantage when nymphing. Skues advocated the use of
glycerine, mud, spit, or leaves or grass rubbed along the leader
point to help it sink quickly, even as he did for annointing his
rather light nymphs. I seldom need such aids, but on occasions
after I have caught a fish I will smear the slime from his body
along the cast points and also rub some of this on to my artificial.
This does help in sinking both nymph and cast points but it has
a second function in making the nymph taste better to the fish.
Or so I have found. A fish taking a nymph so annointed is not
quite so quick in ejecting it and one gains a fraction of time
for hooking.

Elsewhere I have written of my preference for a light line and also the importance of fine cast points. The thicker a cast point is the more buoyant it becomes. The straighter the cast is laid on the water the greater the resistance there is for a nymph to pull it under. Just to bring out my point, let us imagine we have a length of wood, say a stick three feet long. At one end we attach a weight. If you pitch the stick into the water, heavy end first, it drives down quickly to the bottom. Throw it in flat and at once the difference is noted. The weighted end sinks slowly. If a stream is flowing the stick passes a considerable distance downstream before it becomes vertical, or before the weighted end reaches the bottom. The larger the stick used with the weight the more slowly the sinking. You may think this to be a very crude example but it conveys the meaning.

To make the nymph pitch and sink quickly the best method I have found is to stop the rod on its downward stroke in casting, and check the running line passing through the left hand just when it is extended horizontally over the water. This check has the tendency to make the nymph curl downwards with the cast and then to penetrate the water before the line falls. Actually the nymph and its following cast points have an almost vertical entry, the nylon or gut, following the nymph down through the water, finds little resistance and the artificial quickly sinks to the desired level. My own nymph patterns are all streamlined, and have no hackles or fibres sticking out to impede progress.

It is easier to pitch a nymph with a light line, for when checked the line hovers in the air long enough to allow the nymph to swing down to the water and then, as it falls, there is little disturbance when the line touches the surface. But with a heavy double taper, or forward taper, I find the weight of the line invariably beats the nymph to the water. Generally, the check with this weight, brings the shooting line up with much too sudden a jerk and the nymph loops back on to, or beneath the line. For my cast, or leader point, I prefer about two feet of the finest gut or nylon I can use with safety, such safety being judged by the size and strength of the fish I am after. This last link is the most important part, as well as being the weakest, in the whole outfit. All I can say, is to use the finest point within reason. Two feet is ample, and then I gradually taper the whole leader back to the line where the attachment is roughly eighty per cent of the line point. A complete leader should be about the length of the rod one is using. Though I use light lines, some greasing is essential. This enables a very quick pick up for recasting; as well as acting as a tell-tale, and increases the speed needed in hooking.

Because a rod will cast a straight and accurate line it is not necessarily a good one for catching fish. The test comes in the hooking and in the handling of the fish afterwards. Your rod is but a lever. Depending on its length, it can only tighten a certain length of line and at the same time move an artificial in the closed mouth of a fish and give to the jar as the hook takes hold. The fine casts we must use in our deception cannot withstand any sudden strain and so a sensitive tip to a rod is very necessary. Only continued practice can give one the exact touch needed, and only by having a complete mastery of your rod can you bring this touch to the best advantage. Not one fish in a hundred will hook himself when you are fishing upstream with nymphs. Neither will many be hooked securely unless you have the rod held in readiness for precision action. Oh, the hundreds, no thousands, of times I have seen good fish missed through bad rod control, and the numerous occasions I have had to answer the question: " Well, what did I do wrong then?"

It would take too long to say all one can do wrong. Far easier to explain how to do it correctly. There are lots of things to think about after making a cast. This I do with a slack line so that the nymph has an immediate entry and can sink quickly. I pitch my nymph just far enough ahead of my fish to give me time to gather in all slack with my left hand before the nymph can be sighted by the fish. I find the easiest way to gather in line is to crinkle it backwards and forwards from thumb to little finger in a figure of eight coil, or let it fall to the ground at my feet. When once the hand has been trained to do this it becomes automatic and it is surprising how quickly one can gain control of a drifting line. So, by the time my nymph has drifted sufficiently close for the fish to see it, my cast and line are straightened on the water and I am in direct communication from the tip of my rod.

By that time all ripples caused by entry of the nymph have spread clear and the artificial has sunk to the level of the fish.

Now comes the time to expect him to take. A slight lift of the rod tip gives a movement and a lift to the nymph and this immediately attracts the eyes of the fish. The lift of the rod point to move the nymph brings the rod into a comfortable position in the hand and you are ready just as the fish moves to take. You see the mouth open and shut. Your line is tight and just a flick of the wrist to move the rod is enough to set the hook. If you have a rod designed like mine, especially for this kind of fishing the slightest twitch of the wrist on the butt brings the tip into action. The tip of the rod need only travel backwards a few inches before it exerts a pull on the nymph and so reaction is almost instantaneous.

This precision hooking of fish can only be done when the rod is held in the proper position. The wrist is only flexible and sensitive if it has a comfortable grip on the rod butt with the thumb uppermost, a grip taught by most of our casting experts, but for a different purpose. To use a rod to the best advantage when hooking, the flick of the wrist should be sideways with the rod moving in the same plane as the back of the hand and not upwards.

Chapter Ten

NYMPHS VERSUS GRAYLING

For and against grayling as quarry : Their differences from
trout : Extra difficulties in hooking them : The importance
of depth : Tactics with unseen grayling : A bet well won.

_____

IT IS EASY to be irritated by grayling. They invade waters which
should be sacred to trout; keeping their numbers down is a constant preoccupation for every river-keeper; and time and again
some uninvited grayling intervenes to ruin a carefully planned
stalk after a long-sought heavyweight trout. But if we are honest
in our recollections, and look back to our days as beginners,
there will not be many among us who do not feel a sense of
gratitude to the occasional grayling which were not a nuisance
but which made a day, a memory, or perhaps a lifetime's
contentment.

Many an angler has become enthusiastic and started a career
of fly and nymph fishing after catching a grayling. In fact, I
think, were it not for grayling in the upper Avon a good number
of would-be fishermen would have given up in disgust after their
first few attempts to catch a fish in days gone by, when trout
were fewer. And as we know so well, there are interludes on days
throughout the season when trout are dour, when it is only the
occasional grayling popping up which disturbs the surface of
the river. A grayling often saves the day and I must confess that
there have been occasions when I have blessed and looked
kindly on them for being silly enough to continue to be deceived.
The best way to get a man interested in fishing lies in letting him

catch a fish. I know this may sound the wrong way round to start, but repeatedly I have found that there is no real enthusiasm to learn the technique of casting until the pupil has had the thrill of hooking and landing a victim. In the clear chalk streams where trout are wild the chances of a tyro catching one are indeed few, but where grayling are plentiful, well, anything can happen. For those of greater experience, grayling provide valuable practice in the technique of fishing the nymph.

Grayling, for the most part are bottom feeders. By this I do not suggest they are for ever grubbing into the river-bed for their food, but simply that the greater part of it is taken from or very near to the bottom, and in mid-water. It is true they rise persistently when flies are on the surface. Even the big ones do this occasionally. But if you wish to offer grayling something they are looking for, then offer it beneath the surface and as near to the bottom as is possible.

Unlike trout, a grayling is not scared for any length of time by the presence of a fisherman on the bank or wading the river, by the fall of his cast and fly, or even by being hooked and lost. Each fish therefore gives more fishing, and needs less stalking, than a trout. Grayling can be frightened severely, and yet be on the feed again in a few minutes. Many times I have hooked a fish, lost him and then had him again shortly afterwards. One I remember very well. I was using a killer bug trying for a fish of 1lb. and I broke when tightening. The grayling was in my view plainly and I could see him shaking his head and trying to rub the lure free by pushing his nose into the gravel. The artificial was sticking out on one side of his mouth and no doubt uncomfortable. I put on another, exactly the same, and when I offered it to him he took just as eagerly as he had done in the first instance. This time the cast held and I landed him. Though the fish was in my sight all the time, he did not see in me, or what I did, anything which aroused his suspicion. However, easy as they are to approach and difficult as they are to scare, grayling do not let the fisherman have everything his own way. If they did, there would soon be none of them left. Though greedy and less shy than trout, grayling are extremely nimble in getting rid of anything they take in mistake for insects or crustaceans. And though they may take the same artificial half a dozen times in quick succession the chances are that the angler will fail to hook every time unless he is quick with the rod. The smaller the fish the more nimble he is. If you have fished for grayling you will know something of the yearlings, those fish of about 7 inches or 8 inches long. I often say that if a fisherman can hook and land one of these small grayling for every twenty which rise to the fly, he is doing very well. With a nymph the chances are better but even then a complete co-ordination between rod hand and eye is very necessary.

Grayling take an artificial much faster than trout and with the small fish the take and the spitting out is a split-second performance. Unless one can tighten the moment the mouth has closed the chances of hooking are few. The large ones, fish of from 1lb. and over, are not quite so active but even with these the angler has to be ready. Were it not for the fact that grayling are greedy and can be deceived time and again with the same artificial, so giving several chances to hook them, I feel sure many more fishermen would return home with an empty bag. A few fish may be unfortunate and hook themselves, but scores and scores of times I have watched grayling take and then be missed in the hooking. Whether large or small the take is similar. A check of the fins when the nymph is sighted, then a quick surge forwards, or to one side or the other, to take. Then comes the sudden snap which just a moment exposes the inside of the open mouth and following, comes the quick shake of the head, a twist of the body and the artificial is out again.

Grayling must have a very highly developed sense of feeling or of taste. Perhaps both these senses are extremely acute. They are attracted by movement, which gives a fisherman a decided advantage. A dragging nymph which would scare a trout will make a grayling lose what little caution it has. My method of turning these characteristics to good account is this. Once I have spotted a grayling or a shoal I try to move into a position where the clearest view of the fish can be obtained. On bright sunny days and when the water is clear and unruffled by wind this is not difficult, but sometimes when the light is bad a concentrated effort is needed. You may just see a vague shape, perhaps just the white base where the fins join the body, and if you move your eyes from the spot even this seems to have disappeared when you look again.

I have not yet discovered a nymph pattern to beat my pheasant tail which represents the olives, when fishing for grayling in the shallow waters. This nymph is also effective in the deep pools but only if one can get it to sink to the required depth. You can pitch and draw a nymph about all day over the heads of a school of grayling in deep water without attracting one of them, if you do your fishing near the surface. If, however, you can get the artificial well sunk and near the river-bed, well then the answer is somewhat different. It is true, of course, that grayling rise to floating flies. Also they will take hatching nymphs, but generally speaking their eyes are searching for movement near, or rising from, the bottom. It is quite impossible to make a representation of an olive nymph so that it is heavy enough to sink quickly through 4 feet or perhaps 6 feet of water, and at the same time looks like an insect and can be controlled with a rod. So for deep-water fishing I devised the bug which I think is taken by grayling in mistake for a shrimp, and which I have already described.

Nature has given grayling a coloration which merges extremely well with a clean gravel bed and often enough, though one may be looking very closely, it is not until a fish has moved for one reason or another, that its position is located. One has an advantage, however, for grayling never hide themselves in the weed-beds or under banks as do trout, and on bright sunny days with water clear, if you are careful and search diligently, it is possible to find them whether they are in the depths or the shallows.

In every grayling river there are pits and pockets, pools and hollows. These are the homes of the shoals, because the deep parts give them a feeling of security. Each pool or pocket is tenanted by a certain number of fish and at periods during the day they may all be gathered in the one small area. When movements of insects or crustaceans are expected the shoals break up and scatter to various feeding positions upstream and downstream of their pool, and the smaller the fish the farther they range. Generally speaking, however, the large grayling stay in the pools or in choice runs as are nearby. When big grayling are scattered away from their holt they are really on the feed, and if you can see an individual it is almost certain that he will take the first well-presented nymph you may throw to him. You must bear in mind the fact that there may be others in the locality and I find it is an advantage to make a close study of the whole area of river-bed around, before making an attempt to deceive the first fish I have located. Keep quite still and watch for a while and a shadow will lift here, another there, until in a few minutes you will discover that there are several fish within easy casting distance and all on the feed.

Tackle the nearest one to you first and when he takes, hook him and keep a tight line to stop him from running up and alarming the others. If he is lying upstream of a pool this is not difficult as when feeling himself tethered he will bolt downstream to the fancied security of his home in the deep water. Alarm and panic quickly spreads through a shoal of grayling, but if you are careful one after another can be taken without scaring the remainder. I know it is very tempting to cast over a small fish to reach a really big one and sometimes you are lucky. Usually, however, a falling line is quite enough to make the smaller fish suspicious; if he is scared, panic is conveyed to the larger grayling and away goes your chance of getting either or both. A big group of thirty or more grayling can be on the feed about a shallow, but if you are unlucky and scare one badly the whole shoal will stop feeding and congregate like a lot of frightened sheep in their pool. There if you watch them, the unrest is very noticeable, for the whole lot, large and small alike, will mill round and round, here and there, in a very agitated manner. If you are unwise and give them further cause for panic your chances of catching any for an hour or more are very few. When I disturb a shoal I stop fishing immediately and watch quietly until the milling stops and one by one the fish return to their former positions.

Though I now treat grayling with scant consideration, nevertheless, I realise fully that they are fish which can give the young angler and the old beginner an interest in the arts and mysteries of fly and nymph fishing. By some, grayling are considered to be the lady of the chalk streams—perhaps so, but I think a very greedy lady and a flirt. It is true they are nicely shaped and good to look at. To my mind they are just fish to interest one in idle moments—playthings, in fact, which give freely all that is asked until one becomes satiated with the ease by which they can be duped and then has an urge to try deception on something with more experience.

Years ago grayling were plentiful in the upper Avon. We had thousands of them, from tiny tiddlers of 2 inches or 3 inches to fish of well over 3 lb. There is some record of grayling of 4½ lb. being taken at Netheravon in the early part of this century. The largest I have ever taken myself was exactly three pounds. The heaviest caught and recorded since I have been keeper was one of 3 lb. 6 oz. taken at Figheldean in 1947. However, during the years when we had many large grayling, they seldom rose to surface food and few over 1lb. were taken with dry flies. The smaller ones up to 1lb. were forever active, and bags of up to three and four dozen were not unusual during the months of August and September. But this did little towards depleting the hordes of really big ones which were to be seen in every pocket or pool about the fishery. These were the spawners, the fish which each spring scattered their thousands of tiny eggs about the shallows to ensure that their progeny would live and become a nuisance in future years.

It was in the season of 1928 that I first saw a grayling caught with a nymph pattern. Our secretary at that time, Brig.-Gen. Carey, was the fisherman and he was full of ideas. He had just started to use nymphs after reading The Way of a Trout with a Fly, by G. E. M. Skues, who, of course, was very much alive in those days. General Carey explained the technique to me and it interested me considerably. I had permission to fish for grayling in my spare time, yet, though it is true I got some fair bags with dry flies, the big fellows always remained after I had gone home. While watching Brig-Gen. Carey in action I had seen that the big grayling were attracted to his nymphs when they were fished deep.

Gone now are those days when the upper Avon was full of big grayling for in one way and another we have reduced the numbers considerably. Gone also is my old friend Brig.-Gen. Carey. He died in 1944. But he showed me how to make nymphs and that grayling could be deceived with them. In the years which followed on from 1928 my interest in nymph fishing grew. I evolved patterns of my own and what I have learned in

catching grayling has helped me considerably in the taking of
trout at the present time. I feel sure grayling fishing helped me
to develop a methodical control of rod, line and nymph, and at
the same time a synchronisation of hand and eye which now
allows me to appreciate and be ready for everything which
happens beneath the surface.

There is a lot of good sport to be had in grayling fishing with
a nymph and what is more, it is a method by which certain
control of their numbers can be made. Though I have written
quite a lot about the taking of visible fish, grayling can be
caught just by fishing the likely places. The main thing is to
know the river and where the shoals are congregated. I well
remember an afternoon some years ago when I won a bet of
twenty cigarettes from one of our members. It was a hot afternoon in early August and not a fish of any kind had been
moving at the surface. I met him on one of the bridges and
listened patiently to his tale of woe, I agreed with him that there
was no hope of taking either trout or grayling with a dry fly.
And then he went on to say that he considered it to be impossible
for anyone to get a fish with a nymph. This was something of a
challenge and indeed it riled me a little. " Well," I said. " Would
you like to make a little bet? I think I could get a grayling from
that pool." " Done." He replied. " Here's my hand on it.
Twenty Players if you can get a fish in the next half an hour."

Maybe there will be some who will say I took an unfair
advantage but I did not see it that way. I knew that pool well,
and its depth. And I also knew that in it were a score, or more,
of big grayling. He gave me his rod and I changed his fly for a
Pheasant Tail nymph I had stuck in my hat and then went into
action. As I have said, I knew the pool was deep, so I cast the
nymph well up into it and allowed it to sink well down. There
was little current and it went down quickly. Then I slowly lifted
my rod tip and imparted a drag. The response was immediate.
The floating cast drew and I flicked the rod tip. Shortly after
a grayling well over a pound was in my landing net. I got three
others in less than ten minutes and then judged it to be time to
make my departure. I left him with the grayling but took the
price of the cigarettes.

I have recounted this episode just for a lead into the art of fishing blindly for grayling. Previous to this I had caught many hundreds in this same way and have caught many more since. No one need ever be idle on a river where there are grayling even if the conditions are such that the fish cannot be seen. It is true you catch trout occasionally but generally if there are a number of grayling in a pool any trout get little chance to take. The important thing is to know just where the shoals are, and to be inconspicuous in approach. But even this is of little avail unless you expect what there is to happen. The well greased line and part of the leader is important in all nymphing, but never more so than when after grayling which you cannot see. Placing the nymph so that it sinks to the required depth is also a must but concentration is the key to success. Lifting the rod tip to impart a movement serves to tighten the line and any take of the nymph by a fish is registered. But it needs quickness of the rod hand to make a connection.

In some fisheries, as indeed is the case here on the upper Avon, rods are allowed to fish certain stretches for grayling after the trout season has finished. But sport in the autumn with grayling depends to a very large extent on the weather and general river conditions. But some years the river may remain low and clear throughout the months to Christmas and when this happens grayling can be caught. They are not put off the feed by frost, or indeed by snow and ice, but once the river rises and becomes dirty by rainfall or thaw, there is but little hope of getting a fish.

So far I have written only of experiences with the Pheasant Tail nymph when after grayling and this is a representation of swimming nymphs of the Ephemeroptera. With this pattern I have every confidence in water up to around two feet in depth. But for deeper water fishing I devised a lure which at the time I thought was taken exclusively in mistake for a shrimp. Years of experience in using this and also a greater knowledge of other aquatic creatures has led me to believe that with the one pattern I had made something which might well be mistaken by fish for one of several animals which form part of their natural food. It has a good resemblance to a shrimp it is true, but it also serves well as a representation of a beetle larvae and also for the hatching nymphs of the brown Silverhorn Sedge. Both of these latter are plentiful in the running streams, but there are far greater numbers in lakes and reservoirs where they are taken very freely by trout. In these lakes and reservoirs the artificial has proved very attractive and it was because of this and also because the shrimp pattern has been successful in waters where there are very few shrimps, that I came to think it served several purposes. At the time I evolved the pattern and for many years afterwards I called it my grayling lure. But when I found it could also be very effective in taking trout in the lakes and reservoirs I decided to alter the name and instead call it the Killer Bug. This was a name suggested by one of my American friends who had taken some back and tried them in the States with deadly effect. So Killer Bug it is and no doubt the name will remain.

Though it is a very simple creation and one very easily constructed this pattern took me several years to perfect. My aim, as I have said, was to construct an artificial shrimp but time and again I was beaten. Though I got the correct shape of the swimming shrimp I failed to get the right colouring until finally I used a natural wool which changed its colour completely when wet. None of my nymph patterns have anything incorporated to suggest legs. I consider legs to be unnecessary and indeed an encumbrance.

Chapter Eleven

THE CASE OF THE KENNET

A change of view : A dry fly proves the argument : A puzzle about grayling : Contrasts with the chalk streams : Some reflections on stock fish.

MEMORIES OF days fishing with old friends on other rivers are always pleasant to recall and there have been many of these I have spent with my old friend Doctor Cecil Terry on the R. Kennet at Hungerford. Regularly for many seasons I have fished with him at Mayfly time and again at the end of September. These have been days to look forward to, and days to look back upon. Springtime is exciting on any Mayfly river and there on the Kennet these big insects are always a part of the river valley during the first fortnight in June. There is so much going on during the appearance of mayflies that to my mind the catching of fish is but a part of the stage setting. It is true I fish, and true also, that I catch some good trout, but at such times as these the same excitement, the same eagerness, the same madness, you might say, enters into me, as it does into the birds and the fish, and indeed, all else along the river valley. It is a time when I get far more joy in watching, than ever I do in fishing, and I spend far more time sitting, than in using a rod. The Doctor loves mayfly time too and has fished on the Kennet for more than forty years. His pride and joy is the possession of several of the real old Leonard rods, one or other of which he uses, just to show the fish he still has a mastery over them, no matter where they may rise. The slow rhythm of his casting and the placing of an artificial fly shows an artist of the old school, for

such rods as these are not favoured by many now, even if they
own one.

On the Kennet the trout are well known to be slow takers. By
this I mean they take much longer in absorbing an artificial
from the surface and in realising they have been deceived. Slow
thinkers one might call them, more especially the large trout.
They do in fact, give one plenty of time to hook them and
because of this the slow action of the Leonard is no handicap,
especially with the big mayflies. Why this slowness is manifest
I cannot say but it is not confined to the Kennet fish for I know
a number of waters where you can be quite deliberate in the
hooking of fish. The Avon I look after is not one of them, as
indeed the Doctor found, when trying his Leonards there. He
found too that nymphing with such rods is a somewhat different
story.

During the first few years of visits I made to the Kennet, dry-
fly only was the rule throughout the season, but the ruling was
changed in more recent times and the use of nymphs is permitted from the 1 July. This I think is a very fair ruling for such a
water as this, for during May and June there are plentiful small
fly to attract the fish, and also the Mayfly. The dry-fly can then
be very effective and no one would wish to use a nymph in
preference. But from July onwards the conditions change, for
by this time most of the fish have seen a variety of artificial flies
and indeed many have been hooked by them. I was pleased when
this decision to allow nymphs to be used was made, for, though I
love the spring and the mayflytime, the greater attraction was
then at the end of September when I could try for really wily fish
which had defeated many of the rods who fish this water regularly. For the most part the Kennet is slow running. It is a limestone river and trout in it grow big. But for some reason, again
unknown to me, these big fish seldom seek cover in weed-beds
after being hooked. This is so different to the trout in the Avon,
whose only thought it would seem, on being hooked, is to dive
headlong for the nearest cover and tie themselves up firmly in it.

It was on the little R. Dun, a small tributary which runs into
the Kennet by Denford Mill, that I had the longest session I
have ever had after an individual trout. I marked this fish rising
at about eleven o'clock in the morning and fished for no other

until I caught him at seven in the evening. This was on the last day of September and before the use of nymphs was permitted in this fishery. It was not a monster compared to others I had taken but I thought, by the limited views I was able to get of him, and by the size of his rise form and movement of water around him, that he was at least a three pounder, a worthy fish indeed for anyone to get at that time of year. He was rising in a position under the far bank from me. Owing to herbage on the bank and bushes behind me, my casting was limited to a small gap, and to make matters worse, the fish was in a small eddy with a fastish stream of water my side of him. At intervals throughout the day, this fish rose steadily but though I scanned the water closely I saw nothing on it which could keep him occupied so regularly. He took a few upwinged duns and occasional spinners but the main supply was a mystery. I rose him, or thought I rose him, to a little red spinner soon after I started to fish for him, but got no connection when I tightened. I rose him again much later to a small pale watery dun and pricked him, but this did not stop him rising. He was the most tantalising fish I have ever tried to catch with a dry-fly. He would rise consistently for perhaps ten minutes and then stop completely for a while, for no reason known to me then. One would have thought such a free rising fish as this would be bound to make a mistake but it was not until the shadows were lengthening as the sun went down, that he took my offering firmly. Throughout the day I had tried him with a great variety of dry-flies, large, medium and small, and of all different combinations of colour. Many of these I had left with some of my leader points in the tops of bushes behind me, and in the drooping herbage on the far bank. Light was failing as I searched in my box for a further fly to try. I was beyond any calculated thought by this time and, after trying to thread two patterns I selected, which had the eyes of the hook blocked, I found one I could thread easily, a very tiny nondescript pattern which had been battered out of all shape and symmetry. It dropped perfectly and he had it in a flash. After a good fight he came into the landing net and my patience was rewarded. He was indeed a good fish, a few ounces over three pounds, a brownie in very fine condition.

It was not until the following morning that I was able to discover the mystery of his rising. All through the day I had thought I would have got him easily had I been able to use a nymph but after an examination of his stomach contents I felt extremely doubtful if a nymph would have succeeded any better than the dry-flies I had tried. The stomach was full of a mush of pellets which, unknown to me, had been floating down to him periodically from the trout farm which lies on this little river, upstream. I suspect the little dry fly he took, battered and nondescript as it was, deceived him into thinking it was just another pellet, for the colouration of it was somewhat similar.

I have recounted this episode just to bring out the point that when fish have their minds set on a certain food supply it is extremely difficult to interest them in anything else. Something very closely resembling the food they are taking is needed to deceive them. Trout in the Kennet are much less shy than those in the chalk streams. What is more they are always far more conspicuous and lie out in the open whether on the feed, or not. This is typical of most of the tributaries of the Thames as for example the River Coln, River Leach and Windrush. All are good Mayfly rivers and excellent for nymphing during summer and autumn. The Kennet holds quite a number of grayling of sizes up to two pounds, some perhaps over this weight. But, though I have found the majority of trout to be fairly easy prey with a nymph, the grayling are inclined to be dour. On my water on the Avon if I see a grayling on the feed, or know where a shoal is located, I would be willing to bet I could take such fish with a nymph, or with a bug. I thought this might be the same on the Kennet, until I tried. It is true I got a few but there is not the eagerness to take, that I find on the Avon, and indeed in some other waters. Why this is so I cannot say. The fish feed in mid-water and many times I have seen them routing into the bottom but, getting them to take artificials is not an easy task.

At Hungerford I fished once or twice with Howard Marshall. When I told him of my experiences with the Kennet grayling he invited me to visit his stretch on the little River Lambourne which is not far distant from Hungerford and which indeed, is a river which links up with the Kennet. According to the

information he could give me, his Lambourne fish were far more
dour than the grayling in the Kennet. Trout were fairly easy
but the grayling had posed a problem he could not solve. He
wished to reduce the numbers he had for this Lambourne is a
lovely little trout stream where grayling could spoil much of the
sport. I left this visit until the summer, to a time when the
weather was clear and settled and then, with Howard, I went
to his stretch to begin the attack, as I thought. The grayling
were there in numbers throughout the water he owns. None
were really big but some I could see were up to a pound and a
half in weight. Most of them appeared to be much darker than
those we have in the Avon, or in other chalk streams and these
I think were mostly males. Though the water was perfectly clear
and the day a sunny one without wind, these fish were in no
way scary. None were really alarmed by my presence on the
banks or by my casting to them. But I soon realised what
Howard had said was true. I had gone well prepared with
nymphs and bugs in different sizes and with the finest of casts
I thought to be capable of holding the fish. To cut the story
short I fished the whole of the afternoon and got but one small
grayling of about half a pound. Those fish just tantalised me.
They had every appearance of feeding, indeed at times one or
another would rise and take something from the surface. The
queer thing was that if a trout happened to be amongst a shoal,
this would take without any trouble. The grayling disregarded
all I offered.

Later that same year I was invited to another part of the
Lambourne, which is farther upstream, by an owner who also
had grayling trouble and wished to get rid of some of them. He,
apparently, had the same experiences as Howard Marshall and
myself. He was a good fisherman both with dry-fly and nymph
and he thought that perhaps between us we might arrive at some
solution and find a way of taking these fish in a sporting way.
They could have been taken quite easily by netting or with the
use of an electrical machine, but, like Marshall, he had no wish
to upset his stock of trout by preparing for netting, or by shocking the fish with electricity. Again it was a day when conditions
were perfect for fishing nymphs, and grayling in this water were
just as plentiful as in the reaches where I had fished before. It

was the same story. I got three, and yet must have cast a nymph
or bug to at least a hundred. My host tried worms, and then
maggots, then small pieces of bread paste, with no better result.
I confessed to being beaten. "Was there no other way?" he
asked. He had come to hate having these fish in his water and
not being able to catch them and I then told him he could
snatch, or snare them, if he felt so strongly about their presence.
"Show me," he said, at once. So I decided to rig up a snaring
outfit.

Nearby were some good straight hazel rods and one of these
I cut about twelve feet long. In the fishing hut I found some
fine stranded wire with which I could make up a snare to go
on the end of the stick and, with the outfit prepared, I went into
action. It is a sorry thing to have to admit but, to be quite
honest about it, I too had got rather sick of trying to catch
these fish in a sporting way. I concentrated on taking all the
large and the dark ones and, after taking the first half dozen
and examining them, I could see they were indeed old male
fish which were in poor condition and long past the stage when
if hooked, they could give much fun on a rod. During the next
two hours I caught fifty-two, as I explained to my host, one for
each week of the year. Then I turned the outfit over to him to
carry on. He had seen enough to become proficient with the
snare and seemed to enjoy himself as he took a further dozen.

Opening up several I found each stomach was empty, not a
creature of any kind inside them. How they had managed to
exist is still a mystery to me.

At one time and another I have fished nymphs in all the chalk
streams of the South Country which of course includes the
famous rivers such as the Test, the Itchen and the Frome. Then
there has been the Wylye and the Nadder both of which are no
great distance from the Avon. I have fished in the Wensum and
the Wissey and in the little Babbingley stream which is one of
the boundaries of the Sandringham Estate. There have been the
very pleasant hours I have spent on the Welland and on the
Gwash, and then farther north to the Dove. All, and many
others, have given me great pleasure in showing that nymph
fishing can be most sporting and successful and in doing so I
have made many friends and converts. The greatest joy is when

one is invited to go again but the sad part is that I seldom have the time to do it.

The Test, the Itchen, Frome and Wylye are all first class waters where it is a great joy to be along the banks. No one can think of fishing on the Test without also thinking of the Lunn family who for so many years have been keepers and managers of the famous water at Stockbridge. I did not know old William Lunn of whom so much was written by Major J. W. Hills, but I did know his son Alf, and Michael, or Mickey, as we call him, his grandson. To them both I owe the privilege I have had in fishing in the Houghton Club water and in waters adjoining, such as Leckford and Mottisfont. Both grand fellows, with the interest of their river at heart, and both good fishermen. All those who fish, would like to say they have taken fish in such waters as these, for they are well known throughout the world. The joy of being beside clear water rippling over a bed luxuriant with the growth of aquatic plants can put a thrill into the heart of any true fisherman even though the fish are in no mood to rise, or to be caught beneath the surface. For most of my fishing on the Itchen I am indebted to my friends Mr. and Mrs. Dermot Wilson who for some years have had stretches of water in the upper Itchen valley. Test and Itchen trout have much in common which is at variance with the fish in my native river, the Avon. To put it plainly, they either rise or rest. You can get periods of great activity and then a blank for hours with nothing to be seen or to be tempted with either fly or nymph. The Frome, and the Wylye which again are really true chalk streams, are much the same in this respect. It is true you can get grayling at any time for these are always in evidence and on the feed, but the trout retire and for the most part, keep well out of sight, unless there is a good hatch of fly available.

This is typical of all the chalk streams I know and have fished, but here on the Avon and indeed in many limestone waters, fish can be seen sitting out and feeding on something or other throughout most of the day. The Avon is not a true chalk stream for much of the water supply in the upper reaches comes from greensand country. But it is a very good combination of the two, and a water which produces an abundance of insects of many kinds which are in and about the water throughout most of the fishing season. This accounts for the continuous activity with the fish, and perhaps, in some of their eagerness to take artificials.

Unfortunately there are few rivers left in this country where a wild stock of trout are sufficient to meet the demands of the present day fishermen. Most of them are stocked annually with hand reared fish, something we do ourselves now on the upper Avon. But I never feel comfortable anywhere when I catch one of these for I feel I am taking an unfair advantage. You would too, I think, if you had to rear them and feed them daily for a couple of years. It is in the very early stages of a trout's life that he learns the art of self preservation, to distinguish between enemies and friends. It is then too he learns how to find his food supply and the most nourishing types to take. Fish which have been fed and tended by man never have any fear of him afterwards and though they may learn to fear and to avoid, the lines, leaders, lures, and general artificials we use to try and deceive them, they are in no way scared when a human is seen nearby. Such fish are not used to the running stream or to the vegetation which grows in a lot of fishing waters. They seldom hide for in their early and sheltered life, there has been no need for sanctuary. They get into a habit of looking for food at the times when they have been fed regularly and where fish are fed by automatic feeders they are on the look out all the daylight hours. Just because these fish have been fed regularly does not mean that they give up a fight easily when hooked. Often indeed they fight better than wild fish, but they are very easy to deceive.

Leaving stock for a while, as some do, before fishing for them, makes no difference. They are still the same easy prey even if left a month, or even longer. And they remember the kind of food they have been accustomed to. One year I put a hundred large rainbows into a small lake where there was a very good natural food supply for them. These had been fished for regularly for three months and many of the hundred had been killed, others hooked and lost. One day, just out of curiosity, I threw a few handfuls of pellets on to the water. The response was immediate and in less than five minutes quite thirty trout were feeding eagerly. As I have mentioned these had been fished for regularly and with a great variety of arti-

ficials, both flies and nymphs. Yet these fish took the pellets with
complete freedom, with the knowledge, no doubt, that they
could not be harmful to them.

Stocking has to be done, but I do wish there was a way by
which one could make the fish really wild before putting them
into fishing waters. With hand reared pheasants this can be
done by running a few trusted dogs amongst them, but short
of hooking and releasing fish, there is no other method known
to me. Often the public get an entirely wrong impression of
certain fishing waters where really big stock fish are introduced
periodically. Also I fear there are fishermen who get an entirely
wrong impression of their skill when catching these. It matters
little whether these are browns or rainbows. For two years perhaps these fish have taken food without fear of any deception
and many get no chance to learn, after taking a hook.

Stocking in some waters has to be done or there would be no
fish worth catching in them. But when one hears of really big
trout being caught in places where the natural food supply is
too sparse to support fish more than a half pound in weight, I
wonder if this sort of thing is not becoming something of a
farce.

A trout can only grow big if it has an abundant and constant
food supply. If this is not present, then, unless one is prepared to
feed artificially, it is a great mistake, to say the least, to introduce
big fish where they are bound to starve if not killed quickly by
fishermen.

Chapter Twelve

EXPERIMENTS WITH SALMON

Frustration on the Test: An upstream tactic breaks the deadlock: An experiment succeeds on the Avon: And an eventful failure in Ringwood town.

IT WAS almost forty years since I caught my first fish on a hook that I received, and was able to accept, an invitation to join a friend and spend my first day after salmon. Until then my experience of salmon fishing was limited to what I had read and been told, and it was with a feeling of intense excitement when, equipped with a double handed greenheart of 12 feet long, I threw my first fly with the intention of luring one of these game-hearted fish from the depths of the Test below Romsey.

The river looked very inviting. It was a morning in early July, showery, it is true, but to my mind a very good fishing day. My excitement increased when a fish of quite 30lb. broke the surface just downstream and then a smaller one showed a little farther on. The rod belonged to my host. It was an old slow-action one, but still capable of throwing a fair line. Though I tried it I just could not manage it double-handed, and being fairly strong in wrist and arm, found it to be much easier to use one hand for casting, the other for line control. My friend had selected a fly he thought might be useful. He had a second friend to share his spinning outfit and while they went upstream to try the reach above, I was " turned loose ", as he termed it, to try the lower part of the beat with fly.

Away I went, quite happy, to be alone and all keyed up at the thought that at last my dreams had come true. Here I was on a salmon beat, with salmon tackle and half a mile of lovely river below me where already I had seen two good fish on the move. The rod felt a bit unwieldy after my light trout tackle, and rather hard on my arm. " Fish across and swing her down with the stream ", my host had advised, " wet-fly style, you know, not dry ". So, trying to carry this into effect, I started, while with a wave of the hand the other two members of the party went off with high hopes, upstream.

Across and down I fished, pitching the fly well in, and then letting it swing across the current. But though I fished, tensed and ready, I went on past the point where the big fish had shown, and then past the smaller one. Needless to say, I tried the positions thoroughly, but not a move resulted. A third fish rolled fifty yards farther down. I fished him deep and shallow but he was not interested any more than the other two. It was then I decided to change my fly. My thoughts were on grayling. Well enough I knew how little notice they take of a nymph when it passes well above their heads in deep water. So I selected a blue and silver affair on a heavy hook with the thought that at least I should be able to get this down to mid-water, if not lower.

Heavy though it was it still would not sink as deeply as I wanted, and then it occurred to me to try the nymph tactics I find useful for grayling in deep pools. Instead of casting across and swinging the fly downstream I went below my fish and threw my fly upstream and well beyond where I had marked him. At the same time I pitched it in with a shepherd's crook cast and with plenty of slack cast and line. The fly sank like a stone, drawing the nylon down with it and then, when I had judged it had reached the locality of the salmon I took up the slack and lifted my rod point. As my rod lifted still higher I could imagine the fly starting a journey up from near the river-bed, and describing an arc towards the surface. Many times I have found this to be a deadly cast for grayling and apparently it was equally deadly for one salmon.

As I tensed with rod held ready there came the pull I expected. Back flicked the old greenheart and then came the thrill as the hook took hold. My first salmon started to fight. I had no fear that the big hook would lose its hold or that cast

or line would break. But the rod? I have been accused of playing
fish hard. Actually I don't think I am unduly rough, but I do
like to make a rod do its work. Run after run, the big fish made,
and as I tried to control him, the old rod bent to the shape of a
horseshoe with the tip about level with my nose. Though fearing
every moment of stress that the old greenheart would break,
control him I did, and in ten minutes exactly I drove my gaff
home in a lovely fresh-run fish of 14lbs.

Grayling tactics had defeated that one, and thinking once
more of grayling, I cast again. It is, perhaps laughable, but do
you know, I fully expected a second fish to take at once and
was disappointed when it did not do so. And though I fished
the remainder of the day my hook hitched into nothing more
solid than weeds. That fish was the only one caught that day
on fly throughout the Mountbatten water at Broadlands. Two
others were taken on spinners, but neither of my friends had
any luck.

When one considers some of the strange lures and hefty flies
which salmon, commonly supposed not to feed in fresh water,
are expected to accept (and indeed frequently do accept, as my
story has proved) the possibilities of catching them on the nymph
will appeal to anyone with an inclination towards experiment.
Not that the idea is new; several of the smaller, lightly dressed
low-water flies are as likely to be taken as nymphs as for anything else. But whatever is in the mind of the salmon, I suspect
that the intention of offering a nymph is seldom in the mind of
the fisherman. It was not in mine until a day came when, happening to be near a beat on the lower reaches of my river, the
Avon, which is of course famous for its salmon run, the keeper
remarked that there were three salmon in the bridge pool and
that they could not be caught. To most of us, I think, those
would be challenging words. It was not long before I was on the
parapet, peering downwards into the water.

What the keeper had said was true. There were three fish in
the pool above the bridge, and there they were in plain view.
" You might see the biggest of the three sitting with his tail on the
front of the bridge pier at the right hand side," he had told me,
and it was to this place that my first glance had been directed.
The big fellow was there sure enough, poised on the fin not

more than eighteen inches beneath the surface, but he was not alone, for there, below him, one above the other, were the other two. As I looked, so the silly thought of the three bears fairy tale, came to my mind. Father bear, mother bear and baby bear. The big salmon, a fish of about twenty-five pounds, was at the top, then came a smaller one of fifteen pounds or so, and beneath this the baby of the three, who I estimated at about nine pounds. It was a lovely morning in mid-September. The sun shone from a cloudless blue sky and the light was just right for a perfect view into the river. Looking down from the parapet of the bridge made it easier and I had no difficulty in distinguishing every feature of the three fish and every movement they made.

The bridge pier runs to a point, and each of the three salmon were poised with their tails almost touching this apex. Each was at a respectful distance below the other, a matter of about two feet. The lowermost being approximately the same distance from the river-bed. The sight fascinated me. These three fish had been in the pool for a considerable time. Many a fisherman had tried for them without success. Not a fish had been taken for more than six weeks, and according to the keeper the chances of getting one at this time of the year were about one thousand to one against. Still, as he had said, I could have some fun trying, for it happened that I had my salmon tackle with me in the car.

However, I was in no hurry. The sight of these three salmon lying in positions one above the other was an unusual and fascinating one. It would be a pity to scare them, and the good light and my position gave me a wonderful chance for observation. It amazed me that these big fish could hold their positions so easily. The fins of each were moving lazily and the tails waving slowly from side to side, very much like a trout when he is poised near the surface waiting for flies. But there was something different, and not for a long time could I see what it was. Then suddenly it struck me. The eyes of the fish had no life in them. They were just dull and unintelligent. There was no glance to right or left, no scanning of the surface. The beat of the fins and the wag of the tail continued in monotonous regularity. It was plain to see that neither of the fish was waiting for food. All they were doing was lazing away the bright autumn morning.

In the car was my salmon tackle. I also had a trout rod and a box of nymphs. It was a Monday. My wife had some business in Ringwood so, on condition that I could leave her in the town and spend a few hours on the river about Ibsley, I had driven her down. Monday was the day my old friend Dr. Neighbour had a beat on this Somerley water, and he had given me the invitation to fish his beat at any time that he was not available. I had called at the keeper's house to make sure. My idea was to try for some of the big chub in this Ibsley water, hence the trout rod and nymphs. My salmon tackle was but an after-thought as nobody but a fool, it had seemed, could expect to get a fish with conditions such as they were then. The river was low and full of weeds.

My thoughts as I looked at the three salmon were mixed. Should I have some fun and try to get one to take a pheasant tail nymph? I might tempt one to open his mouth and do some-thing more than yawn, as the top one had done on several occasions while I had watched. Even as I was meditating, the big fish moved to one side as though to intercept some creature and in a flash I changed my mind about trying a nymph with my trout rod. What sense was there in hooking a fish such as this with a size No 1 trout nymph on 3 x nylon. In my box were a few of my " Killer Bugs " which I use for grayling and lake fishing for trout. One of these was an outsize I found useful for fishing down to the bottom of deep pools. It was weighted to sink rapidly.

Quickly I put up my spinning rod and then tied the bug directly on to the 0.30 mm. nylon I had on the reel. I could not cast this with the spinning rod, but with a swing I dropped the bug into the water a few feet upstream of the big fish, let it sink to his level and then moved it at right angle across his nose. Immediately the artificial started to swing across, the big fish became interested. He moved to it and just for a moment I thought he was going to take. Thinking better of it he resumed his position. Interested him, I thought. Try him again. This time I swung the bug farther upstream with the intention of allowing it to sink more deeply before giving it a sideways and upwards movement. Down it went to more than half the depth of the water and I judged it time to lift.

As I lifted so all three fish came to life, so to speak. As it so happened the bug was nearest to the middle one and like an outsize grayling she took. The view was perfect. I saw the mouth open and close, as I have many thousands of times with trout and grayling. As it closed so I tightened, and home went the hook. In a moment all was confusion and commotion. Up into the air went the hooked fish and, as though in sympathy, up went the other two as well. For a split second all three fish were in the air at one and the same time and, with a great splash, which caught the eye of a passing motor cyclist, they all went back into the water.

Here I repeat that only a fool could expect to kill a fish in those existing conditions. Upstream of the bridge the river was full of weeds, long trails of pond weed, twenty feet or more from root to tip. Into a bed of this went the hooked fish and there she stuck. By this time the motor cyclist had joined me on the bridge, as excited as a school-boy. " Was that a fish you hooked just now, that made that splash?" he asked. " I thought someone had fallen in." Quickly I explained what had happened, and then told him there was not a hope of landing it. To emphasise my words I leaned the rod against the parapet and lit a cigarette.

Ten minutes passed with the two of us chattering and then a movement of the rod showed that the fish had started to struggle again. To my surprise she came back downstream out of the weed-bed and once more I was able to have a tight line on her. Under the bridge she went and in a moment I thought it was " just out of the frying pan, into the fire ", for downstream the weeds were even thicker. Putting on all the strain I could manage, I stopped the downstream run. Up she came again and once more headed into the weed-bed. This time, however, she was much nearer to the bank. We could see the fish quite plainly from the bridge and that she had tied herself up firmly amongst the weed-stems. Pull as I might nothing would give. How the monofil stood the strain was more than I could understand, a braided line would have broken with half the pull exerted.

A voice at my elbow broke into my thoughts. It was the keeper. " Don't tell me you've hooked one of the beggars. You

must be a magician." From the look in his eyes I feel sure he
thought I had foul hooked the fish and I quickly explained
about the ".bug ". "Have a try from the bank," he suggested.
" She might move from there." So, letting out line, I scrambled
to the end of the bridge and then down to the water's edge,
while the keeper went after my gaff. But though I levered until
my rod was in danger of breaking nothing would give. So putting the rod to one side, I took the nylon in my hands and gave
it a series of short but sharp jerks. In a moment the fish started
to plunge. Weed strands came to the surface. The line cut
through them like a scythe blade. Foot by foot I brought the
salmon nearer to the bank by pulling as hard as I dared and then
letting her kick herself free from the weed-stems. About six feet
out she stuck firmly and then turned on her side. In went the
keeper up to his thighs and in a flash he had the gaff home.
Out to the bank he scrambled and with him the fifteen
pounder.

"Well, I'll be damned for evermore," were his first words
when he saw my bug fixed firmly inside the top jaw. " Fancy
getting her to take a thing like that, and then to land the blighter
in a mess like this. You must mesmerise 'em. Not bad condition
either, is she? A bit red, it's true, but she won't eat too bad.
That's some fun. Do you know, Frank, when I saw you put up
your rod I thought you were just plain crazy. Still, it proves the
old saying that you can never tell with fishing. Look at it. Hook
and land a fifteen pounder in a place like that at this time of
year. I shall have a tale to tell some of them." He was pleased
in more ways than one. That fish was the last but one caught
in the 1955 season by salmon fishermen, and it was, I think,
the one which broke the record total for the fishery.

This incident in catching a big salmon with a nymphing
technique gave me plenty to think about. My opportunities to
fish for salmon have not been very frequent and though since
my first day I have killed a fair number ranging from ten to over
thirty pounds, most of these I caught on fly or spinner. The
chance to see fish and try for them with a bug did not come
again for several years. But one day in 1960 such a chance did
occur. It was one of the most amazing and exciting days in my
fishing career, even though my luck was out.

Friends of mine have a beat on the lower Hampshire Avon about Ringwood which is a few miles downstream from Ibsley. On this day the beat included the bridge pool in the town of Ringwood—a pool well known to fishermen and indeed to the public. Some years, after early June, when the water is low and clear, it is possible to see salmon in this pool from the bridge. It was on this occasion. We arrived at the pool about 10.30 a.m. The sun was high, the light good, and no wind. My first glance showed me two fish and then after closer scrutiny I saw five more. These varied in sizes from one of about ten pounds to a really big fish estimated by the keeper to be between thirty-five and forty pounds. These seven fish were well known. They had been in the pool a long time and on most days one or another of those who had beats, had tried for them with the usual methods, including prawns and shrimps.

I had come prepared to try these fish in the same way as I had fished at Ibsley and with me I had my 10ft. 6in. greaseline oufit, a rod built on the principle of my Trout Nymphing rod which I had used mostly for sea-trout. A No. 4, D.T. trout line and a cast tapered to 8lb. breaking strain, made it complete. Light tackle is necessary in any form of nymphing and it was this method I wished to try. With me, I also had some of my " Killer Bugs " made up on No. 3 low-water salmon hooks, and with one of these knotted on securely, I went into action. Maybe, in view of what followed I will be condemned for using such light tackle. My excuse is that this was in the form of a experiment, for I wished to prove what I had long suspected, that stale fish such as these are not impossible to catch on sporting tackle.

From the bridge parapet it was quite easy to cast, for the pool is on the downstream side. The fish were lying well up in the water and my plan of attack was to drop the bug well upstream of a fish, let it sink down and drift to a point just in front, and slightly below the level of a salmon, and then lift the rod point so that the artificial was pulled upwards to swing past the nose of the fish. I concentrated my efforts on one of about fifteen pounds which was clearly visible and lying high in the water, not more than two feet down. This fish was interested at once and just for a second I thought he might take the first cast

I made near enough for him to see. Time and again he moved forward, then suddenly, after I had tried him quite twenty times he moved quickly forwards and took with a snap. The hook held but he was a lively fish and after three or four minutes of excitement he went around a well known snag in the middle of the pool and the cast broke. This was the start of a day of success and failure.

Five of the seven fish took the bugs in much the same way and these included the monster of the pool. He, like the 15 pounder, took very suddenly after I had been tempting him and another one much smaller, which was lying close to him. Just a quick movement forwards and a snap of the jaws. I think I deserved to kill this big fish. For just over half an hour I had complete control and had there been a place where I could have got him near to the bank and near enough to reach with my gaff, all would have been well. As it was, a large group of onlookers, including my two friends, had a perfect view of the tiring out of a big salmon with a light rod.

He was beaten and on his side when I tried to tow him over a wide fringe of weeds to the only landing place. The strain was just too much. My light rod bent almost double and owing to a barbed wire fence a yard or so behind me, I could move him no nearer. Down went his head and he bored downwards into the weed and my cast broke near to the eye of the bug. The keeper had not exaggerated. I think the fish might well have weighed forty pounds and to have landed such a one on an 8lb. breaking strain cast point, would indeed have been a triumph.

Disappointing as it was, that day gave me plenty to think about. As I have said I hooked five of the seven salmon which I could see in the pool. Three were only lightly hooked, and after only a moment or two which gave me the thrill of feeling their first strong pull, came unstuck. Maybe I needed a slightly larger hook, or perhaps did not strike quite hard enough to get the barb well in. The thing which matters most, is that each took the bug and I feel sure that here is a technique which might well be developed and which may lead to good sport with fish which for so long have been considered as hopeless. As I have indicated in my Chapter on construction, I use the same colour wool for the salmon as for the trout, grayling and other fish. It is very important that the correct shade is used.

Fishing through the years with nymphs for trout and grayling has taught me just what a fish expects to see, and though the correct colour and construction of nymphs and bugs is necessary, far more important is the manner of presentation. In this lies the secret of success. As I have said, my experience with salmon is limited but to me it appeared that the salmon, like many trout and grayling, were only really interested when something drifting in the water suddenly checks and appears to swim towards the surface. The instinct to snap and to catch seems to be irresistible and the angler has only to tighten at the right moment.

My view in this case, from the parapet of the bridge was good. It was possible to see the fish and to judge the exact moment to check the artificial and make it swim. It was easy also to see the fish move forwards and the opening and closing of the jaws. It was very much like nymph fishing for visible trout but with such big quarry, far more exciting. Perhaps this made it simple, but I do think, though as yet, I have had no chance to prove it, that in pools where a number of salmon are congregated, that one or another could be caught by fishing the bug blindly. By this I mean to cast out, allow the bug to sink well down, then give a lift with the rod point and watch for the draw of the cast, in much the same way as I fish for brown and rainbow trout in the lakes and reservoirs.

A well-greased line and a long cast tapered to a fine point, are essential. It is necessary for the bug to sink quickly. It can only do this on a light-weight leader. An outfit balanced to meet all requirements is also a must. Most important is a rod with a sensitive tip with which one can strike sharply and firmly without danger of breaking when the hook takes a hold. The rod too, needs to be single-handed and light.

Though this technique is very similar to nymph fishing for trout and grayling I think it doubtful if the salmon take the bug in mistake for any creature to be found in fresh-water, most certainly not an insect and, being so much larger, it cannot be for the freshwater shrimp. Maybe they just see it as some familiar food they have been accustomed to taking in the sea and are goaded into taking when they see an appearance of life. Perhaps there will come a time when I can try the same methods again and then find out more.

Chapter Thirteen

LESSER QUARRY

Coarse fish on the nymph: An experience with Kennet chub: Nymph succeeds where dry-fly fails: Chub in the trout positions: Watching the rise form: The delicate art of nymphing for roach and dace: Season and weather for this: A trick for attracting these fish: The chances of picking out a prize specimen: More fun than float fishing: Taking a big carp: Expelled through a gill.

THOUGH NYMPHS are mostly used for the taking of trout and grayling, they have attraction for other fish. That chub will take them I proved one summer when I spent a very interesting hour or two in the middle reaches of the Kennet. It was a lovely morning. The sun shone hotly from a cloudless sky and there was not a breath of wind to ruffle the surface. Here the water was beautifully clear and the good light made it possible to see fish from one side of the river to the other. An occasional trout and a few grayling were on the move, but mostly the surface activity was caused by chub. Big schools were everywhere, well up in the water. Some of them were large—fish up to 4lb. and 5lb. I did not go there with the intention of fishing for chub, but since they were the only fish of any size likely to give some sport, I decided to try to catch one or two.

I had a French-built rod with me and wondered if it would be up to the task of handling one of the big fellows. But first I had to hook one. There was little on the surface to attract them, but now and then a big fish rose to take a black gnat or a midge. But I could see they were interested in something beneath the surface. One hefty chap was feeding very much like a nymphing trout. Several times I saw him swing to one side or the other, cruise forward a foot or two, and clearly I saw his mouth open as he took some insect. Then he rose twice in succession, taking, as I thought, a black gnat.

I have not fished much for chub—we have none in the upper Avon—so I tried this one with a black gnat, then with a tiny midge. Then I tried, one after the other, all the dry flies I had with me. But no, one after another these chub treated my best efforts with disdain. The big fellows slowly sank down and out of sight, and then led their school off to fresh feeding grounds.

" Not as daft as they look," a friend remarked, quite unnecessarily I thought. Apparently he had the same experience with flies.

Well, I hate to be beaten and treated disdainfully by a trout or a grayling—to have this happen with chub, well! Some years earlier I had had some fun fishing my killer bugs to chub in the Thames at Clifton Hampden. The Thames chub seemed to like them and I had some in my bag. There I had fished from a boat drifting down the river and had taken a number by pitching the bug under the banks and beneath the overhanging branches. So I tied one on and pitched it out to the next sizeable fish I saw. One look as it drifted to him and he bolted. So did half a dozen others soon afterwards. It is true I got a brace of grayling, but these gave me little consolation.

Then it occurred to me to try a nymph. I had some of my pheasant tail patterns with me. Big fish, big nymph, I thought and selected one on a No. 1 hook. From my previous experience I found I had to be just as accurate and delicate in placing my artificials as with trout. The nymph fell nicely just in front of the next big fish I found up in the water. It fell to one side of him, but at once he was attracted. As it sank he moved just as if to take, then pulled up in a hurry and turned away. The performance was repeated and I tensed ready to hook him. But once again he refused at the last moment.

When trout do this I change to a much smaller nymph of the same pattern. I thought it wise to do so now. So on went a pheasant tail ooo. He took the first offer without any hesitation and a few moments later he was on the bank. I got another smaller one with the next cast and then others from the same school. But so far I had not caught a big one and was delighted when, farther upstream, a four-pounder showed his back fin above the surface. He had another with him even larger. My little nymph pitched just in front, drifted to him, and my cast checked in its drift.

That big fellow fought as well as any trout I have hooked. It is true I did not try to hold him hard as I had no wish to ruin my rod. Also I had on a 4 x point and the tiny hook. He gave up very suddenly after a strong fight and gave me no trouble to land. His companion was still in view and I was eager to have him also; it was some moments before I could try though. That tiny ooo hook had hitched into the leathery jaw as though to stay for ever. I had to cut it free with my knife. After all that, the nymph should taste good, I thought, as I pitched it in to chub number two. I could see him clearly as he moved to intercept and waited for his mouth to open and close. No movement of his mouth showed but my cast drew under. I was caught napping and struck like a novice. The strain was too much for the cast and with a plunge which sent a wave from bank to bank, my friend number two went off to think over his mistake.

Let those sneer at chub who will. Since that day I have come to think far more kindly of them than in the past. With a light rod, light line, a 4 x cast and a tiny nymph, these fish give one plenty to think about and some very fair sport. They are no man's fool and truly " not as daft as they look ".

Several years after this I was invited to spend a few hours with one of the Members of our Association who owned a short stretch of a sidestream of the Avon at Breamore. In this he said were a number of really big trout and he would like to see me try for these with a nymph. Apparently these fish had defeated him time and again with dry flies and with his own efforts at nymphing. It was early July. The water was low and clear and the morning a sunny one. He took me along the stretch and pointed out the feeding positions of the fish. Occasional small flies were hatching and I could see at once that each fish had chosen a place where a good drift of floating insects could be expected and I watched closely the area where the first fish had his home. A dun drifted along and down it went into a small bubble of a rise and I could just discern the shape of a really good fish. Though my host was anxious for me to try him at once I was in no hurry. I wanted to see him rise again and be quite certain of his position. We did not have long to wait. A second fly disappeared into the same quiet dimple but I saw no sign of the nose of the fish. My suspicions were immediately aroused. It was a queer kind of rise for a trout to make in taking a floating dun, it must be a really big one, I thought. I had on a leader tapered to 4 x and a o sized nymph and so I substituted this with a 3 x and a No. 2. Pheasant Tail nymph. It is never advisable to try for really big fish unless the tackle is strong enough to hold them after being hooked.

Again I saw the loom of the big fish as he moved near to the surface and then pitched the nymph a foot or so upstream from the position. It sank, dragged slightly with the current, then the drifting cast checked and I struck into something really solid. The stream was fast and away down he went with a mad rush and I let him run. But that was all. With the first run over there was no more fight and I knew then that this was no record trout. And so it proved. It was a chub of just over five pounds, the largest I had ever taken on a rod. The look on the face of my host was amusing. " Do you think the others might be chub too?" he said. " That is something I cannot answer," I replied. " But there is a way of finding out and I would like to if you don't mind."

During the next two hours I caught six more big fellows. Neither was as big as the first but weighing between two and three pounds. They took the nymph very readily and indeed gave me some very good fun. All the fish had been in positions at the far side of the sidestream. Big chub and big trout are not unlike at a distance and my host was not the first, nor will he be the last, to be mistaken in their identity. These fish will take all the best feeding positions in a trout water and bully even the big trout away from them. Watching the rise form can often be a clue to identity but even this is not infallible. Usually, however, a trout will show his nose above water as he takes a floating fly whereas the chub just suck in water and fly. Often, too, the chub will make one or two bubbles. When chub are nymphing, unless you are near enough to see the fish clearly and the forked tail, I fear no one can be certain.

This is what I told my host. I could quite understand his failure to get either of the chub to take a dry-fly for most of the fish were in small eddies and backwaters and to reach them meant casting across the streamy part in the middle when a drag was immediate. With the nymph it was much easier. Providing it was pitched in so that it sank quickly and somewhere close to the position of the fish, the drag had attraction but quickness with the rod in hooking was the main thing.

One point, however : though I proved they take a tiny nymph very readily, they do so in a manner much different from trout. If you watch to see the mouth open and shut, well, you won't. These chub, large and small alike, suck in an artificial with very little movement of the jaws. If you try for them with nymphs, just concentrate on the floating cast and tighten the very moment it checks. Chub can suck, they can also blow, and the time taken between one and the other is very little. The take is slow. By this I mean there is no hurried movement through the water to intercept, just a leisurely amble forward and then a check as the nymph is absorbed.

Only when you examine the stomach contents of roach and dace is it possible to realise fully that these fish eat a considerable number of immature fly larvae and nymphs. When a big shoal is in a pool, few insects can move without attracting the eyes of one or another. Usually they feed near the bottom, and therefore, excepting when in the shallows, which is not often, it is difficult indeed to catch them with anything but a weighted leader and a baited hook. I have caught roach, big roach and dace, when fishing deeply with a weighted grayling lure, indeed the heaviest roach I have ever caught with rod, a fish just an ounce short of three pounds, came in this manner. But generally speaking, with few exceptions, these coarse fish are prey for the bottom fisher.

The exceptions are during the summer months, from mid-June until the end of August. On hot afternoons the big shoals lie up near to the surface to bask in the sunlight and enjoy the warm upper layer of the water. I have seen them hundreds of times. There they are, scores and scores of fish of all sizes from tiddlers no larger than a minnow, to big, deep fellows of 2lb. or more, all lying with their backs so near to the surface that dorsals and tails often show above. When coarse fish are basking the bottom fisher might just as well bask also, for he will get little sport with his bottom tackle. The fish are not up in the water to feed, though most of them cannot resist taking insects from the surface. Should there also be nymphs they take these as well. And this brings me to my point.

Many times I have had some very good fun with a basking school of roach and dace. They like each other's company, it would seem, and when fishing for them with a nymph the catch is about equal. A light line and fine leader is essential and they prefer tiny artificials. Caution in approach is important and also it is a great advantage to fish with the sun in your face. Shoals are easily scared by shadows. The shadow of a falling line and leader will quickly put a whole school to flight. A tiny nymph makes very little disturbance when it is thrown delicately, but with these fish lying so near to the surface, the take is usually instant and one has to be prepared to tighten quickly. Though they take freely the hooking is not easy. Roach and dace take an artificial very much the same as chub. Their tiny, rounded mouths are adapted for sucking in their food, rather than biting on it in the manner of, say, trout, salmon, pike or the snapping take of a grayling.

On many occasions I have seen roach and dace take my artificial, blow it out, then take it again. Also I have seen their mouths working on the nymph as though feeling or tasting it. These fish are not scared by drag. Movement of a nymph horizontally just beneath the surface is a great attraction. At times I have watched half a dozen or more roach and dace have a race to see who could be first to take. And I have known one fish take, blow the nymph out, and another have it straightaway. It is very, very difficult to be quick enough. One needs a rod with a fast tip and a quick hand and eye to go with it.

Both roach and dace take a dragging nymph while they are in motion. By this I mean the fish take and continue to swim with the nymph in their mouths. So this means there is no check to the cast, no twitch to be seen, and no pluck or pull to be felt. The only way to know a fish has taken is to watch its mouth.

The little white flash of the inner jaw shows plainly if you are watching intently, but watch you must.

Fish after fish can be caught, as time and again I have proved. Some care must be taken after a fish is hooked and the faster he is coaxed away from his companions, the better chance to get others. Immediately I hook one I drop my rod point low to the water and keep it low until I have my victim away from the shoal. This stops him from skittering on the surface and gives no alarm to his companions. Amongst the shoal will be one or more of exceptional size. If you want a prize fish all well and good. Make an individual effort to get one of the big ones and then be satisfied. These are the leaders. If you hook one, panic will at once spread through the whole assembly and the basking will be done for the day.

In still waters such as lochs, lakes, reservoirs, ponds and canals, where these kind of coarse fish abound I am sure there is far more sport to be had using a fly rod and a tiny nymph and casting to visible fish than there is in any kind of float fishing. And it is not only roach and dace which are attracted, for I have taken many really good sized perch, bream and tench as well. On one occasion I took an eight pound carp. On this day I was coaching a number of boys in casting in one of the smaller lakes at Longleat, near Warminster. In this lake were a number of these big fish and the boys were excited as these continued to swim around just beneath the surface. I had been teaching dry-fly casting and several times had shown the boys how to place a fly on the water just ahead of a cruising fish, but none had shown the slightest interest. But I thought this to be a good opportunity to demonstrate the placing of a nymph and sent one of the boys to my car to get my nymph rod which was already assembled and rigged with a fine leader and small Pheasant Tail nymph. He was quickly back, and taking the rod I explained what I intended to do, thinking the lesson might be of some use if ever the boys were after visible trout in a lake.

The big fish was easy for all to see as it cruised slowly along about twenty yards away. My little nymph pitched in about two feet ahead but about a foot too far. But immediately the fish turned towards it and I saw my cast draw. I must admit I was surprised but as I tightened so there came a mighty upheaval in the water and then a great bow wave as the fish ran for the middle of the lake. I let him go thinking he might come unstuck, but no. Back and forth, around and about, the big fish lumbered, always near to the surface. The little hook held and the 4 x leader point stood the strain until I knew I had him beaten. One of the boys got my landing net, and a lesson in netting a big fish, and we had him on the bank. Quickly I bent to take out the hook and return the fish to the water, when to my surprise I found the hook embedded in one of the pectoral fins close to the body with the cast leading through a gill cover and out of the mouth. What I think had happened was this. The carp had sucked in the nymph and then expelled it with water through the gill. As I tightened the hook caught in the fin. This was the first and indeed the only carp I have ever caught with a nymph, but the manner of its fight astonished me. To control and land a fish of such size was rather amazing on such a fine leader but maybe this was because all the fighting took place at the surface, caused, no doubt, by the gill cover being held open. The boys all enjoyed the episode which though unexpected, did indeed give them all a certain education.

Chapter Fourteen

THE NYMPH IN STILL WATERS

Variations in presentation: Detecting the territory of a fish: Fishing over weed beds: A trial in a gravel pit: Adventures on the Chiltern chalk: A swarm of bees join in.

TRADITION GOVERNED the methods of fishing lakes and lochs as rigidly for many years as it dictated what was proper and what was not on the chalk streams. The drifting boat, the cast of wet-flies, and enough wind to give a fair ripple are a fair enough design for sport in Scotland and Ireland, as on wide open, upland water in England and Wales. But more and more fly-fishermen are now fishing the many newly-stocked reservoirs and lakes in the whole country. They must take conditions as they find them, and often they find them thoroughly unfavourable to the conventional wet-fly method; a flat calm, with the water surface an unbroken mirror for the cloud formations above, is an all too frequent experience. Beautiful as it is, the sight is an irksome one for the fisherman, who soon desires only that it should be shattered by the rising of fish. As in similar conditions on a stream, the nymph has a part to play with prospects of success. Again its successful use depends on the fisherman taking himself underwater in imagination, and on his forming an accurate picture of what goes on there.

Lakes, ponds, pits and reservoirs are not places where you can expect the same big hatches of insects you get on rivers, or all the same kinds. Nymph fishing for the most part depends on the activity of creatures which in rivers may be found in the deep and slower running reaches. But, though they live in the sluggish deep stretches and in trapped waters, this does not mean that the nymphs are always to be found on the bottom. Few nymphs of the emphemeroptera, care to live on the bottom in deep water, for seldom is there a food supply there for them. Only when vegetation reaches from the bottom to the surface, or near to the surface, are many of these to be found in really deep water. Generally one could say that still-water nymph fishing depends mostly on representations of the pond olives and the chironomids in the small fly class; and on representations of the larvae of beetles and the hatching pupae of the varying sedge flies, water boatmen or corixa, in a slightly larger class. Some lakes may produce an abundance of a certain type, as was my experience in Sweden. This is exceptional.

Usually, until weed growths have become established most of the small creatures are to be found in the shallower parts, that is, in water up to about four feet in depth and, during the early part of the season, these shallower parts are the most likely place for nymph fishing. It is usually around mid-summer, or later, when there is any appreciable growth of deep water vegetation and when this occurs, then there is a migration of nymphs and other creatures to make a home in the weed tops which are well above the bed. There they live and frolic amongst the weed frond within two feet of the surface and often right at the top. Migrations from place to place happen frequently as the creatures travel about in search of food. Swimming nymphs can move very freely through the water and at times, in passing from one weed-bed to another, will glide across several feet of open water. The journey is made within a few inches of the surface and the quickly moving insects provide attractions which soon catch the eyes of feeding fish. Trout know the habits of these swimming nymphs and often enough a good fish will establish a beat in a pocket amongst the weeds. It might be just a tiny place, a square yard or so of open water, again it could be an area of twenty or thirty square feet. There he will cruise around, perhaps two feet beneath the surface, forever on the look out for the activity he knows will take place.

Trout do hunt in the actual vegetation where of course it is almost impossible to present an artificial. At times I have seen fish which appeared to be deliberately tapping the stems of the weeds with their noses with the intention, I suspect, of flushing the nymphs or other creatures above them. And there are occasions, more especially during a hot afternoon—when a trout will work systematically through a weed-bed and take the creatures from where they are perched on the fronds very near to the surface of the water. At such time, if you watch very closely, it is possible to see the weed strands being lifted by the nose of the fish, and to hear a distinct sucking noise each time a victim is engulfed. To see trout feeding like this reminds me of times when I have been after woodpigeons in the late evenings during winter. Often, with gun held ready, I have stalked through covers of Scotch fir or spruce, peering intently into the tops for the dark blobs on the branches. I have kicked the butts of the trees and then waited an opportunity for a shot as, with a clatter of wings, the birds move from their perches and pass into a clearing. I think of myself then as a trout amongst the weed-fronds.

To introduce an artificial nymph into such underwater surroundings and, by making it imitate not only the appearance but the behaviour of natural nymphs, deceive a chosen fish is, to me, a fascinating achievement. Perhaps I may be forgiven for confessing that it is all the more satisfying if it is accomplished in the presence of an unbeliever.

On one occasion, many years ago, I gave some live coarse fish, roach and dace and a few grayling, to the owner of a chain of disused gravel pits at the headwaters of the Anton, near Andover, Hampshire. Several of the locals bottom-fished these pits for trout, and the owner thought a few coarse fish would add greatly to the sport. He told me there were big trout in the pits and that quite a number, up to 4lb. were taken each year with live minnows. Would I care to see the pits? If I wanted to fish I was very welcome at any time throughout the season.

Though I thought of it occasionally, I put off going until the August of the following year and then taking my fly rod and a box of flies and nymphs, I visited the pits. Some of them are an acre or more in extent, some larger, with water up to 12ft. in depth. Soon I could see that there were indeed big trout in them. The pits had been roughly dug and difficult to get around but, as I stealthily moved along the edges, some very good fish moved out from the banks and into deeper water. In one of the pits a brace of two pounders were cruising about the middle and rising every now and then to take midges. The water was perfectly clear and it was quite easy to see the bottom in many of the deepest parts. George, the owner, was there with his threadline outfit. His intention was to use live minnows lip-hooked, and he had a supply ready. Would I do the same? Well, I don't care much for live-baiting and this I told him. Had he, or any of the others, tried these fish with a fly rod and an artificial nymph, I asked, and, getting a negative reply, I said that before using minnows, I'd like to try a few casts with one of my nymph patterns. " Please yourself," he answered. " Some of our people have tried them with dry-flies but without much success."

As I put up my rod I watched the two fish cruising around and the tiny dimples they made as now and then one or the other broke the surface. George had tossed his minnow into a likely pool and kept an eye on his float while I prepared to make a cast. A dimple showed some twenty yards out and then I saw the fish as it came heading towards me. It turned broadside on about fifteen yards away and I pitched my nymph (my favourite, the pheasant tail body, on a No. 1 hook) a yard in front of him. That fish sighted the nymph the moment it touched the water. I saw him accelerate his movements, and, before the artificial had sunk six inches, he took it. He took leisurely and without the slightest suspicion, and I had a perfect view as the jaws opened and closed. He fought strongly and deep, and, after a really good battle I slipped my landing net beneath a lovely conditioned trout of exactly two pounds . . .

While we were examining him I saw another fish cruising along near the bank towards us. Here the water was about eighteen inches deep. He stopped and tilted up with nose in the bottom, and, as he regained an even keel I could see his jaws working on something he had taken. Obviously he was on the feed and without moving my body I flicked the nymph to him and watched as it sank. Down it went and almost touched the bottom 1ft. or so in front of him. He made no move to take it, so lifting the rod I gave the line a slight pull. The nymph moved upwards and at once the fish was attracted. The cast gave a twitch where it entered the water and I drove home the hook. Within a few minutes he also had the net slipped beneath him, a smaller fish, but in the same first class condition as the two pounder. He weighed 1lb. 7oz.

George's float jiggled now and then as the minnow made attempts to free himself but George was no longer interested in it. " Here," he said, " let me have a look at those ' gimps ' of yours." I gave him the box with the various patterns in it. Then he was amazed that I had landed such fish on 4 x points and could control them with the little rod I had. Before I left he was trying to do the same himself. He had even stopped talking about " gimps " and had begun to call them nymphs. That day was one of many I had fishing these pits and several of the four pounders George had spoken of, became victims to the nymph.

Of course, things do not always work out so well. All fishing knowledge is gained by experience, and experience sometimes deals us a blow which puts us in our places, just when we think we have begun to be sure of the answer to another problem. The afternoon I spent fishing the gravel pits at Andover was the first time I had tried nymphs anywhere but in the running streams and when a year or two later, I had an invitation to spend a day with a friend at Blagdon, Somerset, in early October, it was with every confidence that I included a supply of nymphs in my tackle. Naturally I had heard and read a lot about Blagdon and indeed had seen some of the first class brownies and rainbows which had been caught there. I must admit my imagination had been given full play.

The late Harry Hiscock, my host, was an expert wet fly man. He was one of those seemingly tireless individuals who never give up until it is too dark to see. He had fished with me on the Avon and we had talked about the merits of dry-fly and nymph fishing. Now it was his turn to show me something of his skill with the wet-fly. He loved Blagdon, for the water and the scenery around it is alone well worth a journey. I had visualised it and had seen photographs but when I arrived on the day and saw the great expanse of the reservoir I must confess I felt rather doubtful about fishing it with a nymph on a 4 x cast.

Harry had a friend staying with him and the three of us were to fish from a boat waiting for us at the jetty. Soon our rods were ready and away we went to where a first drift could be started and, incidentally, to where Harry thought we might find some trout on the move. He and his friend had on teams of three flies on 2 x casts, but though offered a leader made up the same, I said I'd like to try the fish with a No. 1 Pheasant Tail on 4 x. If I hooked a fish I had a long line and plenty of backing. There were acres of water in which to tire him out.

My two companions fished the water in wet-fly style, throwing their flies well out and then playing them along near the surface. Occasionally, well beyond reach, the head of a fish would appear and leave a fast spreading ring where he had risen, but, try as I would, I could see nothing of a fish nearby. I had been told that at times, when Blagdon fish are really on the move, it is possible to see them cruising around taking insects from, and just beneath the surface. I can see into water fairly well and knew if I spotted one I could put my nymph near enough for him to see it: If he took it, all well and good, if not, well I could try another pattern.

My two friends worked hard and enthusiastically, but they had fished for well over an hour before a fish was interested enough to take. Harry had been turned towards me telling me a story and at that moment a two pounder slashed at his tail fly. He must have felt the pull for with a quick flick of the rod he had him on. Blagdon fish fight hard and as I watched the battle, once more I was assailed with doubts as to my tiny nymph and fine cast. But he had no snags in which to get entangled and no weed-beds in which to plunge. After a minute or two he was in the boat to be duly admired and toasted, as he deserved, being the first fish of the day. Again I was advised to scrap my nymph and put up a cast of wet-flies. But I had seen nothing yet to convince me that Blagdon fish would not take my nymph. One fish proved nothing. But I had got tired of peering continuously into the water and so started to cast in the hope that I might be lucky enough to place the artificial in the view of some unsuspecting trout. Well, we drifted here, then drifted there. Not a fish showed the slightest inclination to give me a chance of sport. I tried, one after the other, all the patterns I had with me.

Yet it was great fun and though I caught nothing I enjoyed

it. I knew big fish were in the water and as I watched my well-greased cast and line floating on the surface I expected every moment to see it draw under as I had done so many times elsewhere in the past. The sun had gone down and darkness came over the lake before the second fish of the day decided to give himself up. I say this out of no disrespect for wet-fly fishermen. Again it was Harry's tail fly which proved the attraction and this as he was lifting it from the water for a recast. The fish actually leapt and hooked himself as he took the fly in the air. All credit was due to Harry as a wet-fly fisherman. He most certainly showed me that fish can be taken with wet flies when the use of a nymph is hopeless. Luck, or no luck, he was the only one of the party to get fish. I left the next morning with a feeling that Blagdon fish had not enhanced my reputation as a nymph fisherman. Few fish were on the feed that October day, where nymphs would attract them.

The following year there came a chance when I was able to get a contrast and see all I wanted to see in lake water. Then the fascination of lake fishing, when fish may approach from any angle, instead of lying in positions against the run of a stream, came out in its full power. In Buckinghamshire, where I went to give professional advice about a seven acre lake, I met Mr. P. R. Goodearl, who had the fishing rights, and his son, both very keen and enthusiastic dry-fly, and nymph fishermen. Mr. Goodearl was anxious to know if improvements could be made to improve spawning facilities and if possible to increase the fly life situation. It was a beautiful morning in late July with little wind and the water was exceptionally clear. In a very short time I could see he had a really first-class head of brown trout in this lake and in its feeders and outfall. The fish were mostly four year olds and during the two years or so they had been in the lake many had reached a weight of over three pounds.

The little lake is in a very lovely setting with trees all around to form a delightful background. It is fed by three small streams and through the gin-clear water, which came from the spring heads nearby, it was possible to see fish at great distances, and see them on the feed. The lake is artificial, as indeed most lakes are in this country, and stepped up with a 15ft. dam at the lower end. Here the excess water tumbles over to pass on down a widened channel to join the old river course. We wandered around the fishing until lunch-time and then to my delight Mr. Goodearl invited me to try and catch a trout during the afternoon. Usually, if in the fishing season, I take some tackle with me when visiting strange waters to give advice, as I like to catch a fish or two to see their condition and to find out what food they are taking. I had my rod and a box of flies and nymphs in my car on this occasion.

We went to the outfall after lunch. Trout were rising occasionally to midges and to that tiny pale watery pro-cloeon rufulum, a fly I had good reason to know well as we get plenty of them at late evening on the Avon. I could see several good fish cruising around in one pool in the centre of the outfall channel. One was over 3lb. I am sure. He rose as I watched and I tried him with a small pale watery pattern dry-fly I find good on the Avon, then a midge, then in desperation with a large red sedge, but neither he, nor any of the others, would take. They did not appear to be scared so I asked if I might try a nymph. Getting permission to do so I knotted on my small spurwing representation. But still I could get no response. I tried a larger pattern with no better luck, and then put on a pheasant tail on a No. 0 hook. First cast, the big fish moved towards it as though intending to take and then went off to the other side of the pool. I decided to leave him and go on downstream.

A couple of hundred yards brought us to the natural course. Here the water had been diverted by groynes into a narrow channel in the centre. In this channel Mr. Goodearl said there lived a four pounder. Though I looked closely I could not see him; but the fish saw me and out he rushed and away downstream. I watched the bow wave he made going away in the distance and then, within easy casting distance, I saw a second fish coming towards me. There was scarcely any current and so, quickly getting out line, I cast my nymph. He must have seen it as it sank down within inches of his nose but he made no move. Then just as I was about to withdraw and make a second cast, he tilted up almost vertically and I saw his jaws move. Up went my rod point and in a moment that fish was away. A long run down for twenty yards, then up into the air three times in succession—up and past me, and then all about the little stream jumping like a mad thing. Flannel weed was floating everywhere and soon my fish was dragging great loads about with him on my cast. This slowed him down a bit but made it impossible for me to land him from the bank. Fortunately the water was not more than two feet deep so I waded out. Mr. Goodearl threw me a landing net and I waited my chance. Still the big fish bored here and there but as luck would have it, a lump of flannel weed slipped down the cast and over his eyes. I pulled him slowly towards me and into the net and then staggered to the bank, just in time to meet a horde of angry bees which my companion had unknowingly disturbed in moving near their hive. One stung my ear, another my cheek, before I had a chance to throw my fish and rod to land and use my hands to beat them off. I came ashore some distance upstream and then crept stealthily down to see just what kind of fish I had caught. There he was in the net with the flannel weed still over his eyes, a short thick beauty which weighed 2lb. 14oz. The tiny hook was in the extreme end of his nose. The sight of it enabled me to understand why he had been so energetic.

As we moved on I forgot about my bee stings. I was quite sure I had caught that fish unfairly. He must have been trying to smell the nymph when I tightened, and by one chance in a thousand the hook took a hold. The water deepened as we approached a set of controls. Good trout were everywhere, but somewhere, I knew, was at least one four pounder. Mr. Goodearl said there were others and I had an urge to catch one. We went to the lower boundary and then, as we returned along the same bank, I saw a noble fish cruising slowly around a deep pool. He was about two feet below the surface, and on the feed. At a glance I could see he was well over 4lb. and I immediately " froze ".

At one side a fringe of scum and flannel weed covered the surface, and beneath this he glided. Now is the time to cast, I thought, and did so just to the edge of the scum and in the direction he was moving. The nymph sank down and my heart gave a leap as the great fellow appeared below it and came slowly up. I tensed and then there was a flash, my cast drew under and instinctively I tightened, but on the wrong fish.

Although Mr. Goodearl had some fine fish, I had not bargained for a three pounder and a four pounder to be attracted to an artificial nymph at the same time. But that is what happened. The smaller fish must have been lying just under the fringe of scum and had taken the nymph almost from off the other's nose. He paid the penalty for his interference. The disturbance caused in playing him out frightened the big one, but sorry as I was to have missed the chance of getting him, I had a brace of trout well worthy of the name.

Later I fished from a boat and though the two brace I got were not as large as those from the outfall they took my nymph very readily. It had been a very interesting and exciting afternoon, and it had made me thoughtful. The artificial I used was evolved to represent olives in the upper Avon but I found no olive nymphs in the lake or in the outfall. I could only think that the fish took the pattern in mistake for a gnat larvae. Chironomids were plentiful in the lake and when examining the stomach contents of one of the large fish, gnat larvae were present amongst the scores of snails which bulged out his crop.

Fishing the nymph in these still waters interested me considerably but at that time my visits to fish lakes was very limited and it was to be several more years before I really became fascinated with the kind of sport one can get in these big waters. The follow up and my experiences can be read in other chapters.

Chapter Fifteen

THE GREAT LAKES

Memories of Blagdon and Chew: Westwards to Durleigh and Sutton Bingham: The art of detecting the take: The fallacy of long casting: Too many missed strikes: Playing heavyweight on light tackle.

ONLY IN THE past twelve years have I come to know and really enjoy the sport there is to be had in fishing the still waters. I must confess that previously I thought that the catching of trout in the lakes and reservoirs was a poor substitute for river fishing. Had it not been that I discovered my technique of nymphing could be most fascinating in these big waters, maybe I would still be of my former opinion, for how wrong I was in thinking there was little skill in the taking of trout from such waters. My fascination for this kind of fishing was clinched for me when I spent the holiday in North Sweden which represents a chapter of this book. There I had plenty of time at my disposal to work out theory into practice and so, when I fished again in the lakes of this country, I was able to do so with a quite different approach and with success fresh in mind.

My wife cannot understand why I like to visit Chew Valley or Blagdon, in Somerset, to travel a distance of sixty miles and then pay twenty five shillings for a day permit to fish, when trout are so plentiful close to my home and in other parts nearby. From her point of view, perhaps it is rather amazing, for no doubt there are many who fish at Chew Valley, and other reservoirs and lakes, who would love to have the chances I have to fish rivers. It is not that I ever take many fish in these reservoirs, for only once have I had my limit at Chew Valley, and never at Blagdon. Perhaps I would have done this on various occasions had I used the popular methods with teams of flies or big lures. But such fishing has no appeal for me and it was only after I found, by much perseverance, that it is possible to get really good sport with light tackle and a single nymph or bug, that I began to class it as a sport equal, and at times, even more exciting, than fishing the chalk streams and other rivers. Trout in lakes will take small nymphs and bugs quite as confidently as those in the running stream. But the whole success lies in the ability of the fishermen to place the artificial where it can be seen by a fish and in such way, that the fish is deceived into thinking it is a natural creature and something good to eat.

Discovery that good fun could be had came in rather a surprising way. It was but a fortnight or so after I returned from Sweden that I went with a friend to Chew Valley and during our journey I had recounted some of my experiences and showed him some of the nymphs I had tied and used with such success. He thought these nymphs might bring the trout at Chew and I gave him a couple to try. In turn he gave me samples of several others he had made up and we were all set up with high hopes when we arrived at the lake and put up our tackle. It was about half past ten on a morning in early August. We had had no rain for weeks and the lake was very low in consequence. Though cloudy the day was very warm and not a breath of air disturbed the surface of the water.

I never have confidence in fishing any water unless I have seen fish feeding, either at, or below the surface, but after an hour of watching this place and that, without a sign of a fish, I decided to wade out and just search in a hopeful way. Hour after hour passed along in trying this place and that and, during this time, I tried all my nymphs and also those given to me by my friend. Neither brought response. By about four o'clock I was tired To my mind the position was hopeless and, so, washing off the mud from my waders, I went back to some clean and high ground to lie down and have a rest. It was hot and humid and soon I drifted off to sleep.

My friend was one of those who will never confess he is beaten and he continued to persevere. I had been dozing fitfully for about half an hour when I woke to see him with his rod bending and a fish splashing about in front of him. This he quickly landed, a brownie of one and a half pounds. I asked the usual question, " What had the fish taken?" He laughed. " This," he said, with another grin. " One of your wooly bugs you gave me on the Avon when we were grayling fishing last year." He had put it on in desperation after trying all his own patterns and thought it might sink a little deeper. These bugs are weighted to go down well, for when fishing for grayling in some of the deep pools it is necessary to get well down towards the bottom if you wish to interest the larger fish. Back he went to the same place and within a moment was into a second fish. This was another brownie of well over two pounds which he landed without trouble.

Gone was my lethargic mood. Isn't it surprising how a little excitement can freshen one up. I had some bugs in my own bag somewhere, I knew. Soon I located these and had one tied on my cast, and had waded out to a position some forty yards to one side of him. If he could catch these fish with my grayling bugs, then I felt I had a good chance to do so as well. As if to give me encouragement, a fish rose. The first I had seen all day and this within easy casting distance. The bug pitched in to the rings he had made, and sank. I watched and waited as the cast drew down with the weight of the bug, then, judging the lure was deep enough, gave the rod tip a lift to give the bug some movement and attraction. A short draw was enough. That fish had it at once and up into the air he went as the hook took hold. I could see it was a brownie of well over two pounds but he gave me no chance. A sunken hedgerow went out obliquely and through this my fish went to make a turn around a stump. A sudden jar on my rod and he was gone with my bug.

A new cast point and a second bug was soon attached and within moments I hit another fish. Straight through the hedge he went too and when a break followed I decided to move. No sense in hooking fish in such a place only to lose them. Still it had been exciting. Splashes to my left showed my friend had a third fish on, a two and a half pound rainbow, which he landed, and not long afterwards he got a fourth, of just over three pounds. He was cock-a-hoop as you may imagine. He advised me to move along to a place where he had seen two fish rise, and this I did. My luck changed. One after another, during the next hour, I took seven big trout, four browns and three rainbows which together weighed fifteen pounds. My friend got another brace and we decided we would retire. Fishing at Chew Valley and indeed in all lakes and reservoirs is a matter of being in the right place and where the fish are. Also success depends on using something the fish expect to see and to take as a food. This was the fifth time I had fished in Chew Valley but the only time I had managed to catch fish.

We had a good laugh together going home that evening. In the morning we had been discussing lake entomology and the tying of flies and nymphs. My friend was an excellent fly-tyer and took great trouble with all his patterns of both flies and nymphs. He had also taken the trouble to procure some materials which were very difficult to get, so as to be able to construct some patterns of nymphs which had been recommended in a book recently published. He had spent hours patiently sorting out and tying in the right feathers, tinsels and silks, to be quite sure the exact colours were well represented, on the right size of hook. All for nothing. For my own part I had spent quite a time in constructing various nymphs and making sure these were balanced correctly. Then to take fish with a bug I had made up to kill off grayling. As my friend remarked, just a miserable concoction of wire and wool, which to the human eye has not the slightest resemblance to any living creature.

In the Avon, and elsewhere I had fished this bug, but I thought the grayling mistook it for a shrimp, but most certainly those fish at Chew did not make the same mistake for there are very few shrimp in this lake. They could have mistaken it for a beetle larvae, but I think it more likely, in view of later success with it, that the fish in the lakes take the bug in mistake for a hatching sedge fly. The attraction to fish comes after the bug has sunk and is then being drawn gently towards the surface in a slow but even glide. With the well-greased line and cast butt, the effect of a hatching sedge can very easily be simulated. There are some sedge fly larvae which leave their cases on the bottom and swim up through the water in much the same way as ephemeroptera.

Since that day I have fished at Chew Valley and Blagdon lakes many times. Also I have fished in Durleigh and Sutton Bingham and in our own, and smaller lakes, elsewhere. The bug, which we now call the " Killer Bug " the tying of which is described in the chapter on artificials, is now my standby for all static waters where there are big fish. But I have never found it to be really successful at late evening, especially when the buzzer nymphs are hatching. At this time I now change over to my buzzer nymph pattern, or to a small Grey Goose or Pheasant tail.

With lake fishing I came to the conclusion long ago that unless fish are showing at or near the surface it is unlikely that any will be attracted to a nymph. It is but a waste of time, and of patience, to cast indiscriminately. To catch fish with nymphs the fish must be feeding in the upper foot or so of water, indeed not below the depth to which a nymph or a bug will sink, and where it can be given the required movement. The important thing is to know that there are fish within reach. In rivers it is possible, in most cases, to see fish and even if they are not to be seen, if one rises you know he is likely to be still in the same position. What is more, in the running stream you know very well in which direction the head is pointing and therefore can deliver the nymph accordingly. In the lakes the trout continue to move when they are feeding and will travel over a very wide area. But their search is a thorough one and it seems possible that each fish, or group of fish will select a certain beat and keep to it for a while. On various occasions I have found that if I mark the area of a rise form and continue to cast to that spot, the same fish can be caught there even though he has many acres of water around him. At times it might mean casting to that one place for ten minutes, sometimes longer, but eventually patience is rewarded.

Fishing a nymph, or a bug in lakes and reservoirs is much the same as fishing these same artificials in the slow running reaches of a river. The key to success is in knowing just when a fish has taken and it is here that I know many anglers fail. Once the penny drops, so to speak, and the indications of a take are noted, the rest is comparatively easy. So many fish with nymphs and expect to get a pull or a snatch from their quarry, in much the same way as one does when fishing wet-flies or big lures. But the technique is different. If a nymph is fished properly, by this, I mean in a way a fish expects a natural nymph to behave, the take of a fish is seldom registered on the rod. It is because of this, because I have seen so many fish missed after taking a nymph that I make no apology for repeating what I have already written several times. For nymphs to be really effective they have to be fished slowly. Fish, really big fish, can take and spit out an artificial without cast or line showing any indication that this has been done. Even the most experienced of nymph fishermen will miss the take of some fish in this way, and indeed on occasions catch fish when lifting for a recast without knowing a fish had the nymph in his mouth. And there are times when an angler will tighten and connect but cannot explain why. This happens mostly when the line and the leader is slack, sometimes indeed when a fish takes as the nymph or bug is sinking. It is because of this that there is such a need for concentration. I tell all my pupils to tighten at the least indication. I repeat there is no time to wonder, is it, or was it. It might be a strand of weed, or a sudden acceleration of the sinking nymph, but tighten, and think afterwards.

On occasions fish will take and hold a nymph in their mouths much longer than at others. This leaves no doubt at all in the mind of the angler for often cast and line will draw in a decided manner. Usually, the smaller the fish the more sudden is the take. It is the slow draw down of the cast which shows that a big one has taken. Once again I refer to the importance of light quick-actioned tackle. I use the same light rods for nymphing in lakes as I do for nymphing in rivers, for the same speed in hooking is necessary.

When using nymphs and bugs in the still waters it is not wise to be impatient. Being selective and casting to individual fish, can at times be just as important as when fishing in a river and the same accuracy and delicacy is required. It is no use flopping out a long line in a series of false casts on to the water to get distance, for by doing this any trout in the locality can be scared out of their wits. Yet often I see it done. Often too I have seen the line, leader and artificials delivered with such force as to cause a decided splash and with line and leader falling together in a maze of coils. In very deep, or water distorted by wave and wind action, this might pass unnoticed by fish, but on those days when there is a flat or but a gentle ripple, far more fish are scared than attracted.

Long casting when fishing small artificials is not desirable. Nothing is gained by it and indeed much can be lost. As I have already mentioned, patience is needed. I know just how tantalising it can be to see fish rising repeatedly just out of reach of even a thirty yard cast and there have been times when I have been tempted to get a nymph out to such areas. But nothing is gained by it, for should one make such casts in a desirable way, the chances of hooking a fish, even if it took firmly are at least twenty to one against. These lake fish are hunters. They cruise here and there when on the feed and if one can control the desire to start fishing and just wait quietly, often enough the search for food will bring a trout much closer to the shore when presentation can be made in a far more natural manner. Chances of getting fish are often spoiled by being too eager. A fish may be well on the feed and will take if you get a nymph to him properly, but the difficulty is in being quick enough to hook him. You see the cast draw and though you may strike immediately, the long line acts as a drag to any quick movement of the hook inside the jaws of the fish. In most cases this results in just pricking the fish, or in hooking him lightly in the fringes of the jaw. In either case it is enough to make the fish wary of taking a second time and most often he stops feeding.

As I have said the chances are about twenty to one against and this means that for every one fish taken by long distance casting, nineteen are scared. It means too that a water has to contain a very big head of fish for the chance of a brace or more of fish to be caught. Watching and waiting is a thing we have to do on the chalk streams. Indeed far more time is spent in observation than in actual fishing. In such waters the ruling is that one must not cast indiscriminately but only to fish which, through sight or movement, indicates they are of a takeable size. One might sit an hour, sometimes longer, especially when using a dry-fly, before being able to mark down quarry which are worthy of attention.

It amuses me sometimes to see anglers start to fish in lakes.

Granted there is enthusiasm. I have seen them have a race against time to put on waders, put up their tackle and attach artificials. Straightaway they go to a favourite point, to a place perhaps where at some time in the past a fish has been caught by them, or perhaps where it is known that bags have been made there by other anglers. Without a pause for reflection out they go into the water, right to the tops of their waders and a searching of the water around them commences. To me this seems to be just hopeful fishing and in no way calculated. It is true some fish are caught in this way and at times with a very first cast, but who knows just what sport there might have been in the same area if a little caution is used. Because these lakes are so big, I think the tendency of many anglers is to forget that trout are still very shy creatures. Such tactics which are adopted by many would be quite hopeless in small lakes and ponds, or in rivers, especially where the water is clear and for the most part unruffled by wind or by current.

It is because of this, and indeed of several other important factors, that so few are converted to the use of nymphs in preference to the usual methods adopted by the majority of lake and reservoir fishermen. Long distance casting with strong rods and heavy shooting head lines, combined with big lures on strong leaders has taken many fish and will continue to take fish but to my mind the real joy of fishing is lost with such tactics. To say the least it is hard work to continue casting with such tackle all day but to many, results are the thing which count most. Often those who catch fish with the distance casting and lure stripping methods, fail woefully when trying to get sport with small nymphs. Usually this is because the same tackle and the same method of fishing is employed.

Fishing small nymphs and bugs is not a matter of casting out and stripping in fast, for this is entirely at variance with the natural movement of an insect, and fish know it. All the nymphs and bugs I use are constructed so that they have an easy and quick entry into water; they sink to a level where fish expect to see a natural creature. But they need to be fished very slowly through the water to be attractive. With the fast stripping method used with big lures, or indeed when fishing a team of fast dragging wet-flies, fish hook themselves. They are felt by the angler, in fact, and though a strike with the rod is made, this really is unnecessary. When a take is registered on a rod, the hook has already made a purchase in the mouth of the fish. This is not the case when fishing nymphs slowly. One has to hook the fish during the brief moment it has the artificial in its mouth, exactly as when fishing a dry-fly. Very few fish would be caught with dry-flies if the angler waited for a pull. An occasional one, perhaps one in a hundred, would be unfortunate in hooking himself, but that is all. It is the same with nymphs.

It is because of this that I stress the importance of light quick-actioned tackle and the need for concentration. Keep in mind the fact that it is something similar to dry-fly fishing that you are doing, and not wet-fly or lure stripping. It is important to have a line and a cast butt which floats and remains clearly visible on the surface. These instructions will possibly bore those who already know all there is to be known about nymphing in lakes and I apologise. But each day others are keen to learn anything which might help them to have good sport and for these I must write with some clarity. It is much easier to fish nymphs in the still waters than it is upstream in rivers, more especially in fast running water. But whether in fast running or static water, if the fish cannot be seen, then the only indication of a take one can see, is that of the movement the fish gives to the floating leader. One fishes with this point foremost in mind. When I cast it is to an area where I have seen a fish feeding and just as delicately as I would if placing a nymph in front of a trout in the clear water of a chalk stream. I watch as the nymph, or the bug sinks, for sometimes a fish will take almost at once. This means a pause of just a moment or two, until in fact you see that about half the leader has sunk, or drawn under. Then, with the rod pointing low over the water, take up all slack line until a slight drag commences. The time now comes to slowly lift the rod tip, at the same time gathering in line. Sometimes the take of a fish is felt, but this is unusual. More often the take of a fish is indicated by a draw on the floating cast butt, or line. This is a kind of reverse of the arrowhead which shows as the free line and leader is moving towards one as it is being gathered slowly in. Quick action with the rod is then essential but this is not as difficult as it might at first appear. By lifting the rod to impart drag and the correct movement, the rod then comes into a very easy position for hooking with the tip, in fact it is already flexing with the weight of the line, so that instant contact can be made by just a flick of the wrist.

With this kind of fishing in lakes it is necessary to use fine cast points. In the first place the artificials are very small in comparison to such things as worm flies, black lures, muddler minnows etc., or any of the bucktails or streamers, which are so commonly used. Secondly, a quick and neat entry to water is desirable. The finer a point can be the quicker a nymph will sink and the more attractive it will appear beneath the surface. But with the fine cast point it is essential to have line and rod of a sensitive nature, a rod actually with a very sensitive tip which will flex to the wrist action when hooking. Some will say that it is not possible to land the big fish of lakes and reservoirs with such light tackle but with this I strongly disagree. It depends on just how one goes about it. One cannot be harsh or firm with such tackle. The moment a big fish is hooked he should be allowed to run if he so wishes. Just hit him, hold the rod up so that it flexes well to the pull of the fish and let the reel run. Usually the moment they are hooked, these big fish will head towards the deeper water well out from the shore. A hundred yards of 10lb. breaking strain nylon does not take up much room on a reel, and this with a casting line of say thirty yards, should be ample to control any fish one is likely to hook. If a fish wishes to run such distance well let him, but it is extremely doubtful if he will. Usually the drag of the long line and the backing acts as a brake and at about fifty or maybe eighty yards, he slows up and turns back. Then a quick recovery of line can be made and a control established. It is seldom a second long run is made. The light tackle means that one has to be careful and the playing out of a fish takes much longer before it is safe to use a landing net.

There is of course reason in everything and though I have said, be careful, this does not mean dilly-dallying about and allowing a fish to do much as he pleases. Though gentle, the playing should still be firm, as strongly indeed as the cast point and rod will stand. I hate to see fish hooked and skull-dragged ashore. I recall seeing one young angler hook and land two fish he had hooked on a big lure. It seemed obvious that most of the fishing he had ever done had been on a sea-shore for, after the fish had hooked themselves he ran backwards just dragging the struggling fish to dry ground, an exhibition on which I felt duty bound to make a protest. I hate too, to see fish hauled in and then kicked up the bank by the angler. This is just slaughter to my way of thinking. Fortunately this kind of thing cannot be done with real nymphing tackle for then a good sized landing net is needed and some skill also in guiding the fish into it.

Feeling and playing a big fish when using light tackle only comes with experience. You must be with them all the time. By this I mean you must be prepared to give line to a powerful surge and ready to reel in whenever a slackness occurs. The give and the take of line becomes automatic and just the touch so necessary to win a battle, can save many a breakage or escape. It is never wise to assume that a fish is firmly hooked and it is as well to remember that small hooks cannot possibly have the purchase that a large one has, or indeed the strength in the steel.

I think the most exciting time with lake fishing is at late evening more, especially in those waters where the big chironomids hatch. The rise of fish to the hatching buzzer nymph is very well known, so also is the frustration which so often accompanies it. Buzzer hatches continue throughout much of the fishing season. Some hatch during the day but normally it is during the last hour or so of daylight when there is most activity with the fish. For many years I made and tried lots of different artificials and ways of fishing them. It is true I got occasional fish but not enough to get a confidence in the patterns I was using. So many fish would by-pass my best efforts and continue to rise and show in a most maddening way. To me it seemed that once they expected to see these hatching nymphs, they were blind to all else. My chances for experiments in the big lakes were not sufficiently frequent to be able to solve the problem of what these fish expected to see. I knew it was not just a good copy of the actual hatching insect for I knew the creature well and indeed every colour and feature of it. I also knew their habits when hatching from the nymph to the fly. I soon discovered that my normal way of fishing nymphs had little

attraction. I fished patterns in many different ways, ringing the
changes in fishing fast, slow, and medium paced. I tried just
casting and allowing the nymph to hang without motion, as I
have said, without appreciable success.

This went on for several years. Each time I made a visit to
fish Chew Valley or Blagdon I took with me other patterns of
buzzers to try, but I made no headway, until we constructed a
series of artificial lakes in our valley here. These we stocked with
big rainbows and in them were some very good sized wild
browns. These little lakes started to produce an abundance of
chironomids of varying species including the big buzzers, and
rises of fish at late evening to take these taxed the patience of
all who tried to catch them. It really was amazing to watch them
and amusing to watch the efforts of so many who tried so hard
to get one or another to take. Seeing how these big fish behaved
made me realise just how hopeless had been my former attempts
in the big lakes. I could see that by far the greater number of
the insects were taken by fish just in or below the surface. Few
are taken in the winged form, that is, after the nymph has
hatched and the fly is on the surface. So this ruled out any
possibility of success with a well constructed dry-fly, whether
fished motionless or skittered lightly along the surface in a
manner these flies have.

On occasions I was able to watch the reaction of fish to the
artificials I constructed and fished beneath the water. Many
times these big trout would take naturals within inches of my
artificial. Some would brush the floating leader with bodies or
tails. Others would take a natural almost from off the floating
line. On one evening I caught a fish which rose and took a
natural which was actually on my leader and he took the nylon
between his jaws. This fish I caught for, as he turned away, so
the nylon point drew through his jaws and the hook took a hold
on the outside.

It became very obvious that the fish were not scared by any
attachment of leader or of line, but there was some characteristic
of the insect which was definite and which so far had eluded
all my efforts to incorporate it in my tyings, or in my fishing of
the artificials. I caught and studied the live insects and at last
hit on what I think might be the solution. It is too early yet to

say that this tying will remain in its present form but during the past three years I have given it a very thorough trial in many different waters. The tying and the manner of assembly for fishing is given on page 63 and I now do my best to explain the most successful way of fishing it.

I seldom use more than one artificial on a cast when fishing lakes or any still waters as I feel little is gained and a lot is lost. At late evening, when the light is bad it can tax one's patience to clear a snarl, or hang up, of a single fly or nymph, and if two, or three should become tangled, very valuable fishing time can be lost in sorting out the mess. Usually this kind of thing happens just when several fish choose to come within easy reach and rise repeatedly, as if knowing you are out of action and often, the faster you work to try and sort out the tangle, the worse it becomes. Another point too. Though it is possible to use the rod and make a single artificial move and swim in a natural way, this cannot be done with two or more on the leader. A feeding fish is just as likely to see a single artificial as he is to notice several and though occasionally one might get two, or even three fish on a cast, this can hardly be termed sporting. In most cases the second or a third fish will take as the first one to be hooked, tows the other flies after him. These of course hook themselves and there can be no credit to the fisherman, though some credit is due if he can land them successfully. Where stock fish have been introduced I feel the use of more than one fly or nymph on a cast, should be banned. These fish have been accustomed to being fed and to following each other about. Excitement of one splashing about when hooked, will often attract others in the locality, when anything moving in the water near to the hooked fish will be taken by a second or third. This does happen with wild fish too occasionally, especially in well stocked waters.

A single buzzer nymph is all one can fish properly, or so I have found. Though some wire is used in the construction of these artificials it is not wise to overdo the weighting with this, for these should be made so that they hang in the water and not continue to sink. The essential thing is a good floating line and a leader well greased for half its length. Presentation should be done in a delicate way, in much the same manner as adopted when casting a dry fly. There is sufficient weight in the tying for a quick penetration of the water to take place. After this the procedure is much the same as when dry-fly fishing. Cast to the area where fish are moving and watch the floating cast from the moment the artificial has sunk. This is a technique which is different to both wet fly and general nymph fishing. No drag or lift with the rod is required. Just cast, get the rod into a comfortable position in the hand for quick hooking and then watch closely. If cast and line has been treated well, only the finer part of the leader should be beneath water with the nymph hanging. Many times I have watched fish sight, and approach the artificial, and take in a most leisurely way. Then comes a draw of the floating part of the cast. This might at times appear to be just a sudden acceleration of the artificial in sinking but more often it is the take of the fish which causes it. Strike quickly in either case, unless it has been possible to see there is no fish in the locality of the nymph.

Patience in this kind of fishing is required. Nothing is gained by continual casting and re-casting, or indeed by throwing to each fish which may show. It was by accident that I discovered the best way to fish these buzzer nymphs. I had been trying out the pattern by casting out, allowing it to sink and then retrieving, in much the same manner as when fishing an ordinary swimming nymph representation. There had been no response. I had made a further cast and decided to light a cigarette before fishing the nymph in. With rod held lightly in my left hand I used the right to flick a flame from my lighter when, just as I was about to draw on my cigarette, so I saw my cast pull down in no uncertain way. I struck as well as I could with the left hand. This knocked the cigarette from my mouth and the lighter from my right hand, but I hooked the fish, a rainbow of over three pounds. My lighter, with the flame still burning, fell into a pile of dried grass which immediately caught fire and spread around my legs. What with reeling in line to get the fish under control and at the same time doing my best to stamp out the burning grass, I had rather a hectic few moments. I landed the fish, put out the fire, but spoiled my cigarette, for in the excitement this was trodden into fragments.

In the next hour I took four more fish ranging from one and a half to two pounds all with the same method of fishing. Each

took the hanging buzzer and the take was shown plainly with
the draw on the cast. It was the first of many evenings of
success. As explained in the instructions for tying, when threaded
correctly on the leader point, the nymph is at liberty to wobble
from side to side and indeed to spin completely around it. The
tiny bit of white nylon wool which represents the celia can also
spin and move freely. A combination of both, deludes a fish into
thinking the artificial is alive. After reading this you will at
once have a question in mind. Can the hook take hold as well
in this hanging position, as in the normal one? The answer is
yes, indeed the hooking is very definite. Again, you might query
if the knotted nylon wool will pull through the eye of the hook.
The answer is no, for of the hundreds of fish I have caught with
this pattern, only one has escaped through this happening and
then I think it was because of a gap in the correct closing of the
eye, a faulty hook in fact.

There is much sport to be had for those who care to try this
method of constructing and fishing the buzzer nymph and for
all, there can be a feeling of confidence when the naturals are
hatching, and the fish are mad to take them. For my own part,
when I fail to get sport when fishing the bug, nymph or buzzer
during a day and evening on a lake, then I leave with the feeling
that no one else has fared better.

Chapter Sixteen

TO THE FAR WEST

A district of improving prospects : Impressions of Cornwall's new lake fisheries : How to make the best of small trout : Some waters holding large trout : How the nymph again proved its worth.

I KNEW very little about Cornwall or its facilities for trout fishing until, in the early sixties, I was invited to Penzance in my role as a fishery consultant, to give advice regarding the stocking and maintenance of a new reservoir at Drift. This is on part of the Trewidden Estate and the owner had hopes that it might become an attractive place for trout fishermen. The site flooded, covers an area of between sixty and seventy acres brought about by the trapping of two moorland streams. My first view of this little lake, newly formed though it was, was one of pleasure, for it already had a character which is so sadly missing from many of the areas which have been used in recent years for the making of reservoirs. Tucked away as it is, in a deep fold in the hills, but for the big dam, which then looked stark and new, this sheet of water might well have been mistaken for a natural lake. Care had been taken to preserve the amenities in the form of scrub and trees on the hillsides and the setting had an immediate appeal to me as a trout fisherman.

The two small feeders which supply the water are typical of the moorland streams of the far west country. These lead away up into the moors and into the old mining areas in the high ground, for the most part scrub lined and neglected, but issuing a good volume of clear, though acid water. In each was a mul-

titude of tiny trout, little fellows with a colouration which
blended with their surroundings, and as wild, as only wild trout
can be. None I saw were more than six inches in length and
most of them much smaller, little larger in fact, than some of
the minnows we have in the Avon. But at once I knew that
here in the two streams was an inexhaustible supply of fish which
could stock the lake and places where, in years to come, the
mature fish could run up to spawn.

Such water as this breeds a multitude of gnats and midges,
mostly chironomids, and the larvae of these, and the insects,
form most of the food supply for fish. At the same time they
keep fish surface minded. In many places along the streams, and
indeed already in the main body of the lake, many of the little
fish, were rising, and when at evening I visited the lake just as
the sun was setting, the sight of hundreds of little trout feeding
at the surface set all my instincts as a fisherman alight. I knew
at once that this little lake could provide some really good sport,
and so it has proved.

This was the first of several visits I have made to Penzance.
That first year no one was allowed to fish the Drift reservoir
and in the second, I was the first to try it with nymph and fly.
My very first cast with a nymph brought a fish of just over a
pound, a monster when compared to the little natives of the
streams. I fished all that day and a part of the next, catching,
examining, and returning most of the ones I caught. Some I
killed to make autopsies. In all I took some thirty brace on
little P.T. nymphs and must have missed hooking at least a
hundred others. These ranged from six inches to the largest
which was fourteen, and all fought like little demons.

This was my first experience of fishing the Drift, but it was
typical of what has followed on through the years. Though much
has been done and a very gradual increase in size and condition
has been effected, this can never be a water to produce monsters.
But for fighting and sporting fish, and also for free risers, there
can be few artificial lakes to equal it. There may be those who
will fish it for the first time after reading what I write about the
Drift and other lakes in the far West but this I must say. If you
wish to get real sport and enjoyment from your fishing, then
use tackle which can provide it. This is not water in which heavy

rods, lines and big lures are needed. There is no need to cast
for long distances for fish are plentiful within easy reach. It is
the delicate outfit and the tiny flies and nymphs which can bring
most fish, and most enjoyment.

It was in those early days at Penzance that I met and became
friendly with Arthur Tomlin and his brother Ralph. Both are
real fishermen and I need say no more. Arthur had been keen
on trout fishing for many years but Ralph, until our meeting,
had his interests in the sea. But he would come to watch Arthur
and myself in action and gradually I could see an interest
awakening in his eyes and in his manner. So I coaxed him into
having some tuition with my rod and a nymph. It was amazing
how quickly he grasped the fundamentals of casting, and when
after an hour or so he hooked and landed his first small trout on
a fly rod, the bug of trout fishing had bitten hard. It is true he
still goes sea fishing, but now the trout are his great love and
he gets far more joy in hooking and landing a quarter pound
trout on his light tackle than in hauling in a ton of sharks or ray,
or in stringing in a line full of mackerel.

As he said, it is something different, something really skilful,
and something which can take one to very attractive settings.
The seas are much of a muchness and, I must confess, have never
had much appeal for me. I like the wild and rugged coast lines
but the sight always makes me conscious of the great power
there is in the sea and I feel puny and insignificant in consequence. Besides I like peace and solitude and hate the sound
of the great waves, battering away at the coast line, and the
scream and squawking of the gulls. So much better I think to be
where the sound of a hundred song birds can give a background
of music, and where the wings of a thousands insects can glint
in the rays of the setting sun.

The Drift reservoir is not the only place in the locality where
good sport can be obtained. One can have some very interesting
hours just fishing the moorland streams. Some are much too
overgrown to be able to use a fly rod, but parts of most have
open places. Creeping along and dropping a tiny nymph into
the pockets and the pools can be fascinating, for to see the
little trout flashing up from deep down to take, is joy in itself.
No one would wish to kill great numbers, even if such could be

caught, but for practice in hooking, there could be no better quarry.

The Loo pool as it is called, is near Helston. This, at one time was an inlet from the sea which linked into a small stream which ran into it from the land in the locality of Helston. By some freak of tide, the whole inlet became cut off from the sea by a great bank of shingle and sand, which piled up well above the normal high tide mark leaving but a narrow channel at one side through which the water from the stream can enter the sea. This has been controlled at some time with sluice gates which can maintain a good level of fresh water in the former sea inlet, and it forms a lake of some forty acres, perhaps more. I had the pleasure of fishing this on one occasion and also to learn a little about it. For a while the water remained brackish but afterwards settled to really fresh water and trout from the stream above entered into the lake and thrived. This is a very interesting water to fish as I found, for trout in it run up to a very fair size for such locality. Many are taken up to one and a half pounds. In it strangely enough are roach, not a fish one would expect in that part of the country, but apparently some were introduced at one time and they continued to thrive. The first fish I took on a nymph was one of these, which weighed about half a pound. Here, as at the Drift, the trout are very free risers, for small insects are legion, and I found they were just as interested in the small nymphs I fished.

To the other side of Helston and not far from the little town of Redruth lies the newly constructed reservoir at Stithians. It was stocked with rainbows and opened for the first time to fishermen in 1968. This is a lake of several hundred acres and from it the records show that rainbows up to six pounds have been taken. It is a lake which so far has little other than water as an attraction as it is rather exposed, with little cover of any kind around it. Some planting around the site is under way, but I feel it will be some years yet before it has any real character. As a fishing water it is hard to judge yet, but I was surprised to find it contained a multitude of fresh water shrimps, proof indeed that it is alkaline. The presence of these did much to explain the size of the rainbows taken. I have fished this lake on three different occasions but took only one fish, a rainbow

of about a pound which fought stronger than many I have
caught which have been treble that weight. This I took on my
" Bow tie Buzzer Nymph " at late evening when the buzzers
were hatching. My experience at this lake gave me little to
record. Few fish were moving at the surface and I had no chance
for experiment.

Stithians, Argal and College lakes, are all controlled by the
South Cornwall Water Board who have come to realise the
great value there is in trout fishing and are doing much to
encourage it. I had the privilege of fishing at Argal on two
consecutive days in the latter part of May of 1969. Argal and
College lakes lie one above the other in the same watershed in
a small valley not far from Penryn and within easy reach from
Falmouth. Both are very attractive, more especially the older
College lake, which was constructed in the early part of the last
century. Argal is about thirty years old.

A glance was sufficient for me to see that the Argal lake
contained a very good head of trout. Hawthorn and black gnat
were all about the valley, and on the water, and from where we
stood at the dam end, it was possible to see the whole extent of
the water, a sheet of around sixty acres. Planting, and the help
of nature, had provided various covers in the form of small
trees and scrub, around the area, but the lake is surrounded
by hills and sheltered from any but very strong winds. A gentle
ripple covered the whole lake but in this I could see the heads
of fish appearing and also the dorsals and tails of others as they
cruised here and there in search of the luckless insects which
had been blown on to the water. Some were feeding on paired
black midges and on chironomids which had been egg-laying,
and were spent. A rise worthy to greet any stranger and make
him feel there were plenty of fish to be caught.

But it was not to be my luck to fish just then even though the
urge to do so was on me, for first I had work to do. My visit
to all these lakes was a professional one in which fishing became
very secondary. I spent a very interesting time looking around
the lakes and checking on the general fauna in them and then
had a good look at the stock producing site. By the time we were
through with it all and had lunch, the weather had changed
and the wind had freshened. Even so an odd fish was still

moving and with any luck I might have repeated my performance at the Drift and taken a fish with my very first cast. Had
conditions been as they were in the morning I would have
fished a dry fly, a black gnat, for it was very obvious that the
fish were taking these eagerly, but as there was then no real rise
I had rigged up a buzzer nymph. The fish I cast to had moved
twice in the same locality and he came at once the moment my
nymph pitched into the water. Perhaps I was a little late in
tightening for I hooked him but lightly. He leapt and was in
the air long enough for me to see it was a rainbow of about three
quarters of a pound, and my chance for fame had gone.
With this fish too went my chances for quite two hours, for the
cold wind had put down everything. Though I tried fishing
shallow and deep, ringing the changes with the various nymphs
and with the killer bug, there was no result.

Arthur and Ralph Tomlin had been fishing too but had not
seen nor touched anything. We then decided to get a boat and
row across to the other side, to where in fact there was a little
shelter in the lee of some hawthorns and gorse bushes which
fringed the lake side. As we approached I could see a weaving
mass of black midges beneath the bushes and could see they were
in the process of mating. I knew too that some of the paired
creatures would soon be falling on to the water. We dropped
anchor and watched. When fishing from a boat I much prefer
to anchor off likely places and watch for a while, rather than
drift. Fish are like birds when feeding and always work upwind.
We were anchored just in the edge of a ripple. The little black
flies continued to weave and congregate then a pair fell here,
another there, to be swept with the wind along the distorted
surface. Downwind, some fifty yards away, a fish rose, then
another and I could see they were heading in our direction.
I had put on a dry fly, a black gnat, which was the nearest I
had to represent the paired midges. A fish rose within reach but
though I covered him quickly, there was no response. Then I
tried another and still others, but something was wrong. Neither
would take. Though windy, the sun was bright. I could see it
glinting and reflecting from my leader and suspected the fish
could see this too, even though they were viewing from a different angle. I changed my point for a finer one and put on a

small pheasant tail nymph.

The response to this was immediate. The fish I cast to had been cruising along showing the dorsal and tail as it rose and as my little nymph pitched in a couple of feet ahead of his last rise form, so the cast drew in a manner which created no uncertainty. A quick flick of the rod tip set the hook and my first fish from the Argal lake started to fight for liberty. I knew at once that it was of no great size for on feeling the hook it went up into the air twice in succession to show me a rainbow of some twelve ounces. This was the first of several rainbows and two brownies which took the nymph very readily, all were much the same size but good fighting little fish. Though attracted to the surface by the fall of the paired midges, they were all very eager to take the small nymph. For a while the sport was exciting. On one occasion I could see four different fish heading upwind towards the boat, spread across about twenty yards of water. All four took the nymph as they came within casting range but I lost three of them before they could be netted.

The black midges were the main attraction, but autopsies proved that when the fish were at the surface then they took other creatures too. A couple I examined had gnat larvae in them and another contained two sedge flies.

The rise form showing the dorsal and tail of the fish is, apparently, a characteristic of the fish in this lake when they are really feeding. I found it quite interesting and fascinating to watch for one could follow the course of the fish as easily as if it was clearly visible and know exactly where to place an artificial so that it could be intercepted. But they travelled along at great speed. It was no use aiming at the rise form and I found, to get the best results, that it was necessary to drop the nymph quite six feet ahead and watch very closely for the draw of the cast. Though I hooked several fish, I missed quite a number of others. Some I just touched, but some were too quick for my reflexes.

The nymph I was using was on a No. 1 hook but, small though it was, I think an even smaller pattern would have been better but unfortunately I had no smaller ones with me. There was no need to let the nymph sink deeply. All it needed to do was to just penetrate the surface when a slight lift of the rod tip could impart a movement and bring the rod to a comfortable position for quick hooking. To catch these fish, light, quick-actioned tackle, is essential. Delicacy, accuracy, and speed must all be combined. A single nymph at the end of a fine leader is all that is necessary.

The rising of the browns and the rainbows were much the same at this time. I would have liked to see more and indeed to fish more, for to get a true background of all that happens in certain fisheries, one would need to fish for several seasons, and in all kinds of weather and water conditions. My experiences on the following day were very similar however, enough indeed for me to know that at certain times at least the Argal fishing could be most fascinating. I think I proved in the short time I was there that one is much more likely to catch fish with tiny artificials than with large ones. This is something I have found to be true in many other places.

The adjoining College lake is said to contain really good brown trout. Some up to six pounds have been taken from it. This lake, as I have mentioned, is much older than its neighbour Argal, and in consequence a much better food supply for large fish is established. Though so old, the College lake bed is in perfect condition, for through the years there has been little organic matter to settle and foul it. The water in it is remarkably clear, as also it is in Argal, and this, in a way, adds to the difficulty in deception with artificials, either on, or in the water.

In many waters I have found that the clearer the water, the smaller the artificial needed. It is a good point to keep in mind. All the Cornish lakes and streams are the same, for most of the water is of an acid nature and general aquatic vegetation is scarce. Though I have mentioned but four lakes, there are others in the far West country. None produce, or can produce, the class of trout one expects to find in really alkaline waters, but what these lack in stature, they make up in fighting value for a Cornish trout of a pound will give a greater battle than a four pounder in a chalk stream.

Chapter Seventeen

JOURNEYS TO ULSTER

Perspective from an aircraft: Small streams and large rivers: Some famous loughs: First acquaintances with gillaroo and sonaghan: Onwards into Donegal: A famous fly-tyer: The nymph versus salmon again.

THAT MY patterns of nymphs and the technique of fishing them, can be effective in still other parts, I proved when I spent a most enjoyable week as the guest of the Northern Ireland Tourist Board in 1967. During this visit I had the great privilege of the company of Mr. Daniel MacCrea, who at that time was consultant and representative of the Board. With him I travelled throughout all the provinces of Northern Ireland. Daniel McCrea is a great fisherman and character, with a very wide knowledge of all the best fishing waters in the six counties. This he was very willing to impart to me and I could have wished for no better guide or fishing companion. He is a writer on all subjects to do with fishing and is very well known by all in this connection. Though I would very much like to write of all that happened during our few days together, I fear this might weary my reader and so, this being a book mostly about nymph fishing and trout it will be on such episodes I will dwell.

Being so much amongst fishermen it was only natural that I should have heard a lot about the fishing in Ireland, of the many loughs, rivers and streams and of the big trout, pike etc., to be caught there. Often I had wished to see something of this island but it was not until March of 1967 that this wish was fulfilled. Then I was invited by the B.B.C. to take part in a television programme about fishing, which was to be staged at Lough Melvin, in Northern Ireland. I said straightaway that I thought March to be much too early to expect much activity in aquatic life, but apparently, the local informants had thought otherwise.

The invitation excited me, not because of the television, for I was quite used to this, but because a long-felt wish was about to be realised. We travelled by plane to Belfast, but I must confess to being disappointed during the first part of our journey by road to the West, which took us to our hotel at Kesh in County Fermanagh. But as we entered into County Fermanagh so my interest began to quicken. To one side or other of the road there came the gleam of water, a small stream, a river perhaps, and innumerable small loughs and ponds. And on reaching the hotel at Kesh I found I had a room with a window which over-looked a delightful little river, where it rippled over the shallow rocky bed nearby, and sent the sound of water music to my ears. Ireland had given me a welcome for the first night at least, and I slept quite content.

From Kesh to our location at Lough Melvin was a matter of some twenty miles and my first journey there set all my fishing instincts alight. The road took us beside that beautiful stretch of water, Lough Erne, and on that morning which was bright and sunny, I began to realise what Northern Ireland had to offer the angler. Truly this is the Emerald Isle, as it was called by someone many years ago who must have been a poet at heart. But he forgot to mention the diamonds which sparkled in the sunlight; great splashes of light about a vast green background. Granted there is beauty in the little green fields, each separated from its neighbour with a hedgerow of hawthorn and blackthorn. Granted too is the beauty of the hills in the distance at either side, but there in the low ground, there in the hollows and in the valleys; there with the little islands dotted about, was what I had been yearning to see. Here was water, untouched and unspoiled as it had been for centuries. More was to come, and soon I was to have my first view of Lough Melvin with its fringe of small mountains around and beyond. Here is Lough Erne's small sister, small only because of the vast area of Erne, for Melvin is over nine miles long and at its widest quite two miles. Again the sunlight sparkled on the water to give me a greeting and let me see through to the rocky and pebbly bed.

But of the television programme there is not much to say. What little hope we had was squashed by a change in the weather, for the weather worsened considerably and, from the Atlantic, came strong cold winds and heavy storms. But even so, with a little luck I might have got a fish during the programme, for though I saw but two small ones rise during the actual time I was fishing, both of these came very readily to the " Killer Bug " I was using, and I hooked and lost each after just having the thrill of hooking and seeing them leap afterwards. So actually I did have a chance to try out my nymphing technique and had the feeling that such a method could give one good sport.

Lough Melvin is the home of what the natives call " Gillaroo " trout. Indeed it was one of these we had hoped to get during the television programme. These trout get their name from their general colouring which I feel sure is brought about by the kind of food they take in the lough. The main part of this is molluscs and these I found to be plentiful even as early in the year as March. There were also hordes of caddis and shrimps with here and there crayfish under the loose rocks. Bullheads too, and a few loaches. In the algae and mosses were the larvae and nymphs of stonefly, with a few pond Olives. But the bulk of the insect life consisted of Chironomids. These were in multitude and I wondered just what sport one could have at early morning or late in the evening with a buzzer pattern, on a nice day in July or August. I saw enough of the animal life on the bed of the lough to know this water had limestone origin and that there was plenty of food to build really big trout. I wished conditions had been more favourable for fishing and for examination of the various fauna, and said as much to Daniel McCrea. Then I blessed my good fortune for the suggestion he made. " Would you like to come and spend a week or so here later in the year?" he asked. " If so, I feel sure the Tourist Board would be most pleased to have you as a guest."

At once I said I would be delighted. I had seen enough to really whet my appetite and knew a welcome back was assured. Dan was as good as his word and in due course I had an invitation to choose my own time and spend a holiday in Ulster as a guest of the Board. Daniel McCrea would be my guide and my host and I could go, look, and fish anywhere in the Northern Ireland Province where such was possible.

Plans were made, but had to be altered twice for one reason and another. Though I had hoped to make the trip in August, it was not until 16 September that I could manage it. My first sight thus of the Irish coast made up for what I had missed on the previous trip. Again I travelled by plane from London to Belfast. I had a marvellous view as we passed over and along the great Strangford sea Lough. There below, the little and innumerable islands looked to me like patches of floating algae, while between them, and around them, the little sailing boats appeared like a hatch of pale watery duns at late evening on the Avon. All that was missing were the rings of rising fish. Then at Aldergrove were the hordes of hares everyone travelling to this airport must see. It amazed me that such timid creatures could take so little notice of the landing and departure of these giant planes. A typical example of how nature can adapt herself to circumstances.

Daniel McCrea had his car ready for departure. The first leg of our journey was Omagh but before going to our hotel we called to see the Chief Inspector of the Foyle Fisheries Commission who advised us that there was a good chance for sport on the Owenkillew river. Sea trout and grilse were up in numbers, he said, and so, there and then, plans were made to go and see this river and fish it.

It was cloudy and wet the next morning as we travelled north to the Owenkillew river at Crock Bridge. This little river flows towards Newtonstewart where it joins the lovely Glenelly and the two then run into the Mourne. Crock is just on the fringe of the Sperrin Mountains which separate the counties of Derry and Tyrone. The little stream looked very attractive but my hopes of catching sea trout or grilse faded almost before I made my first cast. Bearing in mind what the Fishery Inspector had told us about grilse, I was using my ten foot six, greaseline outfit. With this I had a leader tapered to about six pound breaking strain and fished a single killer bug. It is true I caught some fish, plenty of them, but these were little brownies and the largest was not more than six ounces. If sea-trout and grilse were in the little river I feel sure I would have seen one or two at least, even if I could not catch one, and I am inclined to think that what we were told was wishful thinking, instead of fact.

The rain persisted and by early afternoon it was heavy. By this time we had covered two to three miles of the stream. Though I got no trout of size it was very interesting water to fish. This was moorland river and as expected, the food supply I found in it was very sparse, not enough to build trout any larger than half a pound. But it was a first class spawning stream for salmon and sea-trout. In it I saw many parr. Some I caught, I fear. And I would say that a little later in the year it could have held many fine fish.

By late afternoon the level had risen appreciably, and soon the water was too discoloured to go on fishing. I was anxious to see more of the lower reaches, so, packing up our rods, we travelled further north to Plumbridge and then west to Newtonstewart, so having a good view of the confluence of the Glenelly and the Owenkillew rivers with that of the Mourne. But I am a little in advance of my story. From time to time on our journey north we saw local fishermen hastening towards the rivers and tributaries and by the Glenelly we stopped to have a few words with one whom I thought to be a most amusing character.

He was ancient and of disreputable appearance, hobbling along downhill, helping himself with an ash stick some eight feet long, on which were taped some home-made rings and an old, but small brass reel. Up through the rings snaked a substantial cutty hunk line, at the end of which was a good yard or so of nylon, and a hook which could have held the largest fish in Ireland. In his pocket was a tin of big lob worms. "Yes," he said to our inquiry. "To the bridge I be going." "The river's rising, the white trout will be coming and I should have been there an hour agone." One of the old timers without a doubt. I could imagine him awakening from a nap after his mid-day pint and seeing that it had been raining hard. Then scrambling into his old overcoat, which was draped almost to the ground, he hastened to dig a few worms, grabbed up his rod and away to the river to get his supper or breakfast. Asked if he ever caught a salmon the reply was evasive. "Me licence don't cover for they."

Further on was a young angler with a fixed spool outfit in one hand and dangling a small sea-trout in the other. " His only luck," he said, taken about an hour previously before the river had risen like it was now. We saw others too in this same locality. Word had got round, or was it born of experience? The river was rising. The white trout were running. Many a worm ended its life in the river that day, and no doubt many a fish came from it with a hook well planted in a jaw.

I could have fished there had I wished but knew there was no hope with nymph or fly. Worming, though permissible, has no appeal for me. Besides I wished to see other parts nearby. So on we went to see the Mourne at Newtonstewart already swelled and flowing fast. A first class salmon river this and no doubt good for sea-trout too. But it was too big just then to see its real character and this pleasure I had at a later date. Dan McCrea wanted me to have a look at some famous pike lakes and I was very agreeable. So we headed west to Baronscourt, the home of the Duke of Abercon, a large and rambling house with a magnificent view out and over two big artificial lakes. Ireland is noted for its big pike and Dan told me there were some real whoppers in these lakes. This I could well understand and we decided, if we had the time, we would try these lakes later on, for I had taken pike tackle with me. But on this day no one was fishing, even though the charge was but five shillings per day, with boat included. It seemed, when the " white trout " were up, nobody had an inclination to fish for pike, or coarse fish.

Our next stop to fish was on the following day at a point called Bohe Island which is near the north shore of Lower Lough Erne. Here I met with Mr. Jack Suckling and his wife and family who had made a home on this small island. Jack had anticipated the time when the small island would be an attraction for fishermen and tourists and had acted accordingly. To the island he had transported chalets and equipment to fit them up into first class places to live in and to spend a holiday, and it was in one of these that Dan McCrea and I spent a night. Everything for comfort had been thought of and no one could wish for a place with greater peace. Besides, there right on the doorstep, so to speak, was the vast expanse of the lough.

I think this Lower Lough Erne could hold many big trout, but it was not to be my luck to catch one. The weather was fine and I really thought some fish would be moving. We tried a few drifts in a boat in the afternoon, but though we both fished thoroughly, Dan using a team of flies and I fishing nymphs, neither of us had a take, or saw the move of a single fish. Later we used our spinning rods and tried for pike, but again with no success. In the short stay we made at Lustybeg it was impossible to form any conclusive idea of the sport to be had with a rod. Examinations I made of the bed of the lough in several places proved there to be a really good food supply for trout there.

On our trip back to the mainland in the boat the next morning, with all our equipment packed, just as if beckoning us to stay, two really big trout showed plainly in head and tail rises, that slow rolling rise which denotes a fish really feeding in the surface. Both were fish of around four pounds and for a moment I was sorely tempted to alter our plans and stay to fish again. Had a third or fourth fish showed it would have clinched matters as far as I was concerned and I am sure this was in the mind of Dan McCrea too. As it was, it was but a farewell gesture. I left Lough Erne knowing big fish were there for the taking. Only fools leave the " gold for the tinsel ".

We went on to Enniskillen and from there to the little town of Garrison which is on the shore of Lough Melvin. We had just pulled up, and undecided at which hotel to spend the night, when along the road came a group of fishermen. One was carrying a salmon, another a string of three fair sized trout. They turned in towards Casey's hotel nearby and there we intercepted them. One of them recognised me at once and in a moment I placed him too, for we had met at the Game Fair. They had been fishing Lough Melvin for trout. The one with the salmon was full of excitement. This he had risen and hooked on a small fly he had been using on the bob and it had taken him forty-five minutes to land on his five ounce trout rod. The first salmon he had ever landed. We were invited into the hotel where other fishermen were gathered. There the fish, and the fishermen, were duly toasted. His lucky day, he said, and I hoped, as I drank his health and good fortune, that it would be the first of many. It is so nice to see a fisherman really excited with his catch.

For a while the salmon took pride of place but then I was able to see, and to examine closely, some of the famous " gillaroo ". Some up to two pounds had been taken in the past few days. To the Irish the gillaroo is a fish in its own sphere. I knew enough not to say much about them in the presence of so many believers. Why indeed shouldn't they be called gillaroo for the colouring is entirely different to the majority of brownies. But I would say these are similar to some of the trout we get in our own small lakes here on the Avon Valley and that without a question this is caused by an almost continuous diet of molluscs. We could call ours gillaroo too but let the Irish have their lovely sounding name which, after all is very descriptive.

Unfortunately in one way, but fortunate in another, our newly found friends were leaving the hotel that evening. I say fortunate, because we could have the two rooms which were being vacated. I had liked the friendly atmosphere of this hotel the moment I went inside, for truly it was one for the fishermen. Mr. Pat Casey and his wife are both of the homely type and with their daughter, gave us a welcome. Casey's Hotel was to be our base for the next two nights.

We could have fished in Lough Melvin, but I wanted to see something of the famous Bundrowse river, which is the link from Lough Melvin to the sea. Also I wished to see the river Erne which in turn carries all water from Lough Erne to the estuary at Ballyshannon. So first we travelled to Belleek through which the river Erne flows and then crossed the border and into lovely Donegal to stop for a while just short of Ballyshannon to have a look at the big hydro-electric installation. This huge dam controls all the outflow from Lough Erne and I had a chance to examine the fish pass built beside it. This I found was constructed on a similar principal to the one at Pitlochry in Scotland.

I cannot think any of these really long artificial passes are wholly successful and, judging by the number of trout and salmon in the outfall below it, these fish were of the same opinion. Many hundreds of really big fish were there and lots no doubt had tried, without success, to ascend the ladder to the lough beyond, an uphill battle through tunnels and pools which,

I am sure, must exhaust the strongest long before reaching half-way. Still, it was exciting to see so many fish, even if they were baulked in their movement upstream, for it proved beyond doubt, that the water of Lough Erne had a tremendous attraction for both salmon and sea-trout. Though of the utmost value for civilisation, hydro dams are a sorry sight to a fisherman. When we reached Ballyshannon we heard a little of the general local views.

At Ballyshannon we stepped in to say hello to Michael Rogan who still runs the fly-tying business made famous by his grand-father. A native indeed. From him I learned something about the fishing of years ago, and something too of the sorrow that the building of the dam had caused. Seeing so many fish in the river below the dam prompted me to ask Rogan about the estuary. Only a month or so previously I had been in Scotland and fished the Ythan Estuary near Aberdeen, which is so famous for its sport with sea-trout, grilse, and salmon. I was very glad I did. Rogan was pleased to tell us we might get some sport during the ebb and flow of the tide, for just then there were plenty of finnock (small sea-trout) in the estuary. He told us too that the fishery was completely free of any charge or restriction, excepting for the taking of salmon.

We were able to drive within half a mile or so of the water, and as it was rather a rough day, we decided to take only our spinning rods, which I found later to have been a bad mistake. I enjoyed the half mile walk through sand dunes and marron grass and on reaching the estuary and negotiating a bank of sand quite forty feet high, there we were on the beach. And what a beach it is. Sweeping round in a gentle curve from Ballyshannon for quite two miles, it was as clean as a new pin. After travelling over loose sand for a hundred yards or so, we came to the very hard packed bed of the estuary and to the edge of the water.

Along the whole of the shore were but two fishermen, who, later on I found to be a married couple from London. The wind was strong in our faces from the water, but the waves far less than I had thought. As I looked around, taking in the full beauty of it all, a small sea-trout showed in a wave trough within easy casting distance. Soon afterwards another leapt clear, just a silvery flash above the water. This was quite enough to get me excited. Soon my rod was assembled and I was tying a small mepps spoon. Other fish, including one I thought was a salmon, showed, but, try as I did, not a take was registered. Dan McCrea fished too, but it was the same story.

As the tide, slowly though surely, began to cover the beach again, so we moved along to have a talk with the other two who were fishing. I could see he was using a fly rod and just as we reached him he hooked and landed a small finnock of about twelve ounces. On the beach beside his tackle bag, were three others of similar size, one of which had been taken by his wife. They were about to pack up and go. The last fish had been a bonus one, it would seem, for once the water had covered the hard packed sand, there was little chance for more sport. You got about three hours of fishing during the ebb and the flow of the tide. The best time was when the tide was right out.

These two were glad to talk. Each year in September, they spend their holiday at Ballyshannon and for many years had fished this estuary and enjoyed it. I found he had been using two flies. One of these he called the " Gadget " which he obtained from Michael Rogan, the other, used as a dropper, was what he termed a " Golden Olive " just a hackled pattern on a No. 3 hook. The " Gadget " was usually most successful. Just these two flies, and his wife had the same faith in them. She could not use a fly rod, but had a fixed spool outfit with a bubble float at the end of the leader, with the two flies as droppers. Sometimes they would get a dozen fish between them, on occasions more, and seldom did they have a blank.

It is as well to have to eat " humble pie " now and then. If only I had gone along to have a chatter in the first place instead of wasting my time with spinning we might have had some good sport that afternoon. For apparently it is almost a waste of time to spin. You got an occasional fish it is true, but small nymphs and flies at the surface were a much greater attraction, as I found out for myself the following day.

We were at Ballyshannon by about two o'clock and called to see Michael Rogan once more and to buy a couple of his " Gadget " flies which had been recommended by our friends on the foreshore, the previous afternoon. These he made for us while we waited as he was then out of stock, for he explained they were used mostly in the earlier part of the season. I must say these creations were queer to look at and not very easy to construct, but as I have learned many times, local advice is often very sound and one cannot do better than give local patterns a good trial. " Rogan's Gadget " is a name one cannot forget easily.

The tide was ebbing as we reached the estuary. This time I had my ten foot six parabolic fly rod. As we trudged across the sand so I saw several fish show here and there. There was little wind and the water was smooth for the most part, with occasional ripples in the different areas. It was also warm and sunny. Soon I had my rod ready and I decided to use the " Gadget " as a tail attraction with one of my " Killer Bugs " as a dropper. Long before Dan McCrea had his tackle assembled, I had waded out, and with my third cast was into a fish, a very encouraging start for the afternoon. This was a small sea-trout of about a pound which fought hard for liberty. It had taken the " Gadget " and proved straightaway what had been said of this pattern. But once again I had made a mistake in my choice of tackle. My rod was too big. I wished I had brought along my much short and lighter Fario Club, for though I saw, and felt, several fish, it was quite an hour later that I managed to hook and to hold a second sea-trout. This time it was the killer bug, so honours were even. These little trout were willing and, with a lighter and faster outfit, I feel sure I could have taken quite a dozen, for the estuary seemed full of them. It was then I began to wonder just what natural creature, or creatures, these fish were after. At one time I saw quite a score rising around me and then I could see they were after little dark sand flies, which now and then were blown out on to the water. I had not thought to take dry-flies with me, but in one compartment of my nymph box was a fly I had made up with a pheasant tail body and a bluey-brown hackle on a No. o hook. Quickly I put on a new 4 x leader and attached the little artificial. Then for the first time in .my life I fished a dry-fly in the sea. But I was severely handicapped by the big rod. One after another I rose four different fish and missed hooking them all. Those little sea-trout took as fast, even faster I would say, than any small grayling. It was most enjoyable, for though I caught but the two fish that afternoon I learned a lot. As it was, this was more than my companion, for Dan too was using a rod much too big and slow for the kind of fish willing to take. He said he touched a number and missed others completely.

I feel sure the main attraction for these fish in this estuary was small shrimps. There must have been many in the area for on several occasions I found one impaled on the hook of either " Gadget " or " Killer Bug ". And I have an idea that the " Gadget " artificial had been constructed so that when fished it had some sort of resemblance to a shrimp, but not, I thought, a good one. If ever I have the good fortune to fish this part again I will be prepared with something of my own concoction. Also I will make sure I have the tackle which is most suitable.

However, if I never fish the estuary again, at least I have a memory of the wide and golden foreshore as it sweeps around beneath the sand dunes, and of the clear water spreading out into the great Atlantic. To my mind will come the sight of the little silvery trout flashing to the surface, and at times above it, to glitter for a moment in the sunlight. Once again I will see that shoal rising to the tiny sandflies and relive the enjoyment I had in trying to catch some of the fish with an artificial. This part of Northern Ireland is a picture in my mind which can never fade.

Perhaps some who read this will be tempted. Let me give my assurance that such a visit will never be regretted. Rogan told me there is good sport to be had there all through the season, that June, July and August, are all exciting months, when much larger sea-trout are plentiful. Besides Ballyshannon is no great distance from Bundoran and it was there we went the next day.

At Bundoran we called at the well known Hamilton Hotel to collect permits to see and to fish the famous Bundrowse River at the Lareen end, where Lough Melvin narrows to form the river. All the overflow from Lough Melvin discharges at this point, for this is where Melvin ends and the Bundrowse river begins. The river is not very long, maybe eight miles or so, before it enters into the sea at Bundoran. It was there I had my first view of it, tumbling over a rocky bed into the Atlantic Ocean. Upstream from the estuary the river wound away up through a great flat of meadow-land, just a meandering type of river, clear enough for me to see right to the bed at depths of five feet or more, see also the wealth of aquatic plants the bed produced. This might well have been a stretch of the Test or the Itchen, for it was not until a little later when I visited the Lareen end that the real character of the Bundrowse was shown.

This was also a day I will never forget. There to the left of me as I stood, Lough Melvin spread out to either side and stretched back far beyond my view. A great sheet of sunlit water with the wind rippling it into wavelets which glinted like molten silver. To my right was the river. Here, it converged into a stream which I could cast over from bank to bank, was the discharge of Melvin, clear living water, hastening towards the sea. As we wandered downstream, so, many little trout were rising to a good hatch of pale watery duns. Salmon parr too, splashed at the surface and, in a stream to one side, were several really good brownies, one of which I thought to be quite three pounds.

This Bundrowse is principally a salmon river, and what a river it is. I have seen many rivers all about the British Isles and abroad, but for general character and condition I feel doubtful if there can be many in the world to equal it. I had no wish to fish for salmon, even though some, and grilse were in the river, for I much prefer trout fishing and I had already seen enough to hasten back to the car to get my tackle ready.

Thinking I might get hitched to a big gillaroo, I put up my big rod again to try first of all, and mounted a single No. 4 " Killer Bug " on a 3 x leader. Clear though the water was, I found it to be very difficult to see fish lying in feeding positions for most seemed to come right up from the bottom, very much like the grayling do in the Avon. I saw nothing I thought might be a gillaroo, but caught a number of ordinary coloured brownies, which weighed up to a pound. These fish were very quick in taking, and even quicker in getting rid of the hook, and I missed a lot through being too slow. Apparently it was just a little too early in the year for many big trout to be in the river. Usually these drop down from Lough Melvin in late September and October in preparation to spawn there. The Bundrowse had a bed of shale and gravel and ideally suited for spawning and for small fish. Here the big gillaroos lay their eggs and the young thrive, but I feel very doubtful if many fish up to two years old

are caught which have the gillaroo colouring. This alone should
be sufficient to prove that the gillaroo is not a separate species.
Those I caught were lovely shaped little fish, with a cream
coloured belly, golden flanks and greeny yellow back. As they
flashed up to take my bug, or a natural fly, or nymph, so there
was that golden "wink", as Skues called it, in the water.

Soon I changed my big rod for the smaller one, with a much
lighter line and leader, and on this used a size No. 1 "Pheasant
Tail" nymph. The water was very fast running in some places
and in these I cast downstream, using the parachute cast, with
plenty of slack line and leader. This allowed the nymph to penetrate a little deeper into the water before the line straightened
to cause a drag. I thoroughly enjoyed this style of fishing, for
though one could not always keep in touch with the nymph it
was always possible to see the trout come shooting up from the
depths to take. In one place a grilse of some six pounds showed
beneath my bank in a head and tail rise and within easy casting
distance downstream from me. I dropped my nymph in and
let it swing across the position and my heart gave a bound as
the cast drew down to a definite take. I tightened, but instead of
the grilse I expected, it was a half pound brownie.

This fishing really fascinated me. I could imagine this river
with a big run of salmon in it. Those who have fished it will
agree, I am sure, that considerable thought, planning and work
had gone into the making of the fishery, for much of it is
artificial. The Bundrowse has been made up like a staircase, a
series of shallow dams at intervals of some fifty or sixty yards
over which the water tumbles in a maze of swirls and eddies.
The bed is beautifully clean for the fall in level is steep. I would
say quite twenty feet to the mile. At one place a huge natural
dam of rocky bed extended for quite two hundred yards. Over
this the water surges as a rapid. Every pool between the dams
could be a holding pool for salmon. With a fly rod one's joy in
salmon fishing would be complete. This water teemed with
salmon parr so obviously, it is good for spawning too.

I questioned Dan McCrea about sea-trout in the Bundrowse
and Lough Melvin. He told me he had caught sea-trout there
but that there was no big run. This seemed rather strange to me
in view of the numbers I had seen in the Lough Erne Estuary

and river about Ballyshannon, which is only just around the corner, so to speak. I saw none myself, so cannot say one way or the other. There is, however, a trout in Melvin known locally as the "sonaghan". These might well be small sea-trout which have started to feed well in the fresh water and gradually changed colour through such feeding. These sonaghan are mostly small, around twelve ounces, and said to be white bellied and strong fighters. To me it seemed that much research needs to be done in Northern Ireland before any factual statements can be made. At the moment the names of the various "trout" tend to be confusing.

A week soon passes, fishing country like this. Though my great love is fishing for trout, I spent some very enjoyable hours after pike, and many more looking at the various fishing waters throughout the Province. I will always think very kindly of the Northern Ireland Tourist Board for having me as their guest to see and to fish in these very lovely parts. Well enough they might wish to attract fishermen, for fishing is the most valuable commodity they have to offer, indeed to my mind, the jewel of the country. Altogether we travelled just over 900 miles and I was greatly impressed with the friendliness of all I met, and with the hospitality at all the hotels in which we stayed. But above all my thanks are due to my friend Daniel McCrea. His address is No. 1 Cherry Valley Park, Knock, Belfast, and I know he will be most willing to help any who may wish to enlist his aid.

I would have liked to see still more, and to fish in other parts, but there had been sufficient to let me form a really good idea of the general fishing and environment. Also, I had the satisfaction of knowing that nymph fishing can give the same sport as elsewhere. Maybe one could soon get into the same habit as the natives in telling fairy stories, for the country as a whole gives good scope for imagination. But I think the Irish people can be excused for their desire to pass on their enthusiasm, for there are fish to be caught if one goes the right way about it. Perhaps they are not all as monstrous or as numerous as the Irish would have us believe, but this is a way of fishermen, and none of us is blameless in this respect.

As yet the country is free from the ravages caused by over civilisation and little can have changed through the centuries.

Long may this continue. Long may the hills and the mountains weep their supplies of rain into the loughs and the rivers and continue to bring about the wealth of aquatic life which can delight all fishermen.

Chapter Eighteen

SEA-TROUT AND OTHERS IN WALES

My most expensive fish : Big lakes and small streams :
Season in the South-West : Shoals in the Cothi : An experiment succeeds : Local knowledge on the Towy.

PROBABLY THE most expensive trout I will ever hook and land
was the first fish I caught in Wales, but, costly though it was, it
gave me great satisfaction. Though I had been to Wales on
various occasions I had never fished there, until the chance
came when my wife and I paid a visit to spend a few days at
Betws-y-coed. Our son was then at the Gwyder Forestry School
nearby, and it was to see him and to spend a little time travelling
with him around North Wales, that we went. Knowing the
famous River Conway was close by and that there were other
streams and lakes in the locality, I had packed my fishing tackle
into the car when leaving, but I made a promise to my wife that
this should be no fishing holiday, that I would be quite satisfied
to catch one fish, regardless of size or species, a promise I
intended to keep.

Enquiries proved that I could get a permit to fish for trout
in the Conway for fifteen shillings, but I needed a ten shilling
licence as well. I got both, and then, one morning, went to a
stretch just below the confluence of the River Lledr with the
Conway. Just downstream from this I saw several good salmon
and sea-trout in the very famous Black Hole Pool, but the only
brownies I could see in the water I was permitted to fish, were
little fellows of four to six inches in length. I looked closely to see
if I could find something larger and finally settled for one I

thought to be a little above the average. I had on a oo.P.T. nymph and this I did my best to place accurately to him. The Welsh streams are not like ours in the South and I was handicapped with the overhanging bushes. My nymph fell quite two feet to one side, but he spotted it at once, and took with a rush which drew the cast under to the line knot. A lift of the rod, and he was firmly hooked. Despite his size, he was a wiry one, and he skittered and fought all about the streamy water. He was a lean little fellow about seven inches long, with a colouring like brown marble. Still, honour was satisfied, small though he was. I had hooked and landed my first fish in Wales, and I wished him luck as I set him free to rejoin his fellows. Then I packed up my tackle. He had cost me twenty-five shillings but gave me some brief moments I shall never forget.

Since then I have seen much more of the fishing waters in Wales and cast a fly, or a nymph, for brownies, sea-trout and salmon. Wales is wonderful country for sea trout, and perhaps it is because of this, and to the large size many of them are, that brown trout, excepting in some of the big lakes and reservoirs, tend to be despised. To a very great extent, the trout waters of Wales are similar in character to those in the far west country. For the most part the water is extremely clear, and to get results the finest of leaders are needed, and small nymphs and flies.

I have in mind the big reservoirs and lakes mostly, for there are few rivers or streams other than the Usk, the Wye, or the Ithon where there are trout which may run to a weight over a pound. All three of these rivers hold an excellent stock of brownies and in the very clear water, during much of the summer, there is really good sport fishing upstream to individual fish with a nymph. But it is the big expanses of water such as Bala, Vyrnwy, and the newly constructed reservoir at Llyn Celyn which attract most brown trout fishermen.

Though I have fished in Wales for brownies, my most enjoyable hours have been after sea-trout when I had the great privilege of fishing the Towy and the Cothi. My experience of sea trout had been rather limited until then, to catching a few in the little River Axe above Seaton, in Devonshire, and odd ones from the lower reaches of the Avon, Test and Itchen. Also

I had taken a few decent fish from the Lymington River, which runs up into the New Forest. It was in this small stream that I first tried my " killer bug " and got success with it during the day-time.

It was towards the end of July that I spent a week at Abergorlech and had a chance to examine and to fish the River Cothi. I had heard much, and read a lot, about the big runs of sea-trout which come into the rivers along the South West of Wales, but not until I had seen these could I bring myself to believe it was true. There had been an appreciable rise in the river about two weeks previously but, at the time of my visit, the level was very low, and the water so clear that I found no difficulty in seeing the bottom quite easily, at depths of over ten feet. And it was not only the bottom I saw, for there, in every pool, were sea-trout. Many of these were small, fish of from twelve ounces up to about a pound and a quarter, but quite a lot were two to four pounds, with occasional monsters which one could be forgiven for thinking were salmon. All are called sewin by the Welsh people, regardless of size. The names given to sea-trout in different parts of the British Isles are confusing, especially the small ones. In Ireland they were the little white trout, in Scotland finnock, in the West Country they call them peal. Most of us in the South of England call them sea-trout, small and large, and to avoid confusion, it is of small and large sea-trout that I shall write.

The sight of so many fish fascinated me and I spent far more time in studying their behaviour in the river, than in actual fishing. One thing which impressed me very much was their remarkable eyesight and sense of danger, which is so different to salmon. Why this should be so, is very difficult to understand, for both sea-trout and salmon live for the most part in the sea. What is more they are not accustomed to seeing humans, or other land animals. It cannot be that these trout have any memory of unpleasant happenings in the river during their early life to the smolt stage, but scared they are, and very sensitive to anything happening along the river banks or on the water above them.

I watched many different shoals in varying depths and environment, but to do so meant creeping and crawling to the different vantage points. Any quick movement, or shadow would start a whole shoal running to deep water, or milling in an agitated manner. I remember one place very well. Here the banks were very high above the water and overgrown with trees and scrub. I had been studying a big shoal in which there were a number of really big fish up to ten pounds. These were scattered all about the river bed at the tail of a deep pool, and I was screened perfectly from their view by leaves and branches. I was interested in seeing if any of the fish showed any inclination to feed, that is, to make any move to take any floating flies, or nymphs, or for that matter, anything, on, or in mid-water. Though I could see quite fifty fish, not one made a move to take anything. An occasional fish would shift his position, and, now and then, one would make a rush to the surface and leap. But that was all. One big fish, right below me, made a move to one side and, to get a better view of what he was about to do, I moved the screen of branches in front of me. This let a shaft of light straight through, and on to another fish in the middle. Like a flash he bolted upstream and, in a moment, every fish in my view followed him, with others stringing along from farther down-river. The whole shoal surged up the shallows and into the deep pool, where they milled about in great confusion.

This example was typical of many shoals I studied, and quickly I began to realise just why so many people say that in some rivers it is impossible to catch sea-trout with a fly-rod during the day-time. But I could not accept this, and did my best to disprove it. I had already learned enough to know that the stalking and catching of chalk stream trout and grayling was but child's play in comparison, and knew that here on the Cothi all the arts I knew of camouflage and approach, would have to be observed. The stretch of the river in which I was permitted to fish was by no means an easy one, for bushes lined the banks on either side, and rocks and boulders made it extremely perilous to get near to the edge of the water. I gathered from the local people that few fishermen used a fly-rod along this stretch, but fished with worms or with spinning gear, and this, generally, when the water was coloured, after a spate.

At one end of a long pool where the water shallowed to a

depth of two feet or so, I located a shoal of a dozen fish of sizes up to a pound and a half. I had my lightest rod and line, and a leader tapered to 4 x. On this I tied on a small killer bug. Never was delicacy and accuracy needed more, but the encouragement I got from my first cast was enough to get me excited. Owing to the position of the sun I had to cast slightly downstream to avoid any shadow of leader or line falling on the water, and for the first time, I managed to do this without scaring a fish. The little bug sank quickly and I lifted my rod tip to impart a slight drag. One of the smaller fish came up like a bullet and took, but I was much too slow to hook him. My bug and leader went sailing up into the bushes behind me.

You will know just how exasperating it is when this kind of thing happens just when you feel confident of getting a fish. I was far too impatient to get my line and bug clear without moving, and in consequence got well and truly snagged. But I knew if I moved I would scare the other fish, and so a break was inevitable. A few moments of feverish activity and I had on a new leader point, and another bug, and a second cast was made. Care should always be taken when tying knots to attach new leader points, and artificials, for in such cases the old proverb of " more haste, less speed ", can have no truer meaning. As the bug swung across, so a fish of well over a pound took with such force that he hooked himself, then went up into the air twice in quick succession. My cast broke, or slipped, where I had made the join, and that was that. The commotion made by the hooked fish sent all the others scurrying upstream to the deep water.

I was sorry to have broken and left the hook and cast point in a fish but was quite excited with what I had accomplished. One thing I knew then, was that my bug would bring these sea-trout if I could present it without scaring them.

All my fishing in this stretch had to be done in daylight for it was much too overgrown and hazardous to fish at night, or even at late evening. So I persevered for three whole days. During this time I caught three small sea-trout, neither over a pound, and about a dozen small brownies. Each took the bug. Try as I would I could get no response from any of the larger fish I tried, mostly because the majority were in places

where I found it to be impossible to cast a fly, and secondly
because the water where they were, was much too deep, or too
fast, to get the bug down to them properly. A third reason was
that they were scared, despite my best attempts at concealment, and presentation. Then came my meeting with Eric
Coombs.

Eric Coombs is the Local Honorary Secretary of the Swansea
Angling Association. He came into the Inn one evening, and
soon we were talking. I explained to him where I had been
fishing and the tactics I had employed. He was extremely interested and indeed surprised, that I had managed to get any fish
there with a fly-rod. I had told him I had hoped to fish at night
but had found it to be impossible, then blessed him for the
invitation he gave me. Often, he said, he fished with a friend
at night on the neighbouring River Towy, and was going the
following night. Would I care to go with him and try a stretch
or two there? I could tell as we talked, that here was a man who
knew sea-trout fishing, and I thanked him warmly as I accepted
the chance he gave me. To add to this privilege, he said he
would get a permit for me to fish an Association stretch of the
Cothi the following night, and I left him, feeling very excited.
The few nights I had previously fished for sea-trout, had been
alone on the River Axe. Though I had enjoyed doing this, I
would have felt much more content with a companion nearby,
for one never knows what might happen along a strange river
in the darkness. It is nice to have someone within call should
anything unforseen, or exciting, occur.

The stretch of the Towy to which we journeyed the following
evening is a few miles downstream from Llandovery. I could see
at once that this was a somewhat different proposition to the
water I had been fishing on the Cothi, for much of the river is
open along both banks, with pools and shallows, which looked
extremely attractive. Also it was safe to wade along the shingly,
and sandy margins, and where one could get every satisfaction
in casting a fly, or nymph, without danger of being caught up
in bushes, or scrub. A very lovely stretch in a wide valley,
where hordes of insects were dancing in the rays of the setting
sun. At one point we had to wade the river to cross to the other
side before starting to fish. At no point was the water there more

than eighteen inches deep and about the bottom I saw scores
of tiny trout, and parr. This was a river bed with life everywhere on it, and I knew at once that the evening would be
enjoyable.

My experience in past ventures had prompted me to take
only my quick actioned Fario Club rod, with a light line, and
a leader tapered to 3 x. My host suggested I should use one or
other, or both, of two flies, he himself found good for night
fishing. One had great similarity to an ordinary Butcher, the
other a big ginger hackle, with a gold tinselled body. Both he
made himself, and they were constructed to have an easy entry
to the water. It is always a good plan to try local patterns first,
and I was grateful for the offer, which I accepted.

We were lucky with the weather. It was a quiet evening and
warm. We wandered along to a long pool, which Eric had
decided might give us some sport, a long slow glide of perhaps
three hundred yards. Our side was quite clear of all trees and
bushes, and the shingled bank sloped very gradually into the
water. At the far side, the river was fringed with small alders
and there, beneath them, the water ran to a depth of some four
feet, pocketing and shallowing, and here were the lies of the
sea-trout.

It was a little too light to start fishing the pool so, just to fill
in the time, and to have a little action, we fished down a shallow
stretch for brownies. None of the brown trout are big, and a nine
incher is a good one. It was a delight after the past three days,
to be able to cast freely, and to see my fly dancing along in the
water, for I fished in the wet-fly manner, downstream. Little
trout were plentiful, but I knew my fly was much too big and,
apart from a " flick and a promise " from a dozen or so, nothing
stayed long enough to bend my rod. I feel sure these little fish
could give some very good sport if fished with tiny nymphs, and
fine leader points. But it was relaxing. As we drew near to the
pool, so a sea-trout splashed, and my host decided it was time to
fish in earnest.

He knew the pool well, and he knew also where the best
taking points were, and these, like the true sportsman he is, he
showed to me. He had explained that at times the fish came,
but were most difficult to hook. What he called " the dead leaf

take ". Just a touch, as though the fly had come in contact with some floating debris. Truly the "dead leaf take" is an apt description, for the first thing I hooked was a dead leaf, but not the second, even though the touch was no greater. Years of fishing with nymphs has taught me to watch very closely for any indication of a take. Should my cast point draw I tighten at once. It drew with the semi-submerged leaf, it drew in a similar manner two casts later, and my first fish from the Towy went headlong for the deepest pool. With my light outfit I have to be very careful in playing fish but in due course I landed a very nice sea trout of about a pound and a half. Though I was using the black fly, I fished this in much the same way as I would have fished a bug or a nymph. As I have mentioned, the pool was a long gentle glide. My plan was to cast slightly up stream with plenty of slack leader and line. Just allow the fly time to sink, then take up the slack, and gently lift the rod tip to impart a drag. Lifting the rod tip brought the rod into a good hooking position and if a fish took, just a flick was enough to set the hook.

It was not completely dark, and all the while I was able to see my line and leader floating on the water. Also I could plainly see the draw of the cast when a fish took. I got ten. Several I just touched and three others came free after a short fight. The best of the ten weighed four and a half pounds, but three others were over two. This was truly a night of "dead leaf takes". Not one hit strongly. Perhaps this was because I was fishing the fly very slowly, and fish had no need to move fast to take it. Both the black and the ginger flies took fish. There was little to choose between them. The first six I took with the black, and then lost it in a bush on the opposite bank, when I misjudged the cast. Perhaps, had it not been for this loss, I would not have tried the ginger at all. My only regret is that I did not try one of my "killer bugs" for I think the fish were in a mood when they would have taken it readily, and perhaps smaller nymphs.

My host was delighted with my success, but as the moon had then risen he was doubtful if there could be further sport. He had generously given me the best parts to fish, but had got two good fish, one of two, the other three pounds. But he said he had touched quite a number of others and was interested in what I had to tell him about my own way of fishing, which apparently, is a little different to the general style. So ended my first and only night on the River Towy. Sometime I hope to be there again.

I had been looking forward to the night with Eric on the Cothi, which was the last night of my stay. But at early morning it started to rain, and heavy storms continued right through the day, until early evening. Soon the river started to rise and then to discolour, and by the time I had arranged for our meeting, conditions were pretty well hopeless. Both of us knew that the chance of getting a fish was extremely doubtful, but as the rain had stopped we decided to give it a try for an hour or so. It was a very nice stretch of the Cothi my host took me to, and where I am sure I could have enjoyed myself had the conditions been more favourable. Though not as easy to fish as the Towy water, there were several very nice runs and pools, each of which could be covered very well with a fly-rod.

One of the runs I tried, by wading half-way out into the river. The water was not too badly coloured just there and, after covering about twenty yards, I got a take from a good fish which ran out my line to the backing and then got free. With the next cast another took and he too came off. I was just congratulating myself and thinking this evening was to be exciting, when a trickle of water into the top of my wader made me look down quickly, and upstream even quicker. Then I made a hurried scramble for the bank. These Welsh streams rise very quickly once they start. Before I could reach the bank the water was over the top of both waders and I was wet through. Upstream I could see a mass of foam and bubbles, with branches and other debris sweeping along, and knew that further fishing was over. It was a pity. I think, had we been an hour earlier, both of us might have got fish.

My experiences in the two rivers gave me plenty to think about afterwards. With brown trout, grayling, and indeed most fresh water fish, one can learn a lot by making autopsies, and studying the various creatures the fish have taken as food. This can often be a clue as to the right kind of artificials to use. With sea-trout there is none of this evidence, or so it has proved with

all I have examined, which have been caught in rivers. Neither
of the fish I caught in either Cothi, or Towy, had anything in
its stomach. It is quite certain that sea-trout, especially the larger
ones, have little need of food, once they come into the fresh
water. Perhaps this is just as well, for waters which fail to
produce enough food to grow brownies to more than nine
inches long, could not possibly supply the needs of a multitude
of big sea-trout. Contained in both of the rivers there must
have been thousands at the time I was there. The puzzle is why
they take artificial flies, nymphs, worms and spinning lures. The
same can be said of salmon.

Fishing at night proved one thing to me conclusively. During
the hours of darkness the sea-trout are no longer afraid or
sensitive to danger. So it seems very possible that what they fear
is linked very closely with the daylight and indeed moonlight,
but more especially with bright sunny days. On the night of my
success on the Towy, I had no more takes from fish after about
one o'clock in the morning when the moon rose and shone
brightly into the valley. The rising of the moon was directly
behind me as I cast and this might have had some bearing. Had
I been able to see into the water I feel sure the fish would have
been showing signs of agitation at the fall of my line and
leader, and indeed with my movements in the water whilst
wading and using my rod.

There must be some explanation for this sensitiveness to
danger. The only reasoning I can put forward is that their
action is due to an inherent sense of self preservation, caused
by the avoidance of predators whilst living in the sea. The
danger they suspect when seeing quick movements, shadows,
and sudden changes of light, might well stem from experience
in seeing the appearance of fish-eating birds, such as shags and
cormorants, or from gulls. Or it might be from other sources
such as seals, otters, or larger fish. As I have before mentioned,
the fish can have no reason at all to suspect man, or his actions
in fishing, to be harmful. It is not this at all, for to fish, man is
not a predator. But the falling of shadow caused by his line,
leader or fly, or indeed movement in approach and casting,
might well panic the fish into thinking it is something entirely
different, and to be feared. Whatever the solution, the fact

remains that sea-trout are very easy to frighten, and to have any success in catching them, the fisherman must keep this point very much in mind. Once again it brings out the importance of delicate tackle and stealth in approach and presentation.

Chapter Nineteen

THE HIGHLANDS AND THE LOWLANDS

New waters: A blank, but a point proved, on the Ythan:
A lesson on the Don: Keener vision of acid stream trout:
Surprises in a famous estuary.

FOR many years I had the feeling in the back of my mind that
no one could really lay claim to being a fisherman unless he or
she had fished in Scotland. But in one way and another circumstances prevented me from going to the North and I had to be
satisfied with what I could read or what others could tell me
about the fishing and the countryside there. It is true I had
seen many pictures in the different books and papers, and scenes
on television, which gave me a fair idea of what could be
expected, but seeing is believing and when my wife suggested
we should go on a coach tour up through the West Coast of
Scotland, I was quite agreeable. Holidays for us together had
been few and far between. For one thing it was very difficult
for me to get away for any length of time during the summer,
as I had all the responsibility of the fishery on my hands and
secondly, bringing up, and supplying the needs for a family
of four, left us with little money to enjoy luxury or travel.

We knew there would be no chance for me to fish on this
trip but the planned route would take us through some of the
most beautiful parts of the Highlands and where I would be
able to see many of the famous fishing waters. Besides we were
scheduled to stay at various hotels when an evening or a morning could be spent in exploring. And so it was arranged. Until
this trip the names of the famous salmon waters such as the Esk,

Tweed, Clyde, Spey, Dee, Don, Deveron, Findhorn, Tay, Brora, Helmsdale and Thurso, meant little to me. Neither did the names of the big lochs, Ness, Lomond, Leven, Awe, Shiel, etc., etc. The name Loch Leven was most familiar to me, as from time to time, I had hatched trout eggs which were said to have been from Loch Leven stock.

It was mid-June when we went and the weather throughout the whole eight days was excellent and visibility perfect. Our first stop was at Windermere and at late evening as we wandered along the lakeside, the placid waters were broken here and there by the nebs of rising trout and I was able to watch several fishermen doing their best to catch some. None of the fish appeared to be of a size over a pound, but a fair number were rising all about the lake, mostly to midges and gnats, but an occasional splash denoted the take of a fluttering sedge, of which there were a number of different types about the surface, dipping and weaving in the process of egg-laying. I would have liked to try a nymph on some of these fish but it was nice to watch. Next to fishing yourself, is the joy in watching others. With this I had to be content. It was a nice start to the trip, but I little realised that those few trout rising in Windermere, were to be the only ones I would see on the feed, until I returned home again.

Many and varied were the waters I saw as we passed through this most wonderful country, but though I looked closely as we went past loch, river or burn, not a trout or a salmon did I see. It was the same of a morning or a late evening when we watched a place here, or there, in the hope of seeing something exciting. What astonished me mostly was the absence of fishermen and it seemed that when we left the border, we left all anglers too. At a couple of hotels, I got into conversation with some of the local fishermen and remarked on the absence of anyone out after fish. Fish, to the Scots, mean salmon, and in a much lesser degree, sea-trout. As far as I could gather the brownies received scant consideration. No one wasted time in trying to catch these. If there were no runs of the migratory fish, then fishing came to a standstill, as was the case then. There had been no rain for a month. The rivers were all low. There was no sport to be had unless one cared to fish at night for sea-trout.

It was the same story throughout the trip. Our journey took us via Tyndrum to Fort Augustus and on to the Isle of Skye. From Skye to Inverary and then to Ayr and Rothesay. We returned home via Buxton in Derbyshire.

I thoroughly enjoyed this first sight of Scotland and the magnificent scenery and could well understand the enthusiasm of all fishermen who had been there before me. The lochs, the rivers and the little burns all fired my imagination. It is true I had seen a lot of what Scotland had to offer but I wished to see more. Also the urge to catch a fish was on me. The following year my son was married at Aberdeen and my wife and I went there for the wedding. This was in August. We had decided to stay on for a few days at Aberdeen after the ceremony and to see something of the Eastern side of the country. It was then I had my first view of Royal Deeside, to see the upper reaches of the Spey, the Don and the Deveron. We made a trip to see the Findhorn and another to Tomlintoul to view the Avon. And then one afternoon and evening I went fishing.

To be in Scotland without having a rod in hand is akin I think, to going half-dressed into a first class hotel for lunch or dinner. The previous November I had met Alan Sharpe in Paris at the Fario Club Dinner. The name "Sharpe's of Aberdeen" needs no mention from me for this is the most famous tackle manufacturer in Scotland and their shop in Belmont Street is well known to all fishermen who visit Aberdeen. Alan Sharpe is a well known figure and a well known fisherman. When I told him of our arrangements to be in Aberdeen for the wedding, and of my desire to catch my first fish in Scotland, he immediately made some plans. Unfortunately he had to be away himself during the week I was to be there, but insisted that I visited the shop and made myself known to his nephew Harold, who would fix me up with any tackle I required.

He was as good as his word. I was made very welcome by Harold Sharpe and offered a choice of any tackle I would like. As I had but the one afternoon and evening to spare it was decided we would go to try for sea-trout in the Ythan Estuary. Like Sharpe's tackle shop, this estuary needs no mention from me as it is well known throughout the world for the sport it provides. Through the generosity of the owner of the Udny Arms

Hotel, a boat and a boatman was laid on for us at the estuary and it was with great excitement that I prepared to make my first cast into a game fish water in Scotland.

Harold Sharpe had fixed me up with a fixed spool outfit for spinning and a fly rod, together with spoons and flies he thought might be acceptable and similar to the best patterns used in this water. Spinning, he thought, might be the best bet and this was confirmed by the boatman. All about the estuary fish were moving. Mostly these were finnock but some really good sized sea-trout were showing and here and there grilse. I put on a small silver Mepps spoon and soon we were rowed to a likely position. Several boats were out and a number of anglers were wading and fishing from the banks but though so many fish were showing repeatedly, I saw no one with a rod bending to the pull of one. We anchored and fished, we drifted and fished, but not a take was registered. I began to wish I had put up the fly rod instead of the spinning tackle but we had left this in the car. Time after time I cast to where I had seen a fish surface but the expected pull never came. Then I hooked what I thought at first was a piece of weed. It was a flatfish, a flounder of about a pound or so. Fishing as I was, amongst hundreds of game fish, the first I was to land in Scotland had to be a sea-fish, a flattie. Still it made the afternoon for me. I had fished in Scotland and had caught a fish and it was with a feeling of contentment that I sat down by the car to have some tea.

After tea I decided to put up the fly rod. I much prefer to use a fly rod and knew the one I had would be quite suitable as I had used similar ones many times. I had a leader tapered to a six pound point and to this, knotted on one of my size 5 killer bugs. The tide had turned and was running by the time we were ready, and it was decided that the best chance would be at the upstream end of the estuary, where it converges and goes beneath the road bridge. For those who have never seen or fished this estuary, I would like to explain that the actual Ythan is but a small river which carries no great volume of fresh water. The expanse of the estuary is roughly pear shaped and is an inlet from the sea. All around it is bordered by high banks of silver sand and where the tide enters is a great bar of shingle, pebbles and rocks.

At low tide much of this bar is uncovered by water when it is possible to see the main deep run which enters into the sea. As the tides ebb and flow, so the level in the estuary varies accordingly. At low tide much of the beach all around becomes dry and so the area for fishing is lessened considerably. As the tide runs so it is possible to see the main current and it was in this that activity with the fish started. With the fall in level so there came a pull of the fresh water from the mouth of the Ythan.

Sea-trout, salmon and grilse, showed repeatedly, some, especially the small finnock, were flicking well up out of the water. Some were really small, no larger indeed than many of the smolts which are to be seen in the Avon and the West Country rivers. It was exciting to see so many moving and quickly I waded out to start fishing. Wading all around the estuary is perfectly safe, for the bed in most places, is hard packed shingle and sand. The water is wonderfully clear and, when in the boat, I was able to see down to depths of quite eight feet, and to see also the vast amount of marine growth about the bed. It was because of this clearness that I had decided on a fine leader point. Within a few moments I got hitched to a finnock of about a pound and it was joy indeed to see him leaping and skittering here and there in attempts to escape. But escape he did, just as I felt he was mine and was reaching forward with the landing net. This was but another case of success and failure, similar to other episodes I had experienced in different places and with different fish. During the hour and a half I fished I hooked and lost seven more in exactly the same way. Two of these were quite good fish of, I would say, nearly two pounds. The others were about three quarters of a pound. These were the ones I hooked as I thought, firmly, but many gave me just that little flick and a promise, which proved me to be too late in my striking. The rod I was using was nine feet six inches and the line was slightly more weighty than what I normally use. One can only prove points by continual experience. To be successful in taking fish with nymphs or bugs, one has to be really quick with a rod and anything which can slow down this action must be considered. Though I hooked eight fish, none was hooked firmly, which meant that the fish were already open-

ing their mouths to eject the artificial and only a light hold with
the hook was made on the fringes of the jaw. Maybe a larger
sized hook would have solved the problem, but of this I feel
doubtful.

During this short spell of fishing I might well have hooked
and landed quite a dozen fish. As it was I had a blank. But the
most interesting part to me was the fact that to either side of
me on the bank I was fishing, and across the estuary, there were
fifteen different anglers using spinning tackle. None hooked a
fish. Yet these sea-trout came very readily to the little killer
bug. What they mistook it for I cannot imagine as I had no time
to make any study of the small animal life in this water. Neither
can I say what these fish were rising to take. Most of the insect
life I saw consisted of midges and gnats.

A call from my host told me it was time to pack up as he had
no wish to be late getting home. I would have liked to stay on
and fish in the dusk and after dark but all good things must
come to an ending at some time. I was quite happy. I had
caught a fish in Scotland and had learned a lot. Plans were
already in my mind for a return in the future. Fishing in this
very attractive estuary had given me a taste of what I could
expect. My second visit was to be earlier than I had thought.

The following year the Game Fair was held at Blair
Drummond and I had been invited by Farlows to be one of
their team for coaching and demonstrating rods and tackle, as
I had on previous occasions at these Fairs, but not at the first
one in Scotland. My wife and I made plans to go by car and
arrangements to do some fishing in the Stirling area and on the
border Esk. But at the last moment we had to change any plan
for taking the car and went by train instead, which handicapped
me a lot in the choice of fishing tackle I could take. Having in
mind my experience the previous year I decided to take only
my Fario Club with the lines to go with it. I had no wish to
fish for salmon even if such a chance was possible. I had been
bitten with the sea-trout bug and it was sea-trout water I wanted
to fish.

Alas for plans however. I soon found out that I needed a car
if I was to fish any of the parts where good sport could be
obtained. The Game Fair was very enjoyable and I had the

pleasure of meeting many fishermen from all over the country. Many were the invitations I had to go to fish here or there, but none I could accept owing to transport difficulties for I had my wife to consider as well as myself. It was then, just on the spur of the moment, I decided to have a talk with Alan Sharpe. Alan is always a prominent figure at Game Fairs. What is more he knows all the fishing waters in Scotland. If anyone could help it was he. " Why not abandon any plans you have for this locality and come to Aberdeen where you and your wife will be most welcome," he said. My wife was agreeable. She had enjoyed herself on our former visit and we had four days left to see more of the Aberdeen area. And so the following day we took a train from Stirling to Aberdeen, via Dundee.

Alan Sharpe made us welcome indeed. We booked in at an hotel near to the outskirts of the town where he lives and went to dinner with him and his wife that same evening. And what an evening it was. The Scots are well known for their hospitality and we had a very good example of it with the Sharpes. It was in the early hours of the following morning we were returned in a happy state to our hotel and with an arrangement to meet at about eleven o'clock at the tackle shop in Belmont Street, to discuss possibilities of fishing.

There I met Jack Sharpe who is Alan's older brother but who had retired from the business. I liked him at first sight and was delighted when he asked if I would care to go and fish the Don with him that afternoon for brownies, on a stretch not far up river from Aberdeen, and close to the airport. Alan had various work to do and could not accompany us. Being away for a few days at the Game Fair had left him with a pile of matters to sort out but he thought that on the following day we might have an outing together on the Ythan which we would settle later.

My first view of the Don had not been a very inspiring one for this had been during our visit the previous year and looking upstream and down, from the Don Bridge just outside Aberdeen, on the North side. At that time the tide was out and the estuary was in a shocking state. It was difficult to imagine then, that there could be such a beautiful and attractive river leading to it, though I did see this later, and knew it to be true. So when Jack Sharpe mentioned the Don my thoughts went immediately to the upper reaches for I prefer to forget what I saw in the lower ones.

We met at two o'clock as arranged and Jack took me in his car to the road bridge near to the Dyce airport, which is the upper boundary of the water we were to fish. The afternoon was stormy, but in between storms the sun shone brightly and I could see well into the water. A hatch of fly, mostly B.W.O. and pale wateries, well worthy of any hatch on a chalk stream at this time of year, was starting, and trout started to rise all about the river. We wandered downstream for about half a mile and quickly I saw that in this reach there was a really good head of brown trout and some of very good size. Had the choice of banks been mine, I would have chosen the other side for I could sense at once that these fish were shy. Several I saw feeding high in the water, spotted us quite twenty yards away and went down immediately. The bank we were on is a high one and in places ten feet or more above the water level, so high in fact that our movements along must have been clearly visible to fish.

The hatch of fly increased and by the time we reached the place where my host thought we might fish there was a lot of activity with the trout. The Don is well known as a trout river but I had never heard anyone say that the fish were such free risers or that this water produced abundant fly. Neither did I expect to see brownies of such size, for many I saw show, could have weighed quite two pounds. I wished to try nymphs on these fish and for a start thought a Grey Goose on a No. 1 hook would be attractive as I often find this very good on the Avon when the B.W.O. and the wateries are hatching. We had stopped at a wide pool where quite a dozen fish of varying sizes were on the move, several of which were within easy casting distance. Singling out one I thought to be well over the pound, I made my first cast into the Don. The nymph pitched in delicately and accurately and I fully expected a take, for this fish had risen repeatedly. But nothing happened. I tried him again but with no result, excepting that he stopped rising. It was the same story with the next three fish I tried. Each went down. When this kind of thing happens in other rivers, I usually find the answer is to use a finer cast point and so, snapping off my nymph I put on an extra length of 5 x nylon and substituted the Grey Goose for a P.T. on a size 0 hook.

Many times I have been convinced that the trout, both
brownies and sea-trout have much keener eyesight in the acid
types of water, than in the alkaline, for I had found this to be
true in the West Country and in Wales. And though the Don is a
much better trout water, the character of the fish seemed to be
just the same. Fine and small though I fished, the results I got
were not very encouraging and I had put down quite a dozen
more fish before I got one to take. This was a fish of just over
the pound which was rising close under my bank. This one took
very confidently and gave me no trouble to hook and to land.
My first game fish in Scotland but I knew, even as I unhooked
it and returned it to the water, that the trout of the Don are well
able to look after themselves. No need for me to wish this one
good luck as I felt very doubtful if he would be deceived a second
time with an artificial nymph.

My thoughts went back to a time when I had fished the Usk
in Wales when I spent all one afternoon without getting a single
fish to take either nymph or dry-fly. It is true the fish were not
rising as freely as these in the Don but I had to give them best.
I think it must be due to the very clear water and the very
clear light for it was not until moving farther upstream to more
shallow and broken water, that I took a second fish and then a
third and a fourth. This proved one thing conclusively. The
broken water in the river, acted in very much the same way as a
ripple on a lake and distorted the fish's view of the leader.
Maybe too, it gave more animation to the artificial nymph, but
it called for far more concentration on my part. Though the fish
were willing to take, they were more than willing to get rid of
the nymph again and, quick though I was with the rod, I missed
at least three for each I hooked.

Fishing of this class gives me intense enjoyment. Though I
caught no fish over a pound all I landed gave me grand sport.
The hatch of fly petered out after I had been fishing for about
two hours. During this time there had been a really good rise of
fish and I think any fisherman seeing so many moving could
have been forgiven for thinking they would be easy prey. From
the information I was able to obtain through Jack Sharpe, this
water is fished mostly with the wet-fly but some enthusiasts use
the dry-fly upstream. After spring the fish become very wary

and with the water clear, as it was on this occasion, the best sport was at late evening. Unfortunately we could not stay on to fish the evening rise. Had I done so, I think I would have used a dry-fly. Fishing in good light puts a great strain on one's eyesight, in such water as this but in the subdued light at late evening, fishing a nymph can be very tiring for so much depends on seeing the slightest check of a floating cast.

That day on the Don, when I caught my first trout in Scotland, will always be vivid in my memory. It is a beautiful river with fish in it which can be a challenge to any fisherman. Even as the Usk is the trout water of Wales, so I would say the Don holds pride of place in Scotland. I had read much about both these rivers and heard many fishermen talk of them. But I now know from my own experience, that there are times when the fish are not as easy as many would have us believe.

The following day, true to his promise, Alan Sharpe took me to the Ythan Estuary. Again, through the kindness of the owner at the Udny Arms, we had a boat laid on for our use and a very nice young man for a boatman. Remembering my previous visit I had with me my light, quick actioned outfit, on which I decided to use a single " Killer Bug " on a size 5 hook. Alan Sharpe decided to try a spinning rod first and be judged by the results I got, before changing to a fly rod. To do just the opposite was in my mind. Memories of this estuary and the fish in it had been with me for a year. In my mind I had planned many things but fate decreed otherwise. The weather had turned cold and windy and, according to our boatman, only an occasional small fish had been taken. He was rather pessimistic about our chances and with very good reason, for very few fish were showing anywhere. But I am always hopeful. Where fishing of any kind is concerned, no one can say for certain and, in this spirit, I began to cast and to search the water.

Though I got several tweaks which I thought might have been fish it was quite an hour before my hook took hold in something I knew was alive. But this proved to be a small flounder hooked in the dorsal fin. Shortly afterwards I got another, this time, hooked fairly in the mouth which proved it had taken the bug.

In the meantime Alan Sharpe had caught three flounders and

two pollack on his spinning tackle and honours generally were with him. My own spinning rod was all ready and I thought I would try a few casts. I put down my fly rod leaving the bug dangling in the water over the end of the boat to pick up the spinning tackle when out of the corner of my eye I saw the rod tip bend and start to dance. Quickly I grasped the butt and tightened to a solid pull with my heart beating wildly in the hope that it was a good fish. The strong pull was but a disillusionment, for a moment or so later I could see the fish was a pollack of about a pound. This fish had taken the bug and hooked himself. Two flounders and a pollack. Never before had I caught such fish with a nymph fishing technique. Soon afterwards I caught another pollack, this time in fair fishing which proved that pollack too, liked the bug.

But these fish, and the flounders seemed to be willing to take anything which showed sign of life. Alan Sharpe got three more on his spinner. As I have mentioned there were several times when I had touches to the bug with which I could make no connection. In one part this happened three times in quick succession. Then I managed to hook one. It was a finnock, but the smallest I have ever caught, for I am doubtful if it would have measured eight inches. Small though it was, this was the only game fish we caught between us and for me, the first seatrout in Scotland.

Had I caught a big bag of trout in this estuary I am doubtful if I would have had any real desire to go and fish it again. Catching the flounders, the pollack and the little finnock had fascinated me far more, for each had taken my bug. It is because of this, because too of the surroundings there, and the good companionship of all I met, that I would like to go there again. Just to be able to fish such water should be a delight for any true fisherman. The bend of a rod to any kind of fish can bring a lot of satisfaction.

Chapter Twenty

WITH THE NYMPH IN BAVARIA

Swiss Alpine Range : River Argen at Isny : Typical mountain river : Success with the Grey Goose Nymph : Mixed
Bag : Fast work with left hand : Fish in every likely looking
pocket : Reading the river bed : Nymphs on sunlit rocks
and pebbles : Mayflies and Stoneflies : Catching a trout to
identify insect : Unique experience : Fishing the dry-fly :
Water temperature : Meeting with a German teacher :
Taking turns with the rod : Electric fishing and fish
revealed : Notes on the Burbot : Dams and their effect :
Dead branches : Ruined rivers.

MANY TIMES I had listened with great interest when my friend
Charles Ritz had spoken of the rivers he has fished in Bavaria,
but it was not in my mind that such a chance would ever be
mine until, on the occasion of the 1961 Annual Dinner of the
International Fario Club I was introduced by him to Prince and
Princess Paul von Quadt. I was invited by them to be their guest
at Isny so that I could fish and examine the River Argen. It was
with great excitement that I accepted this great privilege for
July of the following year. I had settled for July after being told
it was one of the more interesting months of the season and also
because it is a favourite nymphing time for me.

My journey was by plane to Zurich where I was met and
taken by car to the little town of Isny and there I was quickly
made to feel very welcome by the Prince and Princess at their
home. Both are very keen fishers and both, especially the
Princess, great lovers of nature. Isny lies in the mountainous

district of Bavaria, or West Germany, as it is now called, and away in the distance the snow clad tops of the end of the Swiss Alpine Range were plain to see. The sight of this great mountain range and the snow upon it convinced me at once that there would be plenty of water to fish and plenty of aquatic life to interest me.

The waters of the Argen run east to west. The river springs in the mountains to join the Rhine and thence to the sea many hundreds of miles away. The Prince owned and rented a stretch of approximately 20 kilometres which I was told contained a variety of fish, those predominating being brown trout, grayling and rainbows. The usual method was to fish the dry fly, but wet flies were also used and on my request to use a nymph this was granted without hesitation.

I was asked if I would like to rest after the long journey or if I would like to see something of the river valley before dinner. My arrival at Isny had been at 4.30 and it was a lovely evening. Quickly I convinced my host that it would take far more than a journey of a few hundred miles to make me too tired to see or to fish a strange river in such delightful surroundings as this Argen.

Soon I had my tackle unpacked and ready. During the latter part of my car journey to Isny the brief views I had of the river, together with the general countryside, had given me the impression that there was a great similarity between this part of Bavaria and parts of Wales. My first sight of the fishing confirmed these observations for the part to which I was taken could quite well have been a stretch of the upper Usk or Wye. Typical mountain water flowing fast over a rocky bed not a place I thought, to expect many large trout or to be the habitat of grayling. But about this, and indeed about many other things, I was to be disillusioned.

There in front of me was a pool at the tail of a long gravelly shallow into which the water surged through an assembly of half-submerged rocks. The water, bubbling and in many places white with foam, travelled at a very fast pace and immediately I had misgivings about the use of a nymph. But as we watched, several fish rose about the pool. So knotting on a No. 2 Grey Goose Nymph I decided to give it a trial. It is only fair to say that these fish had never seen a nymph constructed as mine are made, or fished as I fish them, and after taking six fish with consecutive casts I began to wonder if I was dreaming. A mixed bag too, made up of four brownies, a rainbow and a grayling— all this without moving from my position. None was large compared to chalk-stream standards, the best being the rainbow of just over the pound. All fought strongly in the fast water and I was glad to have decided on a 3 x point for my leader.

During the hour or so before dark I must have hooked more than a score of trout and also some grayling. All these fish took the same nymph and despite the fast-running water held it long enough for me to hook them. A rising fish meant a taking fish and plenty were moving all about the river.

Fishing a nymph upstream in fast water calls for considerable quickness of hand everywhere, but here in this rough and tumbling water my usual speed had to be accelerated. Presenting the nymph was no difficulty, neither had one to worry over-much about rivercraft as far as concealment was concerned. Here one waded the river and fish would rise almost at one's feet. But controlling the line after a cast was made was another story. Some fast work with the left hand, or line-control hand, was essential. Both line and two-thirds of the cast needed to be well greased and then I found they floated high and for most of the time showed plainly even in the rapids. I found, if the cast stopped in its drift, that my fish was always there. If in the take the fish appeared to be of reasonable size I would tighten, if small a drop of the rod tip would allow it to get free. So ended my first evening on the Argen. In that short time I had learned much. The river held fish in vast numbers and I knew how to catch them. I went to bed knowing an exciting week was ahead.

The next day, I think, had I really tried, it would have been possible to take at least one hundred brace of fish inclusive of brownies, rainbows and grayling. My thoughts went back to the time when grayling were thick in the upper Avon but I don't think even they were as easy to deceive and catch as those in the Bavarian stream. Perhaps this was because I had learned much of the art of nymph fishing since those days 30 years ago, and my present artificials were of a more tempting nature. I fished, and continued to fish, simply because I wished to form

some idea as to the numbers and the general size. Also I wanted
to find out the proportion of trout to grayling. In this mountain
water, fish were in every likely-looking pocket and, it seemed
to me, these were continuously on the lookout for food. One
could drop a nymph under the banks, behind rocks and in the
fast runs, into the swirls and the eddies. There to take it was a
fish of one kind or another. Many were small, but a very fair
number were between three-quarters and one pound. Several
I got were up to one-and-a-half pounds but these larger fish all
had rather a lean appearance when compared with the well-fed
and lazy trout of the chalk streams of England. Despite their
lean shape these fish were strong and fought gamely.

Both brown trout and grayling are indigenous to the Argen,
or at least there are records which show they were present and
plentiful more than two hundred years ago. Rainbows are a
recent addition having been introduced by the Prince about four
years ago. This interested me considerably because there was
plenty of evidence that generation from this initial stock had
taken place. I caught a number of yearlings and two-year-olds,
and these, especially the larger fish, were in excellent condition
and were first class fighters when hooked. At two years old each
was about a pound, but these wild-bred fish had a colouration
quite different from the parent fish of which I caught and
examined a large number.

What amazed me was that a water of this nature could hold
and support such a large head of fish and so I set about trying
to find the answer.

When one starts to read a river bed the task becomes absorbing and here, in this river, creatures interested me more than
fishing. I have examined the beds of many rivers, streams and
lakes, both in this country and abroad, but never in any of them
have I found a greater abundance of life. The bed of the Argen
was literally alive, a mass of different animals vying one with
another for existence.

All my life I have placed a great value on aquatic plants but
I begin to feel very doubtful if weeds in a river or any water
are necessary for the production of our most valued fly life.
When I fished in the mountains of North Sweden a few years
previously scarcely a weed of any kind was to be seen in the

beds of either lake or stream, yet some species of Ephemeroptera were present in many millions. In the Argen it was the same story. Hordes of insects of every known kind, yet, with the exception of mosses on the rocks in the rapids, there was no sign of vegetation. Mosses were plentiful in all the natural parts of the river for I must explain that, like a large majority of the rivers about the world, the Argen has not escaped the attentions of men in harnessing the waters for power and irrigation.

At various points down the valley the river is obstructed by dams to hold heads of water, in places up to 30 feet, for saw-mills or generating plants. In some parts the water runs off in canals or underground tubes from upstream of the dams, to completely by-pass the original course for as much as a mile or more. For much of the year the old courses remain almost dry and are referred to as " dead branches " which I thought to be a very fitting description for them, for at a glance they did appear dead. Closer examination proved otherwise but of this later.

My interest centred on the parts of the river which were still in the natural form and by looking at these I could visualise just how delightful this river had been everywhere before man started to tether the wild waters and impede the work of Nature. I had expected insect life in fair numbers, especially the Chironomidae, for chironomids are fairly common in most mountain waters even if they are acid. But the Argen is alkaline, for much of the water springs from limestone origin and in this part the rocks were of limestone too. I expected to find some families of Ephemeridae too, but as I browsed and studied the rocks and the mosses it was possible to understand the eager-ness of the fish to take nymphs. Here was a paradise for a river entomologist where hordes of creatures in all stages of their lives could be studied as easily as in an aquarium. Nymphs and larvae were spread about on the sunlit rocks and pebbles on the bed in thousands, while the mosses growing on rocks in the rapids presented a moving mass of different animals as they were lifted clear of the stream. As one walked along so there was continuous movement on the pebbles and gravel as the nymphs sought shelter beneath.

In a week it is, of course, impossible to find and identify every creature in a river bed, or come to know all those produced throughout the year. For many, just a glance was sufficient as they were very familiar, even though I was surprised to see them —for instance, Mayflies. The Argen is not a river in which one could expect to find Mayflies and yet in early July a fair number hatched each day and I found mature nymphs clinging to the mosses in some of the fastest of the rapids. But apparently there is never a hatch big enough to interest the fish.

Those I saw gave the fish no chance to take them. They hatched by crawling up through the moss to the air then took flight in much the same manner as the stone flies. As one would expect in rocky, turbulent water, stone flies were plentiful and here the big creeper of Perla cephalotes, described by Halford in his Dry-fly Entomology, is abundant, with many other species better known. It was a little early for many of the big stone flies to be hatching but I saw several on the wing and did have the good fortune to see one female egg-laying. The eggs were laid by dipping, but what amazed me was the very fast flight here and there to touch the water in the rapids and then away to rest awhile before repeating the performance. Though I would say there is very good food value in both underwater and aerial forms of this big stone fly, I consider it very unlikely that fish get much chance to eat them. Some I think may fall prey to fish while in the last stages of the creeper existence but it would seem they live mostly in the mosses or beneath rocks inaccessible to trout or grayling.

I haven't the space to give details of all the Ephemeroptera I found. All species known to me in the chalk streams were present in greater or lesser numbers. Of them all the Blue-winged Olives were most plentiful, together with the Cloeon and Procloeon types. One fly I came across was unknown to me. Several had hatched and taken flight close to me and though I quickly found the nymphs, it was some time before I managed to get a dun. The rocks in the bed of the Argen are slippery and this, together with the fast-running water, decided me, for my own safety, not to pursue a fluttering fly across the river. But I did get one and perhaps the manner in which this was done will amuse you. One of these flies had hatched and was floating along under the opposite bank. I moved slowly across to intercept it but just as I got to mid-stream a trout rose and down went the fly. The fish settled back to his position on a rock where I could see him plainly, so, getting my rod, I flicked a nymph to him. He was no less eager in taking than the others I had caught and in a moment or two was landed. He was but a half-pounder and I had to kill him as I could see no sign of the fly inside his mouth. Opening him up, there inside his crop was my specimen, in rather a battered condition it is true. It was indeed a stranger to me but after washing it out into some semblance of shape I was able to examine it under my lens. I had suspected the nymph to be the Late March Brown (E. venosis). This dun supported my views. Later I managed to get others for further confirmation and also some male and female spinners.

I found that this Late March Brown hatches in good numbers and is indeed one of the chief attractions for the fish. An artificial to suggest its appearance was taken readily by both trout and grayling.

Caddis also were present in very fair numbers which again was rather surprising, for most of the sedge flies prefer the medium-paced waters where weed growths are plentiful. Most of those I saw in winged form were familiar but there was one very large insect which flitted about like a moth. I was unable to obtain a specimen but feel convinced this was the very big dark sedge, P. Grandis. Though I searched I could not find caddis which could produce these large types and I cannot think they are abundant.

Prince Quadt allowed me the use of a Jeep-type car. This allowed me to travel along tracks and routes where any other vehicle would have been racked to pieces and there were places where I had to cross the river at some very rough fords. In one or two places I drove along the river bed, for though a very fast stream might run at one side of the bed, the other was dry. Here I had the unique experience for me, of sitting on the bonnet of the car and catching fish. And so, though the fishery is 12 miles in length, it was possible to move from the upper boundary to the lower if I felt so inclined. Evening, from about six o'clock till dark, was the best time to fish the dry fly and on each day my hosts joined me at some agreed point to fish the evening rise.

The great thing in this fast-running water was to be able to

place a fly and allow it to float high without drag. This both of
them could do and it was very nice to see the artificial dancing
along and then chopped down by a fish. The dry fly is fished
upstream and downstream, in each case cast with plenty of
slack line, and indeed leader, and in such a manner that invariably the fly was in advance of the leader when it went over a
fish. The fish were quick to take, indeed it seemed to me that
few ever refused, but it was very obvious that both trout and
grayling were much quicker in getting rid of a dry fly than an
artificial nymph. This I think can be explained by the fact that
the dry fly is preferred by most of the people who fish this water.
Also, as it is very seldom any fish are killed when caught, there
is a possibility that they remember being deceived on other
occasions.

Rising fish, during the evening, were all about the river, but
one thing I learned very quickly. All the better-class fish were to
be found in the rapids. At no point was the river very deep, but
at intervals, long flats, much deeper and much slower running,
came between stretches of rock-strewn rapids. At late evening,
with the sun low, it was a joy to see the hordes of different
insects dancing, dipping and pitching about the rough waters.
These were the places all insects chose for egg laying, a fact well
known to the trout, and it was there they expected and indeed
got, their food supply. The flats held plenty of small fish, with
occasional takeable ones at the throat or tail of the pool. Such
waters were of course, much easier to fish the nymph in, as the
slower-paced water allowed one plenty of time to work with
precision. The take of the small fish was very definite.

A multitude of insects egg laying meant of course, that there
was a multitude of eggs. Although it was impossible to find the
eggs of those species which dip or drop their eggs at the surface,
I experienced no difficulty in finding those of the Baetis group
which go down. Every pebble or rock which rose above the fast-
flowing water and so allowed flies to pitch on them were covered
beneath water by layer upon layer of eggs, millions of eggs, and
all where they stood a very good chance of hatching. Here was
fly generation at its peak and no longer was I astonished at
seeing so many nymphs and larvae everywhere about the river.

Many times I have stressed the importance of a clean bed

and fast-running water for fly production. No fly boards were necessary, indeed no artificial methods were needed. The pebbles and rocks rising from the oxygenated water were in such numbers that I was astonished that all held eggs, enough eggs to feed any and every creature who wished to feed on them, and still leave an abundance. It is conditions such as these we should aim to produce in our rivers where the insect population had become so depleted through the years. Stone, not wood, is what these insects need for egg-laying sites, and stone protruding from the bed of fast-running water. This suggestion is not a new one. For many years I have made use of pre-cast concrete slabs to act as egg-laying sites in the upper Avon.

Another surprise I got was the temperature of the water. I had expected, being so near to the mountains, that throughout the year it would be cold. Instead it was much higher than ours of the Avon and indeed any of the southern rivers. My last experience of mountain waters was in the Arctic circle where the water seldom rose above the lower forties. In the Argen, even though the river had such a big fall in levels, the water held steady in the lower sixties. This perhaps accounted for the large number of Ephemerella and Cloeon.

When searching for insects I did of course, find other creatures. Shrimps were not numerous and these were of a much smaller variety than the ones I am accustomed to seeing in the chalk streams. This I would say, is because of the lack of vegetation, as shrimps do feed a lot on decaying vegetable matter and they get plenty of this throughout the year in the chalk streams. But the water-hog louse appeared everywhere and abundantly which again set me in a puzzle as these feed almost exclusively on decomposing organic matter. Also I found crayfish. Not many it is true, as hiding places among the rocks were legion. One big female was carrying her freshly-hatched young and one large trout I caught disgorged a half-grown crayfish as I was removing my nymph from his jaws. Bullheads too, were to be found beneath the rocks but though I searched diligently I did not see any stone loaches. The bullheads were of a much larger type than those known to me in this country, but as far as I know there is only one species, Cottus gobio, and so I would say the large size was due to the very rich feeding available. No doubt these bullheads took considerable numbers of the big stone fly creepers as well as innumerable nymphs which lived beneath the rocks and stones in close proximity.

As I explained earlier, in places the River Argen is dammed either for saw-milling or for generating plants. In one part above a barrage of about 25ft. high, the waters had spread into the valley to form a lake of about six acres. Here rainbow trout had been introduced as two-year-olds. When the river was running high during the last winter a number of these stock fish, as in previous years, had drifted with the water over the lip of the dam and so tumbled to the pool in the lower level. It is impossible for fish to return to the lake after going over the fall.

Many of these rainbows were fish which, when in good condition, might have weighed up to four pounds. Standing on the bridge over the dam, they were quite easy to see. I estimated there were over 50 and quite a number of these were continually cruising about the pool and rising to fly and midges. It was here I met a German teacher. Apparently this man had permission to fish the pool on the understanding that any rainbows caught by him were to be transferred to the lake above—not a very easy feat as I had every reason to know. The previous day I had taken half-a-dozen of these fish and clambered up to the lake with them.

The German had been fishing dry fly without success, so I asked him if he knew of the nymph. He could speak some English and I a limited number of German words, but getting a negative answer to my question I asked him if he would care to see it demonstrated. He would be delighted and would be pleased to net any fish and take them to turn loose in the lake. Perhaps he regretted this for one after another those rainbows took my nymph and after he had scrambled up and down the steep bank for the twentieth time I decided to call a halt. Never in his life had he seen so many fish caught with a rod in so short a time and he seemed disappointed when I told him I was doubtful if any of them would live for another year. They were all old fish, none of which had recovered from spawning. Though transferred to the lake and perhaps richer feeding, few I thought would ever regain condition.

This German teacher was a kindly man I feel sure. He was a very big man, dressed in leather shorts, stockings and light canvas shoes. He wore a rough heavy woollen shirt and no hat, and appeared to be as weather-beaten and rugged as the countryside around. When I came upon him first he was feeding a young fly-catcher he had in a cage—a bird, he explained, which one of his pupils had brought to him. He had brought it with him so that he could feed it at regular intervals for without such attention one so young would most surely have died. The sight of this very big man tenderly offering tit-bits on a pair of forceps to the tiny bird did much to make my day for me. At once I knew he was a naturalist and one who might be a keen fisherman. I knew, even though we might have difficulty with our languages, that we would understand each other. I gathered from his conversation that he often spent a whole afternoon fishing this pool but seldom caught more than a brace. Often he had a blank day. I gave him some nymphs and hope he is now more successful.

For a few hours one afternoon Prince Quadt and I fished together and shared his rod. This was a short, very quick actioned split cane on which he was using what I thought to be a rather heavy forward tapered line. With this outfit he was extremely accurate and very quick in placing a dry fly and indeed successful in hooking a good number of fish which rose to it. With the nymph he was experiencing some difficulty. Quick though the rod was in its action the pick up of the heavy line wasted just that fraction of time which is so important and it was when I explained this that he suggested we should use his rod and fish up the river together. And it proved to be grand fun. A decision was made that each should give up the rod to the other if a fish was missed and, with the understanding that only fish which were visible should be cast to. Both trout and grayling were moving well, the water was perfectly clear and, with an excellent light, we had no difficulty in spotting fish either lying well up in the water, or after one or other had risen and so betrayed his position. This was a lovely reach of alternate shallows and pools with here and there overhanging branches beneath which one had to be extremely accurate to avoid being caught up.

For us both, this afternoon was an education. Often I was in a much better position to see a fish than was the Prince and sometimes it was the reverse and each would have a good laugh at the expense of the other when a fish took well and was missed. On this occasion I had put on a Pheasant Tail nymph on a o hook, tied to a 5 x leader point. Scarcely a fish refused and between us we caught many trout and grayling, picking out all the largest, a number of which were well over the pound. In my case I caught far more trout than grayling. I was handicapped to a certain extent by the unfamiliar tackle. This was one place where certainly the grayling called for much quicker action than did the trout, and we were lucky to have more than one cast before handing the rod over, often indeed when trying for the same fish.

I am sure Prince Quadt enjoyed the afternoon as much as I did. Seeing the failure of another can be very enlightening and there in the very clear water, one could see just how quick these fish were in taking and in getting rid of the nymph. At the end of the afternoon we were both pleasantly tired for this kind of fishing needs considerable concentration. I should have mentioned long before this that few fish were ever killed from this water, excepting at times when some were needed for the table, which was not often. Barbless hooks were used mostly with dry-flies and wet-flies, but as I had no nymphs tied on barbless hooks I used a small pair of pliers and pressed down the barbs. This enabled the release of fish to take place very quickly and without damaging them in the slightest. Being in the water wading, it was an easy matter to coax a fish near enough to grasp the leader. Then by running finger and thumb down and grasping the nymph this could be turned and a slight shake would free the hook. No fish needed to be lifted from the water. I cannot think they suffered any harm and indeed in several cases were not even frightened. I remember one big grayling which I caught three times in less than ten minutes. Each time on release this fish went back upstream to the feeding position where I had seen it first. What is more it took the same nymph.

Towards the end of the week of my visit the Prince engaged some fishermen with an electro-fishing machine to do some parts of the river and give me a better idea of the stock of fish these held. Only then did I fully realise just how big was the head of fish this river carried, and the size to which some grew. One trout of over four pounds was taken. Several others around the two pound mark showed too, but generally, as I had suspected when fishing, the majority of the good-conditioned fish were just over the pound. These were the native brownies and wild-bred fish. Some rainbows of two or three pounds were also present but these were in very poor condition and similar to the ones I had caught on the nymph. Smaller rainbows, yearlings and two-year-olds, were plentiful and seemed to be well established in both fast and slow-running water. The grayling were mostly small. Numbers of them went up to a pound but only one to a pound-and-a-half. These also were in best condition at about three-quarters to a pound.

Every dip of the electrode brought fish. They were using D.C. with what I thought to be rather a high current. But it did show me the fish, for as well as a terrific stock of both trout and grayling, the water held coarse fish too. Where all these came from in the beginning I cannot say for there were pike, chub, tench, carp, bleak, dace and, in two deep pools, barbel, these last fish up to six pounds. Some of the chub were enormous for such water too, as I saw a large number up to four pounds. The pike were not numerous, nor were they large, a fact which rather surprised me in view of the enormous food supply of game fish present. Apparently, it is exceptional to take pike over six pounds from this water.

One fish taken in fair numbers, was the burbot, a fish we seldom hear or read about in this country, but there were no eels. The burbot is much prized as a food fish in Bavaria and every effort was made to take each as it was shocked. Several taken during this electro-fishing were up to two pounds in weight but my host told me it is not unusual to get them twice or even three times that weight. I had never eaten burbot and when the Prince knew of this he had some prepared for dinner. The liver is said to be a great delicacy, but, though I like it very much, I preferred the flesh. This tasted to me very much like eels in their prime condition. Some burbot are still caught in parts of this country, some in the very lowest parts of the Hampshire Avon, though I have never seen them myself. They were

fairly plentiful years ago along the eastern part of England and
then commanded a good market price.

The burbot is truly a bottom fish and lives a life not dissimilar
to the eel as far as habitat and feeding is concerned. But the
burbot spawns in fresh water and in structure is much different.
It hides during the day and feeds at night. There in the Argen
this fish had plenty of hiding places beneath the big rocks, and
one could see holes leading down deeply in many places. The
head is squat with rounded jaws, in appearance not unlike that
of a snake with barbules at either side of the lower jaw. The
head and the mouth are large in comparison with most fish and
I would say the head occupies quite a fourth of the total length.
The fish had two dorsal fins, a small one between head and
centre part of body, then an elongated one which extends almost
to the tail. The tail ends sharply oval. Pectoral, ventral and anal
fins are also present on this fish and it is said to be a member
of the cod family.

The burbot has a striking colouring, with body mottled in
yellowish brown and much darker brown, the whole giving a
kind of yellow marbling effect. The under-parts are similar but
much lighter. To me, this fish seems to be a kind of cross
between several, in which the eel, bullhead and stone loach could
take a part. The squat and somewhat slimy head and body
allows this fish to squirm into places denied to most other fresh-
water types. Not a very handsome fish to look at and no doubt
a scavenger, but I think I would like to have some in the upper
Avon, even though one could not catch them with a nymph.

I found a comparison of the River Argen and my Avon and
other chalk streams of considerable interest. But though I have
mentioned that this river had been trapped at various points to
provide water power, I found when giving it real consideration
that I should write more about this and so give more explanation. In the past I have written at considerable length on the
subject of dams, weirs, hatches and other river controls about the
South Country, and the effect these have in frustrating the work
of Nature. Along the valley of the Argen in Bavaria I found
the same story but one which has to be told in a different way.

In character my upper Avon and the Argen may be said to
be extremes—one a slow-running chalk stream fed by springs

and not subject to any quick rise or fall of water, the other a spate river where the fall in level and speed of flow is at least ten times greater. Whereas in the upper Avon valley it is very exceptional to get a flood which raises the water level more than three feet across the valley, there in the mountains of the Argen valley, a rise up to 20 feet is not uncommon. And so the action of the water on the river bed is very different in each river.

In the slow-running types of river such as the chalk streams any serious obstruction to the natural gradient has the effect of collecting undesirable spoil in the impoundments and through the years to create an entirely false bottom to the river course for a considerable distance upstream. Rushes and various other undesirable vegetation root into these deposits and so consolidate them, until in time the natural river bed ceases to function in producing the more valued fish and other aquatic life.

In the Avon a dam of five or six feet has the effect of creating a flat above it for approximately a mile, so lifting the water to a top flow governed by the lip of the dam. And so it is possible for the channel to fill at the bottom until the drag from the running water keeps it to this certain level. The pressure on the bed exerted by the accumulations of spoil together with the impounded water, acts as a complete seal to air, which in normal circumstances should enter into the river course. In the case of accumulations of rotting vegetable matter, not only is oxygen prevented from entering, but a considerable amount is absorbed by this foul matter from the water travelling above it.

However, as I have indicated, the dams in the spate river have presented another story. In the Argen valley the fall in level is so much greater and so, to hold a sufficient head to be of use for power, the dams across the river course need to be much higher. Here the barrages are in places up to 30 feet high and in the majority of sites, these are constructed across the original river channel. This of course, presented no great engineering problem, as at either side, the natural rocks helped to create the trap. The bed, gouged down through the years by the water to solid and impervious rock, acted as a sound foundation, and while some strengthening to prevent scouring of banks by the overflow in the lower level was necessary, the natural rock in the bed was sufficient to prevent the waterfall from gouging out a great hole. The dam itself is constructed of concrete and natural rock, wide at the base and tapering up to the crest.

I could visualise this when done in the first place—the water trapped by the 30ft. obstruction to rise and then tumble over the lip of the dam; 30ft. of water covering the rocks and loose gravel of the old river bed, and just downstream the compensation water, making just a trickle as it wandered along the exposed rocks and shingle of its former course; the canal carrying most of the waters of the Argen looped around the contours to feed power to a mill or generating plant and then be discharged back to the natural channel. I could picture the river rushing along down the valley obeying the pull of gravity, over fast gravelly shallows and through rock-strewn rapids and then suddenly to find itself tethered, reined up so to speak, when going at a gallop.

The picture faded and I faced the facts of the present day. As I stood on the dry lip of one such dam and looked downstream, the old river course, the dry branch (as it is called in those parts), had altered a little. Overgrown a little perhaps at either side by trees and bushes but still with its little trickle of water at one side or another, with the bared rocks and gravel hot from the sun. Waiting, waiting very patiently I thought, until wintertime, when there would come an overflow from the dam to sweeten it for another season.

Upstream of the dam a very different story was presented. No longer was the river bed 30 feet beneath me. It had been raised until now it was less than 30 inches. Here in this impound was almost 30 feet of clean-washed gravel and rock, instead of water, which extended away upstream like a great wedge to where the flat of the impound ran out and where Nature once again had command. I quote this one instance of several along the part of the valley I visited and no doubt there are many more. Instead of mud as in my own native valley, here was clean-washed gravel, rock and sand which had accumulated over a period of many years.

Nowhere was there mud or indeed any organic matter. In the first place little aquatic vegetation grows in the Argen and any decay from this is quickly swept away by the fast-running water. The same thing applies to the fall of leaves from overhanging or nearby trees and bushes, and also to any spoil eroded from the banks. And yet the effect on the river life was similar in many respects.

Perhaps for a few years after these dams were constructed the deep impoundments held and produced big trout, as does the newly-flooded land of an artificial lake. But as the bed gradually covered with gravel and rose higher and higher towards the surface, so this production ceased.

The flotsam caught on bushes and trees and the scour marks on the rocks and banks told their own story and showed plainly the height to which water could rise. With the river low, as it was at the time of my visit, there were rapids where the water raced along much too fast for me to wade across in safety. And so I had little difficulty in realising just how powerful this river can be in time of high flood with the volume of water perhaps a hundred times greater.

In one place the packed gravel extended up the river course for a distance of over half-a-mile. Clean, bright and level, it was from bank to bank, and solid enough for me to wade without fear of sinking into it. But in this half-mile stretch where there was not a bit of cover of any kind, I saw not a trout over half-a-pound and the majority of the grayling were small also, though these outnumbered the trout by at least ten to one. As I waded along in my thigh boots I could visualise the true bed of the river 20 feet and more beneath me. I could visualise the rocks which had held mosses and provided sanctuary and a feeding place for innumerable aquatic creatures, now held fast in the grip of thousands of tons of gravel, gone perhaps for ever from the sight of man. It was quite obvious that before this dam had been constructed, the river bed had a character exactly as was shown in the dead branch where now it could be studied thoroughly.

Aquatic life on this packed gravel was very scarce and my studies of the insect life proved the majority to be of the midge and gnat families, a fair number of B.W.O. and Cloeon but no Baetis or indeed any of the larger types of insects which were present in the natural parts of the river. Nor did I find shrimp or water-hog louse or any of the caddis group. All that was produced on this packed gravel was small-fish food and in consequence, only small fish inhabited it One might be forgiven for thinking that this great area of clean gravel would have been ideal for spawning trout. It looked nice but no trout had ever used it, or were likely to do so, for here was a bed much too loose and even the grayling shunned it.

My host has spoken of the dead branch as being downstream of the dam. It was not. The Argen was dead above it, for when these dams were constructed a creeping death came downstream to consolidate them. The dead branch interested me far more than the impound for though only a comparative trickle of water passed along it, the animal life in it was a hundred times greater and with infinite variety. Here in the old rocky channel all the natural creatures of the Argen held on to life and the mosses cling wherever there was sufficient water. There, exposed to my view, was the true bed of the river, its pools and rapids, its shallows and glides. In places water was springing in the bed through loose rocks or gravel; in others, various trickles entered into the course from the outsides; water clean and pure and with oxygen entering into it in sufficient quantity to keep the multitude alive.

Indeed there was a multitude present. The bed of rocks, pebbles and gravel showed continuous movement as the nymphs and larvae of millions of insects sought shelter. Every pool, every trickle between the rocks held trout. Some of these had run up this dead branch to spawn during the winter and had remained. There were fish up to one-and-a-half pounds feeding in water so shallow that the dorsal fin would show above when the fish was lying on the bottom. Here one could see the old redds still heaped in the gravel, and in every pool or stickle were trout fry and yearlings—aquatic life production with a vengeance.

This had been called the dead branch and yet in it I could have caught 20 trout for each one in the impound above the dam, and fish at least three times larger. Just coincidence perhaps, but the stretch of the old river course to where the tail water from the mill rejoined it, was almost exactly the same length as had been covered through the years by the gravel upstream of the dam.

I must explain that most of the dams on the Argen are of solid construction. There are some, however, where provision in the form of sluice gates can allow a generous release of water to the lower level in times of flood or emergency. In much the same way as it is done in this country. Here, however, and indeed all about the British Isles, there is a law which prevents an old river course from being shut off completely from its water supply. On the Argen there is no such consideration and the mills or power plants take the whole supply.

I have written this with one view in mind and this is to bring out the fact that regardless of whether covered in by mud or by gravel, the bed of a natural river course ceases to function in a natural way. Though a firm false bed is formed on the top of it, this bed can never be as productive of aquatic life as the old one and this is a thought which might well be borne in mind by those who wish to interfere with a running stream. Any permanent dam which extends across a river course can act as a check to anything moved downstream by the action of the water, whether this be solids or soluble, and once the bed is sealed to exclude the inlet of air or of water from the surrounding land the work of Nature is frustrated.

Though I have used the Bavarian river Argen as an example I need not have travelled so far. We have many rivers about the British Isles where a similar story can be told. Permanent dams have ruined many good fisheries yet they continue to be made.

Chapter Twenty-one

A DEMONSTRATION IN NORTH SWEDEN

Meeting with Nils Farnstrom: Contrast to the South
Country Chalk Streams: String of Lakes: First Trout:
Frustration: Need for Study: A new rod: A strange fly:
Discovering the nymphs and making copies: The Grey
Goose Nymph: Strong fighters and need for more backing:
The hatching of nymphs and the drift of duns: Nils
Farnstrom has success and failure: Spinners at late evening:
Habits of the trout: Further success: The chance of a life-
time missed by carelessless: Nils satisfied he had mastered
the art: Largest trout: Sawyer's Folly: Identifying the
various insects: Christening the new nymph: Confirmation
by D. E. Kimmins.

I FEEL there can be few fishermen in the world today who have
travelled over twenty-five hundred miles expressly to demonstrate a method of catching trout. Yet this I did in July of 1959.

A visit which took me to the Northernmost part of Sweden
was arranged by Herrer Nils Farnstrom, the Editor of the magazine " Sport Fiskaren ", who is also correspondent to one of the
leading Stockholm papers. He and other Swedish fishermen
had read various articles I had written and all were anxious to
know if my method of nymph fishing could be used to obtain
more sport in some of the waters in Sweden. Herrer Farnstrom
is well known as an authority on fishing throughout the Scand-
inavian countries and has fished in various rivers and lakes
throughout the world. His articles, his books, and his word on
fishing is accepted by all classes of anglers, and after meeting him

and spending a fortnight in his company, this I can readily understand.

There is this however. Had I known, or even had an idea, of the class of country into which I was to go, I am doubtful if I would have accepted the invitation. But I am very glad now that I did. My technique of nymph fishing was developed in this country, mostly in the chalk streams of the South where waters are clear and flow gently towards the sea and where there is an abundance of insects which tempt trout to the surface. Here also the streams are easy to approach and can be fished without the slightest discomfort and with civilisation always near at hand.

What a contrast I found. My trip took me to a place where few Englishmen have fished—to a wild and beautiful part of Sweden, far from habitation and where only the most enthusiastic fishermen could be tempted to wander. It was a place high in the mountains near to the borders of Norway and Lapland. Snow was still on the highest peaks and in a most lovely valley, bordered by forest on either side, there was a string of lakes formed and fed by a thousand rivulets tumbling down from where the snow gradually melted on the mountain tops. For sheer beauty there can be few places in the world to equal it. Here is nature untouched through the centuries. Here the elk and the reindeer wander at will and here the otter and the bear, the mink and the osprey hunt for fish. It is the haunt of the dipper and the greenshank and for a variety of wild-fowl—a veritable paradise for a trout fisherman and a lover of the wild. It was for me. I felt very content just to sit and look—to absorb the loveliness around me. I felt part of it all—just as though this was part of the world fitting for me and I knew, after my first glance, that I should enjoy myself.

The lakes we were to fish varied in size from some of twenty or thirty acres to others much smaller and less than four acres. Each was linked to its neighbour with narrow rapid runs down rock-strewn courses, which had falls in level up to thirty feet or more. Tumbling waters entered the head of each lake there to spread out into great flats, some circular in shape but others elongated and bordered with rugged and uneven shores.

My first impression was that Nature had been using rocks as

playthings and then left them in a state of disorder. On every
side of the lakes great masses of stone, some weighing hundreds
of tons, had been cast into heaps and these, through the ages,
had been covered with a drapery of lichen, moss and heather.
Amongst them stunted pines and silver birch fought hard for
existence as they swept up towards the timber line far above on
the mountains.

In the heart of all this lay the lakes reflecting the blue of the
sky and in whose waters were the trout I had come so far to try
and catch. I would like to enthuse still more on the location and
surroundings, indeed to let you see the picture I myself saw and
which will remain forever in my mind. But I cannot. I have
no words to express all my thoughts. And I made a promise not
to disclose the exact position for fear such a paradise would
become desecrated. But somehow I don't think this will ever
happen. Only those who love nature and the catching of really
wild fish, could withstand the privation and the endurance
necessary on such a trip.

I wondered. My host had told me there were many large
trout in this string of lakes, brownies which ranged from tiny
fry to fish of six or seven pounds. In some were char and lower
down the valley were pike. But it was in the catching of brown
trout that he was interested. The lower lakes—some six or seven
are all preserved for fly fishermen—dry fly, wet fly or a nymph.
In others spinning is allowed. The object of my visit was to
demonstrate nymph fishing, and I must confess I felt rather
doubtful if the methods I have found so effective in England
and France would be the same in these wild parts.

Knowing I was to fish in lakes and link between streams, I
took with me a number of my three patterns all dressed on No. 1
hooks. And it was on one of these—the P.T. pattern that I took
my first fish in Sweden. It was a very small one, not more than
six inches long. That first evening, though we went to several
of the lakes and link streams, no large fish were moving. I was
still in a doubtful frame of mind when getting into my sleeping
bag that night.

You should know, I think, that we were in camp. Our camp
equipment (tents, etc. and provisions) was transported over the
mountains by float plane and it was in this plane that I had my

first view of the fishing. The lakes cannot be approached by a land vehicle of any kind, the nearest road or track being about fourteen miles distant. One has only to travel on foot, as I had to on my return to civilisation, to realise why so few make the journey. The lakes are large enough for a take-off and landing by small float plane. Transport of equipment by horse or pack mule is possible, but some enthusiasts do the walk both ways and carry their kit with them.

The following afternoon I got my first fish of size. It was a trout of two and a quarter pounds. I had waded out in one of the shallower lakes to where odd fish were surfacing in a head and tail movement. This fish also took the P.T. on No. 1 hook but I had the feeling that the taking of this trout was more luck than anything else. I was using a new rod made by Pezon and Michel the French manufacturers. This rod, named the Fario Club is 8ft. 5in. long, of split cane and weighs 5¼ ounces. It was the first of its kind to reach England and I had it to try and give my opinion.

With it I used a D.T. No. 2 Kingfisher line with a cast tapered to 4 x. My reel, a Pflueger 3¼in. The casting line and backing was a matter of eighty yards. That fish took out over seventy yards in one rush after being hooked with the little rod bending as it had never bent before. It was only after a long, strong fight that I got the fish into the net.

Catching this first big trout pleased me. Here was proof that such fish could be taken with nymphs but I was anxious to make an autopsy and find out just what types, or type of nymph, these trout were taking, for though I had tried the little P.T. nymph where two or three other fish were moving, I had no response. The reason why was apparent when I examined the contents of the fish's crop. Amongst a collection of caddis were nymphs of a kind I had never before seen and of a size much larger than the No. 1 P.T. I was using. I was at once convinced that I needed a pattern on a No. 3 or No. 4 hook to meet the requirements.

Flies of a kind I had never seen were hatching and that evening the spinners of the same species came to the water to lay their eggs. And I wondered if these were from the kind of nymphs I had found in the trout.

That evening was one of the most frustrating I can remember. The spinners fell spent in thousands to drift on to the lake with the vagaries of the wind. As they drifted so the trout began to rise in the way I afterwards found to be so characteristic to this class of insect. Head, dorsal, and then tail, would break through the surface as fish after fish came on to feed. Trout after trout, a dozen or more in a bunch, rose and took these spent spinners. So thick were the flies on the water that in rising, the fish took one and missed at least a dozen before taking the next.

I tried with my nymphs, with all my small patterns, but they were disregarded. I tried with dry flies, large and small including Mayflies I had in one of my boxes. And I tried with a team of wet flies. But not a fish did I get. My host caught nothing either. He fished with various dry flies. I caught numbers of the spinners. Both males and females were present in equal numbers and each sex was on the water spent.

So thick were the spinners that I knew any exact representation of the natural fly was hopeless. The competition was too great and I knew, as I have found on many occasions elsewhere that when trout have the chance to pick and choose, as these did, it was just a lucky shot if one was tempted to take an artificial. I failed to rise a fish. Nils Farnstrom rose one with an outsize Coachman but failed to connect and I found out afterwards that other fishermen had the same experience.

That night as I lay in my tent I could see in my mind's eye those great trout rolling in the surface. Some of those I had seen that evening were between three and five pounds. And there had been one even larger, six pounds at least. One thing was very certain, I must find out more about the flies before trying for more trout. My show so far had been very unconvincing.

In the morning I was out early. It was not long before I discovered the nymphs, the duns, and the spinners of this particular fly. I had thought previously that these creatures, living as they did in such rocky conditions, must be related to the March Brown. They were of a size similar and I had established the fact that the duns hatched from the rocks and from vegetation at the sides of the lakes. None hatched in the open water. The nymphs I found in my first autopsy were not in good shape and so I had imagined them to be of the flat crawling

type allied to the March Brown of this country. I was surprised
to find I was mistaken.

These nymphs proved to be swimmers of the finest kind, a fast
moving type which could quite easily be mistaken for little fish
as they moved freely through the water. I was very glad of the
insect net my host had so thoughtfully included in his equipment and the plus 8 lens I had with me, I was fortunate. Not
only did I catch a good number but amongst them were nymphs
ready for eclosion. Some hatched in the net and others in the
receptacle in which I was carrying them. Now I had both
nymphs and duns and I knew the spinners. It was, however,
the discovery that these duns and spinners came from a fast
swimming nymph which gave me most satisfaction. Now I had
something on which to work.

Fortunately, I had taken some fly-tying equipment with me
and a few large hooks No. 3 and No. 4. And also I had some
wing feathers of a Grey Goose. These I thought might meet my
requirement. In a short time I fashioned several artificials, some
for myself and some for my host.

With a promise to meet Nils Farnstrom at a lower lake some
three miles away, after lunch I took my rod to a lake much
nearer camp and to the place where I had caught my first two
pounder. A slight ripple was on the water but otherwise fishing
conditions were good. As I stood at the edge of the lake a fish
moved far out, I waded out to the place I fancied. Would the
Grey Goose nymph be effective?

As I watched, a dorsal fin cleaved through the ripples some
twenty yards away and within seconds my nymph pitched into
the area into which I imagined the fish was passing. Almost at
once the cast drew under, a quick flick of the rod tip set the
hook and a moment later my reel was spinning and the rod
bending to what I knew was the pull of a worthy fish. I let him
run. One of the first things I had done after hooking my first
big trout in this water was to attach a further sixty yards of
backing to that already on my line and now I had over one
hundred and forty yards. But this fish, like the previous one
stopped running at the eighty yard mark and I was able to take
control. With the larger nymph I was using 3 x cast point.
After a splendid fight I netted my first fish on the Grey Goose

nymph, a noble fish almost identical in weight to the other I had caught.

Soon I was back again in the same position, a point perhaps eighty yards from the shore and where the water was about two feet six inches in depth. A second fin showed too far off and then I saw another within range. Again the nymph pitched where I thought the fish might be. He was there. With a beautiful roll which showed the whole size of the fish above the water he took, and I tightened as he went down. Over a hundred yards of line and backing followed him as he sped for the middle of the lake. For a moment or two I wished I had added more. But the drag of the long line told. He stopped running and came under the control of my little rod.

I had to be careful. I had taken no landing net with me and my host did not have a spare one. All I had with which to land such fish was the insect net which had a hoop of about nine inches in diameter with a deep fine meshed nylon bag mounted on a fairly stout bamboo handle. As the big fish toppled in head first I breathed a sigh of relief. It was a four pounder. After a while I got a third fish, another of just over two pounds. The Grey Goose nymph was proving its worth and when I was broken with a fourth fish shortly afterwards I judged it was time I set off to join my host.

However, before meeting with him and continuing with the fishing, I would like to make some mention of the locality where I had just taken the three big fish. This was a lake almost circular in shape and I would estimate it as being about fifteen acres. Along one side, the S.W. side is a low grass bank and grasses grew out for ten yards or so into the water. Here on the same side the feeder or inflow entered from the upper lake. The bed is of firm clay, or similar substance and shelved evenly and very gradually out towards the centre of the lake. It was possible and quite safe to wade out for about eighty yards.

I had studied the position here before attempting to enter the water to fish. Excepting a few very small patches of ribbon weed, no plants of any kind grew in this lake. I found that nymphs migrated from the lake to the grass verge I have mentioned, and there hatched in great numbers by creeping up the stems of the grasses to the surface. Large quantities of nymphal shucks were clinging to them. With the wind in the S.W. and with the set of the current some of the duns would drift out into the lake. But as I watched I could see that flies, though hatching and drifting from a four hundred yard front, so to speak, all converged into a drift of about twenty yards wide as they reached an area some hundred yards out from shore. Here trout from all over the lake would congregate and rise. In that one area, during my stay I took eleven trout of over two pounds each and was broken by others. But though I tried other parts of this same lake I did not succeed in moving a single fish.

Several trout were moving in the area of the meeting place I had arranged with Nils Farnstrom but he had not arrived. I sat on a rock quite content to wait and watch as I wanted him to try with a Grey Goose nymph for these. I was glad I made this decision. Though I had proved the fish could be taken, I had yet to see it done by another. I hadn't long to wait.

It was with a feeling of intense satisfaction that I showed him my brace and a half of beauties, but my pleasure was much greater when one after the other he hooked and landed two two-pounders and proved even more conclusively that the artificial was an attractive one and that my demonstration and explanations of nymph fishing had not been a waste of time or energy. I was very happy to watch. Soon afterwards he hooked and was broken by two really enormous fish. Both of these ran until they came to a sudden stop a hundred yards away as the reel was stripped to the drum. The sudden check was too much for the 3 x points to withstand. If only he had another twenty or thirty yards of backing. He put it on next day.

That evening, just as the sun went down behind the mountains there was a congregation of spinners such as I have never seen before, or, I think, am ever likely to see again. They came to the lake from the forest around in thousands, no millions. So thick were they in the air that as I cast, as my rod flexed backwards and forwards, rod and line brought down scores of flies. And my line as it dropped to the surface would cross over dozens of floating bodies. The egg-laying sites for these creatures were in the rapids—in the rock-strewn course where the water was aerated as it tumbled down from the higher-level lake. Here, above the clear bubbling and sparkling water, the spinners congregated—a weaving, milling green-grey haze, dancing, mating and dipping to lay eggs, a haze from which there was a continuous rain of spent to flutter and die upon the water. Helped by a gentle breeze and by the slow movement of the current, these insects drifted into the lake.

It was apparent that the trout knew all about the habits of his fly. I could see big trout starting to rise near he centre of the lake and watched as they worked slowly along towards the inflow. Far out they were much too far for me to reach. As they moved nearer the inflow so the lake narrowed, but how those fish tantalised me. There near the inflow they would congregate, ten, fifteen or twenty perhaps, in a group. It was too deep to wade and we had no boat at hand. Heads, dorsals and tails would show as such a group moved closer and closer, close enough to get a nymph to one or the other, then away out of reach just as one felt certain of getting a monster. That evening I got four fish, the best being one of two and a half pounds.

It was an evening when one could have a cast until tired with a dry fly or even used wet-fly methods, and not had a single take. But I found if I could judge correctly in which direction the trout was travelling as he fed, that if I placed the nymph nicely, the fish would take as the nymph sank or as it was being retrieved very gently after the cast was made. Even with the conditions so obviously hopeless to the dry-fly fisherman, I proved the worth of the nymph and the manner of its presentation.

Further success came the following morning and again in the evening. In the morning I took five trout, three of these were under the pound, one a pound and a quarter and the other a two pounder. This was during a time when few flies were on the water, and these were duns or sedges. In the evening there came another big fall of spinner.

After the previous evening and my experience in the morning I started fishing full of confidence. With my first cast I took a fish of one and a half pounds. Soon after this I came across three fish feeding almost abreast of each other and keeping a fairly steady position. But it was a long cast, almost thirty yards of my casting line, and it was some time before a check in the breeze enabled me to reach the first. The nymph pitched just in front of his last rise form and the cast drew down in a manner which left no doubt in my mind. It was a real beauty, short and thick which fought like a demon, an ounce or so under three pounds. The other two had continued to feed undisturbed. With another herculean effort I got my nymph in front of the second and once again came the unmistakable draw down of the floating cast. As I hit this fish I knew that once more it was a big one. It was, and I landed my second four pounder.

How foolish one is sometimes. I should have changed my nymph and indeed my cast point, but no, I was too excited, I reached the third fish. Again came the draw of the cast. But as I lifted the rod tip there was a sudden jar as the hook took hold —a noble fish leapt high into the air, then all was slack. This was a trout quite as big as the four pounder and I bemoaned the fact that I might well have caught two four pounders and a three pounder with three successive casts, something I may never have the chance to do again for the rest of my life. I got two others after this—small in comparison but both between one and a half and two pounds.

This I think, was the most interesting evening of my trip. The whole lake was aboil with big fish, most of them far out of reach but nevertheless exciting to watch as they rose with a cheerful abandon, safe perhaps with the thought that no fisherman could deceive them. My nymph pattern had proved itself over and over again. Nils got a three pounder and two others similar to the last two I caught. And he was well satisfied that he had mastered the art.

Next morning I fished alone and got one fish of two pounds and several very small ones which I caught just to examine. All fish in these lakes are wild. There is no record of any being introduced. Spawning takes place at late September or early October and plenty of good spawning sites are available. And it was very obvious that regeneration takes place on a very large scale. Growth of trout for the first three years is slow, very slow. I saw numerous fry, the result of last years spawning. Through July, these fry were no larger than our own fry in April and it would appear that the periods of incubation and alevin stage are much longer. Yearlings average about four inches, two-year-

olds six to seven, three-year-old nine to eleven. But from this
stage the growth is rapid.

Four-year-olds were from one and a half to two pounds and
five-year-olds ranging from two to four pounds. Beyond this I
cannot go but I would say the really big fish attain their peak
condition in the fifth to sixth year and may be anything from
four to eight pounds. All I caught were in perfect condition but
were not the deep pink one usually associates with the lake trout
in this country or where fish can get a diet of crustaceans or
molluscs, minnows or sticklebacks. As I have mentioned, none of
these is present in the lakes.

In the evening everything went wrong. My host had a rubber
dinghy in his equipment. This we had with us and I had decided
to blow it up and park myself near a convenient rock within
reach of a place where I had seen two exceptionally fine trout
feeding merrily the previous evening. But I had to wait a long
time, inactive. The fall of the spinner was much later, owing to
a rather cold northerly breeze, which swept the lake during the
afternoon and early evening. But at last a few flies began to
appear and fish up-lake of me started to rise. Nils was soon
casting to these and as I watched I saw him tighten and then
a fish of four or five pounds went hurtling into the air to go
back into the water with a great splash with the nymph stuck in
his jaw and half a yard of 3 x cast trailing behind.

I shouted words of consolation, but just then a fish showed its
tail fin to my left. First cast put the nymph just right. He had it
at once and up into the air went a fish of about two pounds
and the hook came free. Two fish hooked and lost within a few
moments, but more disaster was to follow. Nils hooked and lost
a second, which, like mine, came unstuck but only after a run of
some eighty yards. Then it was my turn again. Just across from
my position and within easy reach a really big fish showed three
times with a head and tail rise, each rise a foot or so in front of
the last, so I knew exactly in which direction his head was
pointing.

He took with a roll like a porpoise showing me the full size
of his head and shoulders and I didn't need to see the cast draw
under to know he had my nymph in his mouth. It was with a
cool and calculating mind that I lifted the rod and became

attached. Fifty yards of line flew off the reel in a moment and
the line became fast. I could still feel the fish pulling but I had
no control with my rod. A few moments and then a sudden jag
sent a shiver along the line, through the rod to my hand, then
all was slack. That trout had gone around a big submerged rock
and I found my cast broken in the centre. This I think was the
largest trout I hooked during my stay on the lakes.

It took a little time to repair the damage. I attached two new
lengths of nylon and a new nymph and shortly after I had
finished this to my satisfaction, the second of the large fish I
had seen the previous evening, came on to feed in a manner
which left no doubt in my mind that he would become a victim.
He was well over four pounds I am sure and it was with the
utmost confidence that I threw my nymph to him. He didn't
roll as did the former one, but took quietly and firmly giving
me all the time in the world to tighten. He felt quite as strong
as the first as he went tearing away in the same direction, then
he too found refuge by the rock. But I deserved to lose this fish.
I could quite easily have cast off my mooring line and floated
to the rock whilst I could feel the fish pulling hard, but no. Like
a fool I stayed put and tried to lever the trout free with my
rod. Once again came the jag and a slack line and another noble
fish went off with a nymph and four feet of cast.

Afterwards I asked my host if he would consider naming this
pool "Sawyer's Folly". Folly indeed it was, for that evening I
had lost a brace of really big trout, when a little clear thinking
and prompt action might well have given me the chance to clear
my line and land both. An evening of disaster. We saw no more
rising fish after this, but we might have had a bag between us
well worthy of the name, instead of which, a blank.

Still it was a further triumph for my new nymph. My host
decided we should re-name it, call it the "Sawyer Swedish". To
this I agreed, but thought we might abbreviate it and call it the
S.S. So the S.S. nymph it is. But fact is often stranger than
fiction. When I agreed to name it the S.S. nymph I had not
the slightest idea what creature the artificial was representing
in the water. But I have found out since. The S.S. could not have
been chosen better for the Latin name of the nymph is
Siphlonurus spinosus.

I think now that I have said enough, perhaps too much, about the successes I achieved. I had others it is true. Altogether, large and small I landed forty-four trout, was broken by six and lost two others when trying to land them in the insect net. Several others came unstuck. In all I connected with about sixty trout and consider I did the part for which I travelled so far.

Though I had taken two other rods, a nine foot six and a ten foot six with lines and reels to suit them, I used neither. The little eight foot five inch Fario Club did all I asked of it. It cast the No. 2 line accurately and delicately and its quick tip action enabled me to hook each big fish which took my nymph. A beautiful rod this and it amazed me even with the distance it would cast my nymph and the perfect control it gave me with such large and strong fish. Much of my success is due to it and I congratulate the manufacturers on its production. Such a rod is a treasure indeed when using the light line and fine cast points so necessary in my method of nymph fishing.

The tackle used by the Swedish and other fishermen I met was, I thought, built more for tournament casting, than for delicate presentation of dry flies or nymphs. And I found most of them using cast points which to my mind were strong enough to hold a thirty pound salmon. Such strong tackle is not necessary and must be very tiring to use. Some were amazed to see the delicacy of my own outfit and that I could hook and handle such fish as these with it. But this I must say. These men are real sportsmen and I was received with every courtesy at every camp.

I feel sure, urged on by Nils Farnstrom, that these Swedish and Norwegian fishermen, possibly others, will find there is an art they had not previously discovered, in fact that nymph fishing as I proved, can be the most fascinating and most profitable method of taking these trout in the mountains. To conclude this already long story I would like to make further mention of the insects which make such fishing possible.

These lakes in the mountains are at very high altitude. In them is an abundance of Trichoptera—flies which live as caddis during their underwater existence. My brief observations led me to the belief that nearly every known species is present. And it is the Trichoptera which provides most of the food for the large fish throughout the year. No crustaceans were in these lakes and very few mollusca, and I saw no sign of minnows or sticklebacks. Plecoptera also is well represented and Sialidae. It was strange to see these alders in July. But Ephemeroptera are few. I found the nymphs of the Lark Dark Olive, B. rhodani, the Iron Blue, B. pumilus and the Yellow May Dun. Heptagenia sulphurea. But neither in any number, not enough to interest fish.

The predominating species is what I have already described as being Siphlonurus spinosus and it is this species which during July and perhaps August, forms the main attraction for surface feeding trout. That the nymphs are of the swimming group and of large size adds much to the attraction a well made artificial can give if fished correctly. The movement of the natural through the water can very easily be simulated with a smooth and slow draw, though often the artificial, if made on the Sawyer principle, will attract as it sinks.

Mr. D. E. Kimmins of the Entomology Dept., British Museum (Natural History), very kindly confirmed my identification of these insects and I was very pleased to be able to present to the museum some of the material I brought back from Sweden. This included both sexes of nymphs, duns and spinners (sub-imagos and imagos) and I gave some detail concerning their habits.

There is a good mention of Siphlonurus in Harris's " An Angler's Entomology ". There it is called the Summer Mayfly. Eaton in his Monograph gives a much better description of this genus and it was after studying his beautiful and most detailed drawings of the nymph and nymph parts that I was able to recognise my specimens.

Once again I have proved that a slight knowledge of entomology can be useful to a fisherman. A study of aquatic creatures, in itself a fascinating subject, can often lead to better sport. I was rather surprised when meeting the Swedish fishermen to find how little they knew of what was going on around them and which was so plain to me. I think I surprised them in more ways than one.

Siphlonurus apparently is a genus which lives only in water at high altitudes, but what sport they could bring if they were present in such numbers in our big reservoirs such as Blagdon,

Chew Valley, Sutton Bingham and Grafham, etc. But this cannot be. This Siphlonurus is a handsome and lovely creature in all three stages, the nymph, the dun and the spinner, and truly an insect which is part of the mountain beauty. And there in the mountains I hope they may continue to live and to thrive. I hope they may continue to thrill fishermen as they thrilled me, and help to feed trout which undoubtedly rank among the most sporting in the world.

Chapter Twenty-Two

NEEDS OF THE WATER

The underwater jungle and its life: Origins of fly life:
Vulnerability of nymphs at weed-cutting time: Deciding
the policy: Effect of weed planting on fly life: Transplant-
ing fly eggs: Experience with egg boards: Effect of winter
floods: Need for caution in interference: Pure water and
its first life: Maintaining cleanliness: Control of water
flow: The need for joint action by fishery owners: Defences
against road washings: An experiment succeeds: Benefit
to fly and fish.

RIVER VEGETATION plays a very big part in producing fly life,
but even so in rivers where growths are prolific there are times
throughout the year when cutting becomes necessary. What one
has to consider is the best way to do the job so that all the many
requirements are met. One cannot use a dry fly or nymph with
any success in a water choked with weeds and even if there are
small runs between the beds where fish can rise, it is very
doubtful, unless one uses exceptional tackle, if a fish of over
1½lb. can be landed even if well hooked. I know I have lost
many a really good trout in a weed-bed and many others in
trying my utmost to stop them from entering one. But if one just
considers fishing, all weeds would need to be shaved off close to
the river-bed; in fact it would mean clearing the bottom of
everything into which a fish could bolt and be lost. But there is
this to think about. Before a fish can be hooked and landed with
a dry fly or nymph there must be insects of one kind or another
on, or in, the surface of the water and in sufficient quantity to

tempt fish to rise and take them as food.

If all weeds are cleared then one sacrifices a multitude of insect life and consequently a large part of the fishing season. Instead of having fish rising every day to something or other, the season becomes limited to certain times—times which coincide with hatches of flies which live in or on the river-bed. For these, weed growths serve no useful purpose. For instance there are the mayflies, the sedge flies and the stone flies, then there are the turkey browns, the claret duns, yellow upright, caenis, etc., all bottom dwellers. But the olives, iron blues, pale wateries, blue winged olives, spurwings and the like need weed-growths to provide both a living and a sanctuary. And these small fly are those which can keep fish active from the beginning to the end of the season.

So in weed-cutting forget all about the bottom dwellers and concentrate on what is best for the others. Some of these no doubt would live even though all weed was cut, especially the blue-winged olives, but the majority have free-swimming larvae and nymphs and therefore, in rendering them homeless they become an easy prey to fish of all sizes as they move freely from place to place in search of food. From a very early stage in life trout will take immature fly larvae of the swimming group, so also will grayling and coarse fish fry. Then we must consider the hordes of minnows, the sticklebacks, loaches, bullheads, etc. —small fish it is true, but nevertheless all fond of insect larvae and all eager to take them when readily available.

My own observations show that these larvae prefer the short growths at the upstream ends of weed-beds, in fact that they thrive where a fast current of water strikes and filters on the front edge of the vegetation. Here the algae is collected on the weed-stems and a continual aeration is produced as the water passes through the fronds. The Baetis group, which includes the olives, iron blues and pale wateries, thrive only in water with a high content of oxygen and so, to help in their production, this arranging of weed-beds to make the necessary environment needs first to be considered.

But there are many other things to be thought of, and one of them is the occasional need for restocking with fly as well as with fish, as when we dammed side-streams for nurseries.

In clearing out one little river I knew we had sacrificed a considerable quantity of food for small trout. I could do nothing about the midge population other than to hope that the clean aerated conditions would encourage them to multiply. Shrimps would soon be abundant again without any help from me. There was, however, one way in which I could assist and for this preparation had already been made.

When the late William Lunn discovered certain flies would lay eggs on the undersides of boards tethered in fast-running water he did us all a great service, and I had been making use of his idea for some years to transfer fly eggs from one water to another. It is the larvae which hatch from the eggs of the autumn olives which are most helpful in trout fry production. There are two species, one larger than the other, but the eggs of both, though perhaps laid in September or early October, seldom produce larvae for many weeks. Often enough the eggs will not hatch until early in the following year, but usually these eggs will have produced countless larvae of minute size which are available for natural trout fry in early April.

Throughout September, indeed while we were working on our nursing, I had a number of boards tethered at an egg-laying site near my home. Here hordes of olives were in the habit of creeping down into the water to lay their eggs on the concrete apron behind Choulston Hatches. By the time I was ready to transfer them the boards were all thickly covered with many millions of eggs. These eggs are quite safe to transport if kept damp. All I do is to wrap them up in wet sacks and then take them in my car. I had one board for each section of the nursery and these I pushed beneath the slope of the concrete slabs of the dams and there penned them down with a few large stones. These eggs hatched earlier than those in the main river, possibly because the water is warmer during winter. By January all larvae had left the boards. Observation carried out on a few large stones downstream of each dam proved the tiny insects to be well and thickly established. I felt quite satisfied that our future trout fry would have some food at least.

Let me now look again at the river's vegetation. Naturally it must be my river, or at least the kind of river I know best, a South Country river. Elsewhere the species of plants may vary,

but the chief principles remain. South Country rivers are suitable
for many kinds of water plants and some of these are much more
prolific than others. Some are what I call summer weeds. These
are plants such as the pond weeds, watercress, celery, ribbon
weed and starwort. In fact many plants grow profusely during
the spring and summer and then die away in the autumn. All
are quite harmless as obstruction to the water flow, for in average
seasons all growths have died away long before there is any
likelihood of increased volume from the springs.

But there are other plants which thrive throughout the year
and of these the water buttercups (Ranunculus) and the water
dropwort (O. fluviatilus) are the most hardy. Both root deeply
into the bed of the stream and each can provide thick tresses
which cushion and divert any direct action of water on the
river bottom. Both have great value; are what I call natives, and
have a permanent function in the life of the river. In the upper
Avon the water buttercup is by far the more common and it had
the greater influence on the run of the stream. This plant thrives
best in shallow gravelly reaches where the water is well aerated
but it does grow strongly in depths down to three feet.

In the natural course of events the beds start to throw out
new shoots immediately after the old fronds have died away in
the early autumn but Nature sees to it that these new shoots do
not grow to any great length until after she has done her cleaning
up. They then quickly spread as the temperature of the water
increases and by early spring the luxuriant tresses are to be seen
spreading towards the surface. Soon the buttercups stud the
fully extended fronds. For a while the thousands of little flowers
add their beauty to the valley but all too soon their annual glory
is gone. Gradually the fronds change colour and then, one by
one, the long tresses die away. The short sprouts of the new
crop show plainly but wait for the command of Nature before
starting to flourish.

Now that is as it should be—as it was planned in the great
creation. It is only when we interfere with the natural events
that trouble arises. In one way we help and in another we
hinder. Too much weed in spring interferes with fly fishing so
instead of waiting for the time of season to thin out the vegetation, we cut it. Our scythe blades slice through the trailing fronds

of the ranunculus long before they have reached maturity, and the great tresses float away downstream.

In cutting these weeds early in the year we interfere with their life cycle. Instead of stopping the growth we increase it for, in shaving off the long tendrils to clear the surface area, the growth on the bed becomes more prolific. Where one stem sprouted in the first place, now comes three or four and, instead of a bed which flowers and then dies away, it remains vigorous and healthy. Soon such beds have to be cut a second time. By late autumn a third such growth has sprung up and this, unless cut clearly, has a serious effect when the winter water starts to clean up the course.

In summer and early autumn thick beds of vegetation can be very valuable to filter and cleanse the water, but during winter they are but a menace to the well-being of a fishery. Some, however, can be of use in directing cleaning currents into desired channels and in clearing a river course at late autumn such beds can be positioned accordingly. If all the short growths are left they filter and retain the very filth we are so desirous of being carried to the sea and much of the labour of Nature is frustrated.

Most men know the best thing to do when spring-cleaning starts and, though few of us can retire and keep out of sight as we would wish, it is simply that we have no chance to do so. River creatures are more fortunate in this respect for when Nature's broom comes brushing along the river-bed in winter each has a sanctuary where for a while it can live in comfort. In deep and shallow, the tiny life of the stream seek their various shelters and, unless conditions become far worse than they have expected, there they remain while the foulness of the course is carried towards the sea.

Each tiny stone on the shallow then becomes a temporary home for one, or another, while insects and beetles, crustaceans and little fish may all live together for a while beneath the shelter of some big boulder. Around them the water surges and gurgles and sufficient oxygen for their need is created as currents pass over the uneven bed. In the deeps the small animals forsake the bed and take shelter at the edges of the river. Each crevice in the bank has its thousands of occupants while any underwater vegetation becomes a harbour in time of need. The edges of the water in a river always remain clearer than other parts and aeration is created as the currents are baffled by the uneven sides.

These little animals are perfectly safe while the racing water carries its sweepings in suspension, but should there be a sudden slackening of the current then they must move quickly or die. Generally speaking, however, this sudden lessening of the current is not likely to occur, especially on shallows which have a fair fall in level, but when, through some interference, it does slacken in speed, any matter hitherto being carried in the grip of the water immediately sinks to foul the bottom. The hiding-places of the millions no longer receive their supplies of oxygen and mud fills the crevices beneath the stones. These creatures sheltering on the shallows are then no better off than their neighbours in the deeps, and must seek similar security.

But in seeking such security, and indeed when such is found, there comes a great loss. Life on the shallows is ten times greater than in the deeps and, when all herded together in communal shelters in times of emergency, only the strongest will survive. I write mostly of the insect life—of the larvae of flies which in later months will gladden the eyes of fish, birds and fishermen. What we must remember is, that larvae of different sizes, some very, very minute, must live in the river during the winter months. Even as the larger ones, these tiny beings must have conditions which they can endure whatever Nature has ordained. The more we know of the everyday life of these river-bed animals the easier it will be for us to know what best to do in assisting their production.

For fishery owners it is important that a river course is kept clean and wholesome, but it is essential that no help is given to do this until it is expected by the occupants of the stream. Even then such help should be given gradually, and while the course has a fast and unrestricted flow.

Before fly life can exist at any stage, and hence before a river can provide the population of living natural nymphs which permits the artificial to deceive the fish, its water must be in a fit state to support insect life. Not only the life but the sport of a fishery depends upon the health and numbers of its stock of flies. Unless this is maintained at its highest level the pleasure of those who fish be they purists or not, can never reach its full quality.

Spring water, though perfectly clear and pure, has no living creature in it when it comes bubbling from the ground. As rain water it seeped into the land, eventually to become trapped, and then to well up in the valleys. In its passage through the earth the rain water is cleansed, and being in perfect darkness, no life can exist as it passes along subterranean routes. But while moving through the earth and bubbling once more to the surface this water becomes oxygenated and purified until immediately it is capable of supporting aquatic life.

As the water is exposed to the light the first life of the river is created, the warmth from the sun strikes on the surface and sides and soon the temperature rises. Then the pure water is impregnated with living matter, tiny animals so small and so shapeless that to our naked eye they pass in the water without detection. Quickly they multiply and spread with the stream, and the initial life which ultimately produces the trout of our rivers has become established. This proto-life can best be seen during the spring and summer months, for then it is most abundant. Much appears only as a slime on the stones and vegetation or as a bloom on the surface of the water. It is here, there and everywhere, wherever the water remains sufficiently wholesome and exposed to encourage its regeneration. Under the microscope a very different story is told for then the slime is revealed to be millions of separate cells of life of every conceivable shape and colouration.

Here then are the first living creatures we need for the natural production of trout and if a river cannot, through reason of pollution or other causes, produce this initial life, then it is quite hopeless to expect any other life to thrive. How all the other aquatic creatures started their lives is not for me even to conjecture. Sufficient to write of them as being in existence to live and to multiply if conditions are favourable. Nature stocked all her streams and waterways with the animals such waters could support. If any certain species was not included it was for a perfectly good reason and it is not wise to introduce them from other waters.

Few river creatures live on vegetation. The majority are
carnivorous, living either on creatures smaller than themselves,
or feasting on larger ones which have died. None can live long
on water alone. That a trout will live for a considerable time
on just one diet has often been proved, but usually some disease
or other brings a premature ending to his life. To be perfectly
healthy and to bring forth healthy progeny the fish must have
a chance to pick and choose; to take that which is his fancy at
the moment, and to what his appetite is directed by nature. He
cannot attain any great size unless he has food which builds up
his body; sufficient good feeding during spring and summer to
more than make up for the energy he has expended in spawning
and for poor winter food supplies. So, to ensure he gets all he
wants, a multitude has to be considered. First and foremost
come the insects. From the very first day he starts to feed, these
river insects in one form or another play a very big part in the
life of a trout.

It is useless to expect a clear and pure drink from a spring if
you use a dirty cup. Yet how often this kind of thing happens.
Each year our springs give their quota of pure fresh water only
for it to flow into a container foul with the poison of years. It
is useless to have a pure water supply if this cannot use a course
that is equally clear, for if such course is foul then soon the
wholesomeness of the water is destroyed. Soon the life-giving
properties are rendered ineffective and the whole cycle of
aquatic life comes to an end. Much depends on the cleanliness
of a river course as Nature indicates to us. She does her best,
but I fear civilisation has put too great a demand on her powers.
We have created conditions which foul our waterways and if we
are to have the best from them then we must give assistance in
keeping them clean. Too often I see banks beautifully trimmed
and yet the bed and sides of the river are foul with the accumulation of years.

It is quite natural for us to get mud in a river, stream, or in
fact, any waterway sufficiently pure to produce vegetation, for
this vegetation flourished in the spring and summer to decay
during autumn and early winter. Usually this decomposed
matter comes to rest upon the river-bed until conditions are
suitable to carry it away. In addition particles of dust and debris

enter the course from the land and all the while there is certain erosion taking place as the water eats into the banks which confine it. And today we have surface water draining from villages and roads, carrying with it tons of silt and various bodies which soon find a place to settle. All an added burden for the work of Nature.

In itself rotted river vegetation and leaves from trees is a deadly poison to most of the aquatic beings, when in bulk. This can be proved conclusively by digging into an accumulation and studying a sample. Take for example a heap of cut weeds left to rot away on some shallow or other. There they remain until nothing is left except a black slimy mass. A few creatures, mostly undesirables, will be found at the top, but elsewhere the heap is dead. Yet gradually the water carries the filth away until the bright gravel shows once more. One such heap may not cause much trouble but when scores are moving at the same time the water soon loses its crystal clarity and much of its reproductive power. Nature does her own weed thinning in a very gradual manner, no great bulks are sent down to lodge and rot and be harmful.

Such heaps moving near the mouth of a river are much less serious for soon the filth is carried out to sea, but when they occur near the source, then it is quite a different story. This rotted vegetable matter can be carried many miles in suspension down a stream, so if the upper reaches are neglected and allowed to become foul, all water downstream must suffer and with it the river life. So all who have a river at heart should be united. Owners with the lower and middle reaches have to depend on those higher up the valley for a pure water supply, and in their own interests they should see that they get it. Nature does her best to cleanse the rivers, for usually the water supply increases during the winter months to such an extent that any sediment from summer and autumn can be carried away. She cleans up her container at a time when the water carries sufficient oxygen to combat the impurities, or at least, to render them less effective. And if we are to help, then we must also concentrate our effort during the time Nature is at work, for if we try during the wrong seasons we do far more harm than good.

Though many are no longer used for the purpose for which

they were constructed, various types of river controls still exist
and are maintained in good working order by their owners.
Some of these have been in operation for two hundred years or
more. They were made in times when there were far less
mechanical contraptions than at the present, yet how well the
underwater work has stood the passing of time and the scour of
a thousand floods. Undoubtedly these old engineers understood
their work and constructed according to the demand Nature
would have upon their labours. Of this we have ample
proof.

I often stand on some old sets of hatches and ponder. It would
seem that the structure and hatchways were made long before
the river course was diverted to flow through them. In fact
they were put in a firm part of the valley where any seepage of
water could easily be controlled by pumps while the work was
on. Some of the sills of these hatches go down several feet
beneath the bed of the channel and are very soundly constructed.
It is obvious these old-time people paid far more attention to
the solidity of the underwater parts than to those above. In
going down so deep they were only preparing for what they
knew must follow the release of any impounded water.

Today we see Nature's work through the centuries. Downstream of each set of hatches a great hole has been scoured—
hatch holes as we call them. Some of these may be from ten feet
to twenty feet deep and the homes of monster trout. These have
been gouged out by the pressure of the water as it pours in concentrated force from one level to another, and the spoil from
them is scattered to form a shallow in the reach below. But for
the deep apron and sill which guards the under part of the
structure, the water would have scoured a way beneath it and
soon the bed upstream would have undermined and collapsed.
Solid wingings extend on either side to guard the banks upstream
and down, against scour. All very clever and thoughtful. These
men knew what they were about. But, thoughtful though they
were, they made one mistake. In constructing these appliances to
control the flow of water they thought only of the water to be
impounded. Their job was to provide heads of water, sometimes
of many feet, by which machinery could be driven and by which
the meadows could be irrigated. They gave little thought to the

parent stream in time of flood or to the flotsam the water must at times carry.

Perhaps our river has widened in the years since the work was done, if so I do them some injustice, but in most places today the structures do not span the river course. But the great mistake was in making the hatchways too narrow and in making the hatchguides too numerous and bulky. To my mind come two sets of seven hatches. Here the width of each hatch is but 2ft. 3in. In between each are guides which measure 1ft. 6in. Actually at these points the river is fifty feet wide, but the whole structure is but half this width. Now if this twenty-five feet could give unrestricted flow in times of flood it would not be so bad, but the flow is impeded by the nine feet or so which comprise the piers. With all hatches open and clear of debris the flow is reduced from fifty feet to little more than fourteen feet. Such sets of hatches need continual attention to keep them clear. Old-fashioned river controls have to be endured and they play a very big part in the well-being of a trout stream as will later be shown.

For a river to keep pure and wholesome and fit for the great family which live in it, it must have an annual clean-up. From November to March is the time Nature uses in doing this cleaning up and any assistance we can give should then be utilised to the full. Often I wish I could wave a wand, like a magician, and eliminate all the old-fashioned controls I have to manage, and at the same time install a design of my own. River controls are valuable, but I would like to have them so that by the turn of a wheel I could set free the whole river as well as being able to stop the flow.

At the present time these old-fashioned structures act as a deterrent to the drag of the current on the river-bed. They are obstructions and any obstructions in a running stream prevent the natural action of the water removing matter which, during summer and autumn, has settled on the bottom. Not only this. Often these obstructions check the flow to such an extent that any mud successfully carried in suspension from reaches upstream is given a chance to settle and consolidate. Mud is the curse of any trout fishery and while there are any large deposits both the fauna and the flora will suffer. Decomposing vegetable matter in itself can be deadly poison to aquatic life, but when this becomes mixed with the various chemicals and impurities which drain to our rivers these days the situation soon becomes serious.

Hatches and the like are valuable assets for impounding and conserving the water supply, but a river was intended to have an unrestricted flow during winter and it is to the advantage of all fishery owners to see that this is what it gets. Water can only clear up its container if it has sufficient speed, first to move the foul deposits from the bed and then to carry them in suspension to the sea. It is just hopeless to move the collections from one place to another and this I fear is what is often done where hatchways are inadequate.

Some rivers must for ever remain muddy for the fall in level from source to mouth is too slight to be of use. Such waters can never produce the multitude of life we need. In others the fall is too great so that continual scouring by a racing stream gives vegetation no chance to flourish and it is too fast for the needful small creatures to exist. Valuable indeed are those which are the happy medium, those neither too fast nor too slow, and having the advantage of increased flow during the months most needed.

Lakes and ponds or indeed any static water, especially if artificially constructed, can never continue indefinitely to be successful for the production of trout, if left to themselves. No matter how large or how small, in time the bottom becomes foul and finally the whole water becomes unfit for the fish to live. All such waters should be drained and cleaned periodically. Some may produce both trout food and trout for twenty years or more, others foul in many fewer. If they are left, soon only the upper layer of water is productive, while the bed is poisonous whenever it is disturbed.

To keep the course from bank to bank the current, or flow, of a river must be distributed evenly so that its action has a drag on the bottom like a great brush. Where there is but one central and main current much of the bed and sides of the course must forever remain muddy. Only by increased flow or by some diversion which breaks up and evenly distributes the main current can such mud be disturbed to be carried in the stream.

Many times I have watched Nature at work moving the refuse she herself has created. It fascinates me to see the smaller and lighter fragments answering to the pull of the stream. It is just as though an invisible brush is sweeping lightly over the surface. Behind the brush tiny currents and eddies swirl around and around, whirling the little particles higher and higher into the water. As the mud moves so the heavier matter sinks to the bottom. Grit and sand, stones and gravel, lie side by side with thousands of snail shells, while the currents filter in between them to seek out the last lingering foulness. Then the heavier fragments are caught in the toils and away they are swept to some pit in the bed where the current can no longer give play.

At times the heavier particles are swept into a heap which forms an obstruction to the current. They have already been cleansed of all impurities and now must play their part. The heaps create a diversion. On them the current strikes and is parted, to send a cleansing stream on to the bottom at either side until such time there is sufficient volume to move the whole lot downstream. No one need worry about these heaps of washed silt being left behind in a river after a flood. They are quite harmless to aquatic life and on them vegetation can flourish. Nature is satisfied that her annual clean up has been thorough for all the impurities have been winnowed from the pure substances, and the winter field is prepared for the harvest of Spring.

Only when one can see road washings trapped in a small area is it possible to realise fully just how much erosion takes place in our modern roads and of what these washings consist. Road washings into the upper Avon in Wiltshire have been a constant worry for many years, for on either side of the valley, roads run parallel and often very close to the river. From these in times of heavy rain I have watched the surface water racing along into gutters and drains which carry it almost directly into the main river or to one if its tributaries. The term "surface water" may be misleading. If it were surface water there would be little to worry about, for there are no impurities in rain water; in fact, clear rain water running direct to a river or steam would be very welcome, from the fisherman's point of view, in these days when our rivers are so low. But the rain water is far from pure and wholesome after it has pattered on to the surfaces of our

present-day roads. As it rushes towards and into the river or
sidestreams, so it carries spoil that is poison to aquatic life. I am
sure that the answers to many of our problems regarding the
well-being of our fisheries lie with road drainage.

On many occasions I have examined the fauna immediately
downstream of a road drainage outfall and I have compared
their numbers and variety with those of the creatures found in
the clean water upstream. I advise anyone who is sufficiently
interested to do the same, for one has no need to be an expert
to appreciate the fact that life is almost nil where silt from a
road covers a river-bed.

Some people I know become greatly agitated if they see oil
or grease floating downstream on the surface. It does look bad,
far worse indeed than it really is, for oil or grease on the surface
of the water does little harm to aquatic life. The harm is caused
when it is carried with other poisons to the river-bed, there to
percolate into the gravel and foul the birthplaces of trout and
many of the insects we value so much for fly fishing. And this
is what has been happening so long with road washings. Oil,
grease, rubber and tar are scattered and ground up by the traffic
to mix with and stick to the pulverised road metalling. Then it
is all swept into the river by rain and, instead of floating downstream to the sea, as it would if a liquid, the poisons are carried
to the bottom, imprisoned on the the tiny fragments of gravel
and sifted and silted into the spaces between them.

On the upper Avon we are less fortunate than some, for the
river runs through the heart of Salisbury Plain, the training
ground for much of our mechanised army. Not only have we
rubber-tyred vehicles on the highways but track-laying tanks
which weigh 40 tons or more, and lumber along crunching and
crushing the road surfaces almost to dust and losing and scatter-
ing some of the large quantity of lubricants needed by them for
easy movements.

The increase of mechanised units is perhaps the cause of much
of the trouble with which we have been faced in the Avon
Valley, for I am quite certain that road washings and their
effect have worsened considerably in the past ten or twelve years.
These heavy vehicles enter roads from the downlands at either
side and between them bring on their tracks tons of spoil. This

shakes free as they advance and then, mixed as it is with oil, tar and other matter, it is left on the roads to be washed into the river by the first heavy rain. The silt washed into the river has slowly spread. Gravelly shallows which once were productive of both trout and trout food have for long been hidden by the deadly creeping layer. To add to our troubles we have villages where the drainage from farms and houses links with the system of road drainage, and the combination, more especially with the increasing use of detergents, has produced anything but a happy state of affairs. I had been worried by it for a long time, and finally tests were made at various outfalls from roads and villages to prove that the river was being grossly polluted. It was unfit for aquatic life and unsafe for animals to drink. Something had to be done, and done at once. My chief concern was the fishing, but there were other things to be considered. T.T. herds feed in the meadows and drink from the river, the main water supply comes from it, and the silting, if allowed to continue, would obviously have a serious effect on land drainage.

I made a proposal to construct a series of catch-pits for road drainage throughout the valley and eventually the scheme was accepted. At this stage the Avon and Dorset Rivers Board was consulted and we had a great encouragement from their fisheries inspector, who wholeheartedly approved the plan and expressed a willingness to do all he could to help. It was impossible to work to any detailed plan, but the main idea was to provide pits where all water from roads and the sullage from the village drains could be trapped long enough for all suspended and some of the soluble matter to be arrested and fall to the bottom. It was not possible to dig pits large enough to hold all the surface water one might expect from a heavy thunderstorm or a sudden thaw of snow, so each had to be provided with an overflow outlet from which the cleared water could pass on to the river. My job was to do what I could to have the pits constructed to meet all requirements, and I was greatly handicapped by the fact that the pits had to be made on waste ground and that near the river the water table is often only two feet or less below the land surface.

But we persevered and all the pits were dug as deeply as was considered safe, for we could not have places which might prove a death trap for any child who fell in. The pits are oblong and approximately 40ft. by 20ft., each being between 3ft. and 4ft. deep. Silt-laden water enters through a channel at one corner and strikes the opposite bank, where an eddy is created. This eddy checks the water just long enough for all silt to fall to the bottom, and then the cleared water is led off at the outlet.

Some of our pits are dug deep enough into the gravel and well beneath the water table in the valley, yet considerable seepage still takes place. For how long this will continue remains to be seen, but, except in severe storms, the trapped water seldom fills the pits to the overflows and consequently all alien matter is trapped. The seepage is clean and wholesome after passing through the subterranean passages to the river. An analysis of samples taken just after a heavy storm from the inlet and outlet of one of the run-through pits showed that eighty-three per cent of suspended and soluble matter was being collected. There is something very fascinating and soothing in looking at a running stream which fits in with every mood. Though there are times when Nature in a valley can be most severe, there is always that little something which turns bitterness into sweetness. A river is not just a drain for the waste waters of the earth, as I fear some misguided people think, but something created for a much greater purpose. In taking away water no longer to be retained in the land, the stream becomes an element which gives life and sustenance to millions of creatures and for us provides endless joy.

Perhaps from some hill or other you can overlook the valley where the little villages and their farms huddle together as though for warmth. In winter, after the bleakness of the downs, the view brings a warm glow to the heart and in spring and summer comes that feeling of everlasting freshness, that of gazing at something new. Unconsciously, one's footsteps hasten down the hill, eager to be there—eager to see more of what Nature has created in this hollow and enjoy to the full this heritage we possess. To the fisherman comes an even greater urge. He absorbs the scenery at a glance for to him such sights are frequent. These river valleys are his life and immediately his thoughts go to what may be hidden beneath the surface of that shining strip he seeks snaking away in the distance.

INDEX